CONFLICT, VIOLENCE
AND MORALITY
IN A MEXICAN VILLAGE

CONFLICT, VIOLENCE, AND MORALITY IN A MEXICAN VILLAGE

LOLA ROMANUCCI-ROSS

With a new Afterword

THE UNIVERSITY OF CHICAGO PRESS
Chicago & London

To my Father, Ignazio Romanucci, in gratitude
To my husband, John Ross, Jr., in love

The University of Chicago Press, Chicago 60637
The University of Chicago Press, Ltd., London

95 94 93 92 91 90 89 88 87 86   5 4 3 2 1

Library of Congress Cataloging in Publication Data

Romanucci-Ross, Lola.
   Conflict, violence, and morality in a Mexican
village.

   Reprint. Originally published: Palo Alto, Calif. :
National Press Books, 1973. With new afterword.
   Bibliography: p.
   1. Morelos (Mexico)—Social conditions—Case studies.
   2. Social conflict—Mexico—Morelos—Case studies.
   3. Violence—Mexico—Morelos—Case studies.
   4. Morelos (Mexico)—Moral conditions—Case studies.
   I. Title.
HN120.M58R64   1986   306'.0972'49   85–24610
ISBN 0–226–72464–6 (cloth)
ISBN 0–226–72465–4 (paper)

CONTENTS

PREFACE vii

1 THE SETTING 1

A Mexican Mestizo Village 1
The Hacienda 6
The Raid on the Haciendas 11
The Agrarian Revolution 14
Post-Revolution Village 20

2 ON CONFLICT 28

Forms of Conflict 28
Levels of Conflict 30
Size of Conflict 31
Stable and Unstable Conflicts 33
Dimensions of Conflict Resolution 33

3 CONFLICT: GROUP AND SOCIAL RELATIONS 35

In-group and Out-group Relations 35
Village Factions 38

The Family Unit 45
    Residence Units 48
    Family Conflicts 52
    A Family Typology 58
Intrafamilial Conflict 61
    The Abandoned Spouse 61
    Issues of Husband-Wife Conflict 62
    Locality 65
    Family Discipline 66
    Sibling Conflict 68
Kinship Beyond the Family Group 70
    Kin and Kindred Fragments 72
Friendship and *Compadrazgo* 74
    Friendship 74
    Compadrazgo 79
    Structure of the *Compadrazgo* Relationship 82
Kinship, Friendship, *Compadrazgo,* and Patronage 84
    The Relational Network 87

4 CONFLICT AND MORALITY 93

Relationship Between Conflict and Morality 93
    Egoísmo 94
    Categoría 95
    Envidia 96
Categoría and Race 97
Moral Status 105
Uses of Witchcraft 108
    A Case of Witchcraft 110
The Moral Record 115
Political Morality 116
    Compromised People in Undermined Roles 116
    Collusive Participation 120
    Real Leadership 124
    Persuaders and *Patrones* 127

5 MORALITY AND VIOLENCE   132

   Violence and Murder   132
         Trends in Violence   134
   Alcoholism and Violence   136
         Alcoholism and Murder   138
   Flight, Protection, and Rehabilitation   138
         Role of the Avenger   141
   Motivation and Premeditation   144
   Violence versus Conflict   146
   Bases of Trends   148
   Village Self-Image   151

6 MORALITY AND THE CHURCH   156

   Moral Codes and Church Morality   156

7 THE CATALINO CASE   167

   Background   168
   The Hearing   173
   An Attempted Settlement   177
   Summary   182

8 SOME CONCLUSIONS   185

   Morality   185
   Social Structure and Conflict   186
   Violence and Homicide   187

AFTERWORD   189

APPENDIX 1   209

APPENDIX 2   214

BIBLIOGRAPHY   218

PREFACE

In 1958 I joined Erich Fromm in what he had begun a year earlier as a psychoanalytic inquiry into a Mexican village. Fromm's method lay in administering a questionnaire, in psychological testing, and in psycho-analytic interpretation of these data. I and my associate Theodore Schwartz assisted in shaping and scoring the questionnaires and administering some of the tests, but our main contribution consisted of living in the village as field anthropologists. Fromm and Maccoby acknowledge the uses of our field researches in the foreword to their book.

> Their observations permitted us to know a great deal about the intimate life of the villagers, to form an idea, for instance, of which individuals were sober or mild alcoholics, which people were the most and least successful, about their mores and married life. All these observations permitted us to judge to what extent the answers on the questionnaires were ideological or corresponded to facts in the lives of the villagers.[1]

The present work is based on three years of anthropological field-work in the village and has grown out of those aspects of field research that reflected my own view of the anthropological experience. I have limited my presentation to explanations and internal analyses of structures and their functioning, which has required an intimate knowledge of personalities interacting within events. To respect the privacy of those villagers who so willingly helped me in this, the village shall be herein unnamed. The names used are fictitious, but the people, places, and events are real.

The text takes up the following considerations: (1) how social stratification occurred in the village during the period of land distribution following the Revolution of 1910 in Mexico; (2) how the multiple bonds of kinship, friendship, godparenthood, and patronage are used in the village to meet various needs in conditions of limited resources; (3) how violence and conflict are defined and related in the minds of villagers; (4) how moral codes are used or construed in calculating the outcome of acts and events; (5) how social images of long duration affect village behavior and social roles; (6) how conflict, violence, and concepts of morality are interwoven in the village structure and reflect the problems and processes of its people; and finally, (7) how the concept of *machismo*, or "manliness," has sustained the emotional tone of the culture and shaped future social change.

The Catalino case, a major conflict, is discussed in detail in chapter 7. Throughout the three years of my participation in the study, this case provided a focus for social, moral, and legal issues that stirred the village and influenced its development as well. Much that is discussed in this work has arisen from events in this case, and there are references to it throughout the text. It has been placed at the end of the book in the belief that the reader will be better able to appreciate it after he has learned something about the village; some readers, however, may prefer to read chapter 7 at the beginning rather than at the end.

Spanish terms have been used only when I have felt that the customary English translation was in some way inadequate. "Small businessman," for example, is not what villagers mean by *comerciante; envidia* is not properly "envy," nor is *categoría* "category." The nicknames of various of the villagers are given in the original Spanish in Appendix 2, and many of these will be found to be very revealing of village attitudes.

I am deeply grateful to Erich Fromm for allowing me to participate in the formulation and analysis of all aspects of his broader study. I am indebted as well to Theodore Schwartz, an experienced field worker who taught me much about systematic inquiry and anthropological methods. I owe a great deal to David Bidney, whose influence as a scholar, teacher, and writer has oriented, and will continue to affect, my anthropological field work. Finally, I am grateful to the villagers. This book is really a product of their confidence and collaboration.

---

[1] Erich Fromm and Michael Maccoby, *Social Character in a Mexican Village* (New Jersey: Prentice-Hall, 1970).

EL MACHO VIVE MIENTRAS QUE EL CODARDE QUIERE

("El macho lives as long as the coward wills it.")

Village Proverb

View from the hacienda rooftop

1

THE SETTING

A MEXICAN MESTIZO VILLAGE

The village of this study is located south of Mexico City in the State of Morelos. It lies in a valley in Mexico's Central Plateau, whose lands are far more fertile than most in Mexico (only 7.6 percent of Mexico's total land area is arable).[1] The climate is subtropical—never cold, yet never tropically hot—and the village is well-known today for its pleasant climate, its sulfur springs, and its natural beauty and picturesqueness.

The buildings and walls of its hacienda, among the first to be built in Morelos, still stand, though the hacienda was burned in the early days of the 1910–17 Revolution in Mexico;[2] a seventeenth-century aqueduct runs through the main street. (Although the aqueduct still carries water to the hacienda, its mill wheels have not turned since sugar-refining operations were transferred to a nearby hacienda in 1896.) Unlike many other towns and villages in Morelos where all the large old trees have been removed, this village retains many centuries-old trees, providing graceful natural beauty as well as welcome relief from the sun.

The *yunta* (yoked oxen)—a traditional agricultural practice

Two dirt roads connect the village with the nearest paved roads, and the dirt roads are in poor condition—potholed and with large sections washed out every rainy season. Repairs are always years in arrears of deterioration, but there has been transportation for the villagers since 1961, when buses running between two large towns began to enter the village. The streets, of either dirt or grass, are all unpaved and are, however charming to outsiders, a source of considerable muddy annoyance to villagers during the rainy season. Village pigs enjoy them, but the villagers dream of paving these streets someday—at least, of paving one main artery.

The village economy is chiefly agricultural: sugarcane, rice, corn, beans, and tomatoes are cultivated in that order of importance. Like other, larger villages in the immediate area, the village has no market of its own. Much of its food is purchased at five small stores in the village; the rest is bought in the markets of larger neighboring towns, all less than an hour away by bus. Crops are normally sold in their entirety—sugarcane, through the cane-growers' cooperative; rice, through the Ejido Bank or other purchasing agents. Although planters may keep some of their corn and beans for home use, this is not the usual practice. Speculative crops, such as tomatoes and melons, are sold in Mexico City, which is three hours away by truck.

Land and its use are central to the history of Mexico, where communal landholding was known before the founding of the Aztec kingdoms and the Spanish Conquest. Although profoundly affected by the four-century tenure of the hacienda system, Morelos was at the heart of the Mexican Agrarian Revolution that sought to end that system, and the present village, its population and socioeconomic form, may be said to have emerged from the Revolution.

Most of the village's 792 inhabitants, or their parents, came from elsewhere in Morelos or other nearby states to take up the village hacienda

Workers in the rice fields

land as it was divided by the post-Revolution government into *Ejidos* and *ejido* parcels. (The large landholding transferred by government edict from the hacienda to the new community—i.e., usually granted to the already-existing nearby village—was called the *Ejido*. The term *ejido* also applies to the land parcel and its special tenure conditions assumed by the individual, then called *ejidatario.*) The average *ejido* parcel is 2.35 hectares (1 hectar equals approximately 2.5 acres); actual holdings range from .5 to 7.7 hectares. Under the system of individual parcels, the *ejidatario* must personally cultivate his assigned parcel; a failure of two years' duration to do so can lose him his land. Although rental and outright alienation of land is formally prohibited, employing others to do the actual labor is acceptable as "personal use" in the village.

Informally, however, land is not necessarily used by the person to whom it was allotted as an *ejido* parcel. We found that approximately one-third of *ejidatarios* rented or shared out their land to others, in whole or in part.[3] The relative stability of the pattern of distribution of land use under informal reallocation is based on a constant core group of nineteen *ejidatarios,* with some concentration of land use at the top end of the scale (where a few already have larger holdings), and some fragmentation of land use toward the lower end of the scale. The *ejido* is actually divided further in use-sharing by the person who is legally entitled to work it with a person who is not so entitled. The "concentration at the top" comes about in the absorption of more "parcel land" in cultivation than the *ejidatario* was originally allotted. Reallocation involves an informal or extralegal transfer of use not only among members of the community, but within the family and its extension as well. There is, however, an alternative that is equivalent to rental. Because sellers in need of cash can always be found, many men purchase crops before harvest, often early in the season, as a form of investment and speculation.

This part of Morelos has attracted immigration from other states because the water supply available for irrigation allows for year-round work. Numerous springs in the valley irrigate all of the village's arable land during the dry season, when valleys nearby have turned brown and become unsuitable for agriculture. There are streams from the rugged mountainous area in the north of the state and from the volcanoes of Popocatepetl (17,887 feet) and Ixtacihuatl (17,343 feet), both snowcapped throughout the year even though they are located at the Nineteenth Parallel.

The rainy season from May to October affects the life of this village less than it does villages in other, nonirrigable areas. Abundant rainfall floods the rice fields, whose production is confined to the rainy season; the sugarcane crop, which takes fourteen to eighteen months to mature, requires water throughout the dry season. Since early colonial times, it has been the presence of water above all that has made the village one of the important sugarcane areas of Mexico.

The availability of water should not be overemphasized, however. There is enough water to irrigate all of the village *Ejido* when this water is well managed and well distributed. Area farmers employ a system of allocation, and water is a subject of vigorous dispute in the village itself and between it and other villages as well. Much of the water, highly sulfurous, comes from local mineral springs. Although supposedly detrimental to crops, it is necessary to use as much of this water as is not supplied by the more distant "sweet" springs. There are several large springs in the village *Ejido*, and the largest of these will be discussed later because it is the crux of the most crucial conflict in the village.[4]

Water has, in any case, attracted both poor and rich to the village—the poor attracted by the year-round work that the village water supply makes possible; the more affluent, to its vacation possibilities. There are in the village at present about a dozen *residencias* built by wealthy Mexicans from Mexico City. A famous Mexican artist had a rustic home constructed here, and at one time the hacienda was owned by an American film star. The village is popular as a weekend spot among Mexico City Mexicans—streams of automobiles bring large crowds of bathers and picnickers on Saturdays and Sundays—and villagers care about all this only insofar as they benefit from it economically.

The *residencia* owner might serve some significant purpose in the community—as a village *patron* perhaps, hearing petitions, donating money to build a road, repair a bridge, or to build a factory that would employ the poor—but he is generally disappointing in this respect. On the whole, the wealthy outsider is important to the village only as an employer of maids and gardeners.

Although a few villages in the area are reputed to be Indian villages still speaking Indian languages, the majority of them exhibit few remaining traces of Indian tongues, except for remnants of vocabulary in medicine, plant names, place names, and words relating to older processes in agriculture. Like most of its close neighbors, this village is not Indian but rather self-consciously mestizo—a mixture of racial and ethnic elements—and exhibits an internally varied culture based upon the partial, diluted, and impoverished remains of both Indian and Spanish civilization.

From 1928 to 1960, the village increased from about 250 to 800 persons through rapid population growth, especially through immigration. In 1961, of the total adult population over sixteen years of age, about 28 percent had been born in the village; about 38 percent, in the State of Guerrero. The specific numbers were as follows: 118 born in the village; 79 born in the State of Morelos but not in the village; 151 born in the State of Guerrero; 41 born in the State of Mexico (none born in Mexico City); 6 born in the State of Michoacán; 3 born in other northern states, and 10 born in other southern states. Of the 118 born in the village, 11 had both parents born in the village; 42 had one parent from the village. Of the 25 people born in the village and over thirty-five years of age, 10 had both parents born in the village; 7 had one parent from the village; and 8 had neither parent from the village.

After the distribution of *ejido* land to formerly landless peasants, the village became almost, but not quite, socioeconomically homogeneous. Early distinctions became highly important in the rapid socioeconomic differentiation of the village population over the next thirty years.

THE HACIENDA

From the very first, the State of Morelos was profoundly affected by the Spanish Conquest. The whole of Morelos was, in fact, part of the Marquesado del Valle, the estate given to Cortez, who built its first hacienda and introduced sugarcane.[5] On this basis, Morelos became a state of great feudal landholdings *(latifundios)* and favored the development of the hacienda system.

Before the Revolution, the village was known as a *real,* which is a smaller unit than a *congregación* or a *ranchería* and denotes a population of peons housed by a hacienda. (After the Revolution, because of its growth, it became a *congregación.*) Its owners, the *hacendados,* owned several neighboring haciendas as well as all the land now divided among the villagers; and although at that time only a few dozen peon families lived outside the hacienda walls near the aqueduct, their families, their parents, and the generation before their parents were all products of the hacienda system.

The hacienda was the large privately-owned estate of the Spanish colonists; the land was either an outright grant of the crown or it could be purchased from the crown. Workers were invited to settle on the estate, and for their labor they were given the right to purchase goods on credit or were advanced small sums of money to be repaid through their labor. Peonage bound and perpetuated the labor supply.

Some of the workers lived on hacienda property in villages fairly remote from the hacienda itself, and many of these were renters who paid for the land on which they lived, and sometimes also for land they might wish to farm themselves, with early morning labor *(faenas)*. Others who lived in the village, then a small cluster of thatched *jacales*, or huts, around the hacienda, owned virtually nothing—neither the sites on which their houses were built nor the land they were sometimes permitted to farm.

None of the people in our study had been independent renters before the Revolution. Some had been sharecroppers, turning over a portion of the harvested corn to the hacienda; but sharecropping had been a supplementary activity at best, and most of the sharecroppers were employed by the hacienda in any case. In towns where land was not owned by a hacienda, a few people owned property on a small scale. Indeed, some were small merchants, traders, and storekeepers.

Workers in the hacienda itself, who were somewhat above the field peon in status, did anything from common loading to supervising the sugar refining. It was customary, however, for haciendas to employ a minimal staff and to meet future exigencies through the use of migrant workers. When cane had to be planted, cut, gathered, or transported, migrant laborers were brought in from as far away as Guanajuato, Michoacán, Veracruz, Puebla, and the states of Guerrero and Mexico. Some of these would occasionally remain with the hacienda or join local communities. Thus, the fluidity of populations and community composition was already marked even before the Revolution and the repartitioning of the land.

From the very outset there were marked status differences between many of the families that had immigrated to the village before the Revolution. The Anclillo family was descended from Negro laborers brought in from Veracruz at a time when the hacienda administrator was himself a Spaniard from Veracruz. The Garzelas and Arquillos families had originated in the free village of Tilzapotla. Doña Benita's family had lived in the village but had had lands in the free village of Tesoyuca as well.

A few of the present-day families are descended from a hacienda foreman *(mayordomo)* or supervisor *(capataz)*, each of whom had had a crew of men working under his direction and discipline. Among the original families of the village, Don Mirando's great-grandfather had been a foreman of the hacienda. (This family was among those that did not claim land after the Revolution, reasoning that when the *hacendado* was re-

The old aqueduct from the hacienda

turned to his former power—as in all likelihood he would be—those who had claimed land would lose it and be punished.)

Some of the most eminent families of the village were descendants of *arrieros* (mule drivers), who had worked as small businessmen carrying grain and supplies between haciendas and between haciendas and towns. The *arriero* was quite different from the peon, who led a very poor but somewhat more secure existence as a part of the hacienda. The more independent and venturesome *arriero* ran convoys of mules through territory subject to bandit raids. Banditry was rife throughout the area, terrorizing peons, townspeople, and the wealthy alike. The chief incitement was the possibility of raiding haciendas for money, precious metals, and jewels. Bandits who "specialized" were known as *plateados* for their ostentatious display of silver ornaments. (The *plateado* is enshrined in romantic novels and folklore as an outlaw, but also as a sometime revolutionary.)

Some families felt an emotional attachment to the hacienda even though they owned nothing. Doña Teresa's family, for example, was from the village, but her father and the rest of the family had been ousted from the hacienda to a nearby village because of a minor incident connected with a card game. Although they were well situated where they were, they were happy when an uncle arranged for their return. They had missed the village because it was their *tierra*—their land of birth.

No one remembers that the village ever had a resident priest; then as now, it was served by a visiting priest. Nevertheless, the church was closely connected with the hacienda and its administration throughout the hacienda area. Gruening documents its ideological service on behalf of the hacienda owners and the existing social class system and points out that the church was often supported by deductions made from the earnings of peons by the administrator.[6]

Although older informants recalled dances at the hacienda and bands brought in from other villages—"My father," said Doña Maria, age ninety, "was a *capataz,* and so he was invited to all the dances they used to give"—there was less *de gala* than at other haciendas, less glamour in which the peon could participate at a distance.

On 13 June, the traditional feast day of San Antonio (the village patron saint), and during the Easter season as well, it was customary to celebrate a week of fiesta. The money for these celebrations was raised through the "corn fund," a practice dating from precolonial and colonial times that involved setting aside a portion of the communally-farmed land and supporting religious ceremony with its yield. Later, a certain portion of the yearly harvest was given for the church, and this fund was known as *el renovo*. Corn could be borrowed from the fund, but it had to be returned in double measure. This institution remained intact until the 1930s.

Our hacienda was not the most important in the state before the Revolution; neither was the hacienda system altogether complete here.[7] When the hacienda of a neighboring village was modernized in 1896 and the sugarcane was sent there for milling, our village ceased to function as a direct refining and milling center of sugar and became instead a kind of field center for the agricultural exploitation of the land around it.

To the peon, the hacienda was both a law-making and law-administering institution, and if it had no support from state or federal government in this regard, it had no opposition either. Most *hacendados* did not live in the hacienda but only visited occasionally. Administrators were always Spaniards; foremen, more often mestizo. Villagers recall the relationship between administrators and their own numbers with bitterness. "Undesirables" were expelled and, through a system of blacklisting, were often forced to leave the state (although it was possible to go from a hacienda to a village unaware of such associations). Severe corporal punishment was common, and peons who in any way offended the *hacendado* or administrator were executed.

Tannenbaum argues that the productivity of the hacienda system was very low because the absentee landlords held traditionalist notions of exploitation—i.e., they expected a certain secure income and did not push their administrators for more.[8] Industrially, the hacienda was primitive and inefficient. Large tracts of potential agricultural land were not exploited but were "let out" in shareholding to peons of villages peripheral to the hacienda village. Much land was not used at all. Post-Revolution land reforms brought about a far more extensive use of land in areas that would previously have been regarded as marginal.

The hacienda economy was, moreover, not a "cash economy." Administrators tried to avoid making payments wherever possible, making payment in kind, payment through privilege (land use or grazing rights), or payment in token to be used at the *tienda de raya* (literally, "salary store"). Most of the crops grown by peon shareholders went for subsistence. When the Revolution brought the commercialization of agriculture, the development of cash crops, and crop speculation, the average peon had had little experience in the management of costs against credit and cash returns.

THE RAID ON THE HACIENDAS

In 1856, during the period of Mexican social revolution known as the Reform, an incident involving the village hacienda had national, and even international, repercussions. The incident is worth reporting in detail because it reflects the attitude of those who governed with respect to civil rights, the position of the *hacendado,* the legal relationship between a servant and his master, and Mexico's position toward Spain.

On 17 December 1856, two men of the village, leading two bands of armed men (some from the village), knocked at the door of the hacienda. When the door was not opened to them, they murdered the caretaker and traveled some six kilometers to another hacienda owned by the same *hacendado,* where they found four Spaniards—the owner among them—and a Frenchman in conversation. The Frenchman was spared when he was able to prove his origin, but the Spaniards and the *hacendado* were killed, in spite of the latter's offer of "much, much money" in exchange for his life. The armed men took money in any case, as well as clothing, jewelry, and horses.

The first break in the case came from village gossip. A woman reported that one of the armed men had been dismissed by the Spaniards on the charge that his animals had been damaging the hacienda crop and that on the day of the crime the man's wife had expressed hatred of the owners. She had complained bitterly that his past worth meant nothing to the *hacendados* and that she "wanted only the consolation to see the Spaniards of the hacienda wallow in their own blood." Of the forty-three suspects apprehended, most were released, but the husband was held as the principal figure.

Among those executed were two servants. Servants were required by law in those days to give their lives for their masters when the latter were in danger; failure to do so meant the death penalty.[9] Because one servant had not locked the door, his conduct was judged "perverse and criminal," and the court charged collusion between the "criminal" and the bandits. Although the defense held that one of the accused had always shown good conduct in the past, the judges were unmoved, it being axiomatic that not all the acts of a criminal are bad; indeed, some criminal acts may be heroic. According to the defense, the accused regarded the crime as an act of reprisal against the assassination of some peons by Spanish owners at the Rancho de los Hornos in 1853, adding that there were thirty-one other men in the village who supported him "in spirit."

Two women were executed who had not taken part in the murders, the court reasoning that not to resist an error is to condone it. A mistress of one of the leaders had committed the error of allowing a fine dress to be found in her home; the wife of the other leader was judged culpable because of remarks she had made against Spaniards. Still another person was executed because he had had an idea of what might happen and had failed to report it in advance.

The prosecuting attorney closed his case by describing the motive as "vile vengeance, desire to satisfy particular personal resentments, and the insatiate code of stealing the goods of others." The report disregarded all the arguments for the defense and refused all rights of appeal, reasoning, first, that there were no judicial records of the assassinations by the hacienda owners (!), and secondly, who had given these bandits the right to seek vengeance in any case? The court would have the accused be like General Nicolas Bravo, who, in the War for Independence, had refused to shoot three hundred Spanish prisoners, even though he had been given this right to avenge the death of his father.

The court then took its own vengeance. Some women were sentenced to ten years in prison; the others were publicly executed in the main square of the *Caballito* in Mexico City on 25 September 1858. Two of the accused men were shot, one was strangled, and three were hanged. Their heads were sent to the two haciendas to be hung on the entrance gates as a reminder and warning to the wise.

The Supreme Court report of 1858 categorically denied that the crime had been provoked by anti-Spanish sentiment or class conflict, although it requires little discernment to see that this completely contradicts the facts of the case. The crime was said to be "absolutely lacking in political character . . . . The thirst for robbery was the only thing that armed the hands of the assassins."[10] Such things were, after all, "more common elsewhere than they are here." The report apologized to Spain, promised to give the offended society satisfaction, and assured the Spanish government that all peaceful and productive foreigners were, without exception, secure in the protection of the law.

Although the dramatic climax and bloody mementos of these events were of no small moment, and although *las ruedas* (storytelling circles) were a common amusement at the time and later, few of the older villagers recalled having heard of the hacienda raids of 1856. Individual questioning, accompanied by substantial prodding, evoked a long, reflective silence, and finally, "Oh, you must mean the *plateados*. Yes, we had many of them in Morelos, but mostly around Cuautla and Jojutla." That there should exist virtually no memory of this incident in the village may probably be attributed to the inculcation of fear by those who governed. Magaña has written of the 1856 raids that

> those tales produced an intense sensation in the Republic, and political passions "ran over" in the form of accusations and calumnies. Anger was aimed at generals Alvarez and Leyva, accusing them of being led by the Spanish. These crimes gave rise to strong claims for damages by the Spanish government against Mexico. Spain even considered war against Mexico along with England and France.[11]

Only one man in the village, Federico Garzelas, had heard of the raids; he had been told of them by his uncle and recognized the events as described to him. The outstanding fact for him, however, was a legend of buried money at the hacienda. He said that some of the villagers had actually dug for the alleged treasure and that one man had even induced the governor of the state to send troops while a large excavation was in progress in the hacienda cellar.

Everyone believes to this day that the hacienda remains conceal hidden treasure. There are said to be ghosts of the Zapatistas and federal troops and echoes of crying babies (a certain sign of hidden gold). Perhaps someone in the village will be lucky enough to find the treasure someday, but probably not. In any event, *"los federales"* (meaning the present government) will never find it. It is commonly believed that a new wealth will come out of the hacienda one day. There are always rumors that someone will start a business or some sort of tourist accommodation and that everyone will have work—that, in other words, the old building will give up its treasure to the people at last.

THE AGRARIAN REVOLUTION

Between 1900 and 1910, according to Magana, 189,070 hectares (of which only a small portion was arable land) in the State of Morelos was owned by sixteen persons. [12] Gruening disagrees:

> Despite a great deal of subsequent revolutionary propaganda to indicate that the usually oppressive conditions in Morelos led to its being the "cradle of the Agrarian Revolt," I have found nothing to justify the view that peonage was different or worse than in a dozen other Mexican states, and certainly not as barbarous as in Yucatan which remained peaceful during Madero's revolt against Diaz. The statement most commonly made is that Morelos belonged to a dozen, or 17, or 27 landowners. There were, in fact, some 27 important owning families, some of them related, which may account for the lower estimates in the number of owners, most of them with many children, some of the estates being divided among the numerous progeny of several generations. The entire area of the State of Morelos—excepting Tlaxcala, the smallest in the Republic, is less than half a million hectares (496,400). The average ownership therefore, could not exceed 40,000 hectares, and making allowance for towns, railways, roads, etc., considerably less. These were large holdings, but other states contained many larger. In my judgment the outburst in Morelos, based on feudal conditions which to be sure existed there but were little different from elsewhere in Mexico, was due to the accident of Zapata's personal leadership. [13]

The facts of the 1910 Revolution have been admirably detailed and documented elsewhere. [14] This section does not attempt a historical reconstruction of its events but presents for the most part the subjective memories and impressions and certain present-day notions of the conflict as these were found in the village.

The Revolution was anticipated in the State of Morelos in the 1909 gubernatorial campaign between General Patricio Leyva and Colonel Pablo Escandón. Leyva opposed *haciendismo,* and it was in his behalf that Emiliano Zapata first became involved in politics in the area of Cuautla. It is said that although Leyva won the election, the government imposed Escandón on the state and that the revolutionary uprising grew directly out of this.

At any rate, the Revolution began in Morelos on 7 February 1911.

At the very beginning of the conflict, when Francisco Madero was the new chief executive in Mexico City, the village hacienda was abandoned by its owners and in 1913 was burned; some attribute the burning to Maderistas, but Federico was told by his uncle that it was done by troops of General Victoriano Huerta, one of the best combat officers in the Mexican pre-Revolutionary Army, who earned his rank crushing revolts in the south, especially in Guerrero in 1890. (At the end of the Revolution, the hacienda was owned by a bank and subsequently passed into private ownership by a series of sales.) It is also known that Madero's troops at some point evacuated the people of the village and reconcentrated them in other villages. The reassignment was done in Cuernavaca over a period of several months. At that time a forced levy pressed many young men from the area into the army to fight in the north.

Later, a government garrison was stationed at the hacienda, but following a conflict with Zapata forces, the village came under Zapata's control and the garrison was withdrawn. Zapata's general headquarters were nearby in Tlaltizapan, and, according to the village secretary who lived in the village at the time, Zapata is said to have visited on occasion. The secretary says that Zapata had a girl in the village who worked at the hacienda store and that he also came to the village for gambling and cockfighting.

Whether battles were fought in the village itself we were not able to ascertain. It has been said that no battles took place in the village, but one old villager insists that five people were killed there in one day, and Doña Isabel describes federal corpses piled up in what is now the village square. Then very young, she vividly remembers that she and others of the village had picked over the bodies for money and jewelry, that the bodies were burned, and that fat ran off them in streams. Doña Benita told us that a major battle between government forces and Zapatistas was fought at a nearby village. Although the government suffered heavy losses in this engagement, the government returned, she said, and drove out the people of that village, who came to our village while their homes were burned.

Most of the people presently of our village, however, had not yet arrived, not even in Morelos, and while their experiences spread over a wide area, they were all affected by the disaster. Those from the states of Guerrero and Mexico report that they were constantly on the run from their villages for about ten years. They speak almost unanimously of the opposing sides being equivalent in terms of the suffering imposed on nonparticipating civilians.

Garrisons of troops were placed in their towns and villages; crops and animals were seized. Everyone speaks of *andando en el serro* (wandering and hiding in the mountains), of hunger, of living on herbs and grasses, of sickness, smallpox, and exposure, and of constant flight. Women routinely fled, if at all possible, at any news of approaching forces. Those whose husbands were away fighting, or perhaps attending to some business that might provide food, hid with their small children in ravines, caves, and other remotenesses to protect themselves against rape. Many women speak of the absolute necessity of hiding girls over ten or twelve years of age for fear of abduction.

Many of our informants had been under fire. Don Pascual and his father (who was with one of the armies) started out from the State of Mexico and moved from place to place until his father died and Pascual was left on his own. Doña Gabriela and her two-year-old son fled from village to village (she had another son, Roque, during this time), selling their pigs, goats, and donkeys. Doña Teresa's family was also relatively well-to-do. Her mother had remarried; her stepfather had fourteen cows, some chickens, corn, and rice, and they were able to buy other things with the milk and eggs they sold. The worst period of hunger, she says, was after the Revolution and their return to the village, when they ate only grasses "without salt."

Filomena (whose brother, she says, was a colonel with Zapata) spent this time in the State of Guerrero and tells of fleeing with the girls of her village at every approach of soldiers; she also reports the rapes and horrors recounted by other women. Occasionally they slept in trees or hid in churches, feigning prayer when anyone entered. They would sometimes exist for three or four days on nothing but herbs or perhaps sweet potatoes. Not until the war was over did they feel it safe to appear in exposed places where government troops were establishing the peace.

Most of our informants declared that government men and Zapatistas posed an equal threat. The majority regarded themselves as *pacificos,* or nonparticipants, and there are many jokes from the period that reflect civilian eagerness to express the appropriate deference to whichever side made an appearance. When the Zapatistas came, one wore *cotones* (traditional Indian pants of handwoven cloth); for the *federales,*

Don Pascual

Ted Schwartz

one changed routinely into *regulares* (federal uniforms). When troops came through shouting "Viva Madero" or "Viva Victoriano Huerta" or "Viva Zapata," citizens had to declare the correct cry in advance at the risk of their lives.

Villagers today have mixed emotions about the Revolution, but almost all dwell on the insecurity and suffering it caused and on the relief found in the restoration of peace and order. The question of what ends were gained will be taken up later, but Doña Benita's reply is characteristic of women informants:

None, none, because only the liberty that there is now of lands and that we now own our own house sites. That is all, but from there on we got nothing out of it, only great frights, long journeys, hunger in the hills, fractures, and all that sort of thing. Because it was a suffering. While the Revolution was being established it was a suffering for us. There was no work. One's little plantings, that's how we got along, don't you know? The Zapatista would come and run off with the *maiz,* the government troops would come and seize the chickens, and everyone came to do us harm.

Don Victoriano alone glories in the fighting. He claims to have been a prominent Zapatista captain and has since then tried to exploit this in his activities in state politics and in a national organization known as the Veterans of the Revolution. Villagers assure us, however, that he is a liar and that he greatly exaggerates his position and participation alike. Don Adolfo, one of the oldest men in the village, who claims to have fought throughout the Revolution, reports no retrospective sense of glory, only much the same memory that others describe—suffering relieved only by the cessation of the war.[15]

Although the majority of the villagers now sympathize with Zapata, seeing him as the source of land and liberty and themselves as his beneficiaries, this view has its dissenters, Abel Arquillos among them. Abel is from the village of Buenavista de Cuellar, in Guerrero, near the Morelos border (at present a town of about three thousand people), where a Zapatista garrison was once stationed. The garrison forced levies upon the men, but the village remained tolerant and *pacifico,* supplying food and cattle for the garrison and Zapata's larger army for more than a year, even though its resources scarcely sufficed for anyone. The breaking point came when the garrison demanded six young girls and the village was given one day in which to comply.

That night, at a meeting in the hills outside the village, the villagers decided to fight. With only seventeen guns, they surprised the garrison, seized its arms, and subdued it. Then they ambushed other Zapatista garrisons and supply trains, and by the time a siege was launched against Buenavista they had about five hundred arms. Zapata's army attempted repeatedly to enter the town, which is located in rugged mountainous country, but the attempts were repelled. Prisoners captured by the Zapatistas are said to have been tortured or mutilated and left in the mountains to die. A request for aid was dispatched to a federal general garrisoned in Acapulco, but this help arrived only after twenty-nine days of siege.

The men of Buenavista joined the government army and aided in the campaign against Zapata in Guerrero and Morelos. Abel's family became Carranzistas, favoring agrarian reform by constitutional means. In many ways a conservative, Don Abel claims that many of the land reform ideas were Carranza's and that most of the gains attributed to Zapata are unjustified. Buenavista provided our village with the influential Arquillos family and some of the relatives of Federico Garzelas. Don Catalino, a relative of Abel and also from Buenavista, is a fervent Zapatista, however, principally because he believes that he resembles him morally and physically.

In general, then, to the people of our village the Revolution meant hardship, starvation, endless flight, the disruption of families, armed violence, and death. For some men it meant opportunism; for others (although this is not characteristic of our village), a dedication to the ideals of revolution. Although one side is considered to have been as bad as the other, there are varying degrees of Zapatista sympathy and a feeling of indebtedness for land distribution. (The Buenavista opposition is a distinct conservative element related chiefly to the personal experiences of the immigrants from that town.) The emphasis on hardship persists in spite of the many patriotic holidays in Mexico commemorating the Revolution.

Villagers tend to see the Revolution as a conflict between Zapata, on behalf of the peasantry, and the government (which they sometimes identify with the present government). At other times they say that it was really a war against the Spanish (gachupines)—an association of the Spanish hacendado, the rich, the government, and the leader of a political faction. Those who opposed the existing system saw their struggle in terms of putting an end to the past and to haciendismo, the residue of feudal land ownership and serfdom. The general notion was that a new government would be formed with the consent of the governed that would devote itself to the welfare of the poor. At the heart of it all, however, was the hope for land.

But Zapata's agrarismo did not offer a utopian blueprint for the future. There was little attempt to spell out the form of a future government, of a new economic system, or even of the relations between men in a new society. If some leaders entertained the idea of the *ejido* or the cooperative organization of rural society, it was neither expressed nor discussed among the revolutionaries who fought under Zapata, nor was it evident in the period immediately after the Revolution when land was actually being divided.

It is said in our village that Zapata did not institute a revolutionary division of land among the peasants, but that many peasants began to seize land (with Zapata's approval) while the fighting was still in progress and before it was legal to do so. The formal division of land had begun under Carranza, who had attempted by a proclamation of 1915 to win over the Zapatistas by means of land partition. Land division did not occur to any appreciable extent, however, until roughly 1919. Don Federico reports that engineers first began to survey the village land for repartition around 1919-20.

POST-REVOLUTION VILLAGE

Although the armed struggle ended in Morelos around 1920, the Revolution itself did not end abruptly. There was a long tapering off of armed violence and disorder, and many years passed before a stable government was established in Morelos.[16] Villages had their own groups of armed men—ostensibly for defense, though they were guilty of many abuses—well into the 1930s. Although the federal and state governments gradually disarmed local militias and "defense corps," the arms of the Revolution supported local factions in some villages, while banditry and armed local or factional conflict remained common until about 1940.

The village population began to reassemble in 1919. Families that had fled began to return, and new families were already being integrated into the village (Don Pio, for example, claims that his family came to settle in the village before many of the original families had returned).

The formal division of land began when the village *Ejido* was formed under the village's own *Comité Administrativo Agrario* in 1924. At that time village residents and early comers had their choice of land, of which there was then more than enough for years to come. Some selected an *ejido*, others did not. Later, because its population was considered insufficient to use and exploit effectively the large amount of land expropriated from the hacienda, the village lost a substantial portion of its *Ejido* to a neighboring village. Eventually only 120 hectares were left to the village *Ejido*, with 90 hectares of the best land given to the hacienda as private property.

Villagers who hold any land at all today hold it by virtue of being *ejidatarios*. The *ejidatarios* who originally received land parcels had all formerly been landless peasants, many of them from areas much poorer and more remote than Morelos. Attracted by the year-round work that the water supply made possible, many continued to work as day laborers even when there was no more land to be distributed.

Although 1927–30 was the main period of land repartition and immigration to the village, by 1926 some of the early immigrants had already arrived, received *ejidos,* and begun planting rice. (The planting of cane and other crops, such as rice, that require careful cultivation and irrigation, was suspended from roughly 1911 through 1935. Corn and beans were sporadically planted between the predations of federal and revolutionary forces.)

By 1930, when the land was almost completely partitioned, the population of the village was 250–300 persons. Those who came later received land only upon the cession of an *ejido* parcel by another family that had lost it, either by not working the land or by leaving the village. Thus as the population increased after 1930, the proportion of *ejidatarios* declined. By 1961, there were fifty-nine, usually heads of families, in a population of approximately 800 people.

Land division is considered to have formally ended in 1935, a year of heavy crop losses for the village but the beginning of a period of greater security for the new *ejidatarios*. President Lazaro Cardenas formed the Ejido Bank, making credit available for the first time to advance planting expenses. In 1935 or early 1936, under the leadership of the hacienda's private owner, the *ejidatarios* began once again to plant sugarcane after an interruption of almost twenty-five years. At the same time, President Cardenas began the sugar cooperative and sugar refinery in a large town nearby. Seed was provided for the first planting for the entire region the sugar cooperative serves, and everyone planted at least one-third of his land in sugarcane.

The first sugarcane harvest in the region was milled and refined by the refinery at Zacatepec in 1938, a period of high hopes that the cooperative would bring cane workers the benefits promised them by Cardenas. Relations with the Ejido Bank were satisfactory, and no thefts of any magnitude had yet taken place. The village, however, was internally divided between those who gave their allegiance to Don Pio, who had become the village's most important political leader, and a group of progressives who looked for leadership to the village schoolteacher and Federico Garzelas.

The only serious conflict to occur between this and another village arose in 1927. The nonsulfurous, nonsalt water that is used to irrigate the valley passes through the lands of a number of neighboring villages before it reaches our village *Ejido*. This water is used by all the villages along the course of the streams coming down from the head of the valley, so that any village can divert the water and use an unfair proportion of it for irrigation.

In 1927, village "T" had virtually cut off the water flowing to our village, and while the latter still had water from the springs, this was inadequate. Indignant, a group of unarmed men from the village went to village "T", where two of them were killed and three wounded. Our village did not retaliate with armed violence, and although the case was brought to the municipal court, there is no record that the men of village "T" were ever punished.

The years 1930 to 1937 brought a certain sense of community, above the subsistence level of existence, to the people of the village, though this was not unaccompanied by setbacks. Assisted by a school-teacher, villagers staged a series of theatricals during these years. In 1935, people from a neighboring village performed a Passion play in the village; but the *maiz de fondo*—the special "corn fund" used to finance the village fiesta on the week of San Antonio—was borrowed from and never reimbursed, and what remained in the fund was said to have been stolen by the man who administered it. Thus ended the old tradition of the church corn fund; thereafter all church activities and festivals were supported by cash collections.

Theatricals were revived briefly in 1942. In the same year a village band was formed under the leadership of Don Pio and the management of Doña Teresa (according to one report, the village itself raised the money to buy the instruments and pay the music teacher; according to another version, the village petitioned the governor for the instruments). Since

Carrying sugar cane to the refinery

1942, the costly main village fiesta has been discontinued, and 1952 is given as the year of the last *jaripeo* (village bullfight and rodeo).

In 1936 the school was under the direction of an influential teacher who introduced basketball and other sports to the village, formed the Youth Club (which has persisted as a sporting club), and began the village's cooperative store, possibly in response to the new wave of cooperatives throughout the area. In 1937 another teacher, much loved and well remembered, took over the promotion of the cooperative store; but in July 1939, in the first of a series of thefts, 200 pesos were stolen from the store, and the thefts of the justice of the peace from 1940 to 1942 put an end to the cooperative. The justice of the peace was only one of a series of managers whose embezzlements eventually left the store without capital.

Although he was brought to court and promised to reimburse the village in part, this promise was never kept.

In 1937 the schoolteacher began planning a more orderly arrangement of the village, and in 1938–39 the reorganization began, with streets laid in place of winding paths among the houses that had arisen haphazardly as new families had joined the community. The prospect of traffic entering the village and of future tourism induced most villagers to accept the change. The meetings and work of rebuilding took place between 1940 and 1942. In 1943, the last man to oppose moving his house to make way for a new street was killed in a gambling brawl; 1943 thus "places" the completion of the village for our villagers. (Although there have been many acts of violence that might have resulted in death, there have been no murders in the village from 1956 to the present.)

In 1937, under the initiative of Don Federico, the village drew up petitions to obtain potable water, acting on an announcement of a government program for extending potable water. On behalf of the entire area, the village called a meeting of a group of villages, but it would take twenty-three years of petitions, fund raising, demonstrations, and trips to Mexico City before potable water was obtained in 1960 with the installation of hydrants and tubing. To this end, the village had raised approximately sixty thousand pesos over the years.

In 1938 the hacienda belonged to an Englishman who owned very large plantations in Veracruz as well. Wishing to sell out in Morelos, he offered the hacienda to the village at a very low price—fifty thousand pesos for the hacienda and the entire ninety hectares (the land was far more valuable than the buildings). But according to those who wanted to buy, it was impossible to enlist the support of the entire village, and a group headed by Don Pio was vigorously opposed to the purchase. The group that wished to buy had three years to pay the full amount and hoped to do so by cultivating the hacienda's total acreage; but the group lacked the money to exploit this large area fully and failed in the attempt. Their idea had been to build a bathing resort (balneario), and this idea would persist significantly among certain elements in the village. At the end of three years, however, they sold the hacienda for ninety-two thousand pesos, and while this represented a profit, the hacienda was then lost to the village, probably forever, because its value and cost multiplied thereafter.

The formation of the sugar cooperative, the building of the Ayudantía (town hall and community center), the beginning of the new school, the introduction of electricity—such were the events defining progress and development in the village. The Ayudantía was built at the instigation of Don Pio in 1939. Under the initiative of Don Federico (then, as now, postmaster and postman), direct mail service began in 1944. The new school, begun by Don Pio with the help of the sugar refinery, was built in 1945—the village raising three thousand pesos, the refinery paying the rest. A fête for the manager of the refinery in 1948 brought a new roof for the schoolhouse.

During the 1946 Aleman-Padilla presidential campaign an important change occurred in the village's internal politics. Don Pio was an Alemanista, but the majority of the village backed Padilla, and Don Federico led the Padilla group. Thereafter, the form of internal factionalism changed in the village, for it was believed that Padilla had actually won the election even though Aleman was given the office.

The village began its efforts to obtain electricity in 1947. In 1949, 17,300 pesos were collected for this purpose; the money was advanced by the sugar refinery and repaid by deductions from the return on cane. But electric lighting was not installed in the village until 14 December 1955, and then only after many petitions and failures. This date—which marks the introduction of electric lighting in the houses and streets and the inception of the radio—has become the "sophisticated" annual holiday in the village, for which a "big dance band" is brought from Cuernavaca.

In 1949 a paved road bypassing the village was begun, mainly for the transport of cane. In 1954 a Rural Welfare Center was initiated under the direction of a rural welfare social worker who had been a schoolteacher in the village. The same year the Society of Ejidatarios built a rice warehouse and rice-drying platforms on the site of the former bullring. A crop insurance program was begun shortly thereafter. In 1960 a new bridge was constructed, the cement and money donated by a politically-motivated businessman from Cuernavaca. In 1961, hourly bus service through the village was available for the first time.

That the village is of relatively recent formation does not diminish its intrinsic interest. If it lacks the continuity of centuries of communal tradition, it still exhibits many of the important dynamic characteristics and future uncertainties of present-day rural Mexico. Land, poverty, and wealth remain the foci of its history and social relations, but neither Hispanic, Indian, nor even Mexican elements will shape its further cultural development. The world itself will decide its future.

---

[1] Nathan Whetten, *Rural Mexico* (Chicago: University of Chicago Press, 1948), p. 7.

[2] We were not able to learn the year of its construction.

[3] For our data and analysis of actual land use, see T. Schwartz, "L'usage de la terre dans un village a Ejido du Mexique," *Etudes rurales* 10 (1963): 37–49.

[4] The Catalino case is discussed in detail in chapter 7. Briefly, it concerns the course of litigation over questions of land and water rights between one man and a group of persons representing the village. The case is significant in calling attention to various moral and legal implications of the agrarian reforms instituted by the Revolution and to the various agencies to which the litigants had recourse.

[5] Cited by Ernest Gruening, *Mexico and Its Heritage* (New York: Century, 1928), p. 115; from Puga, Cedulario, *Provisiones, cedulas, instrucciones de su Magestad-desde el año de 1525 hasta este presente de 63,* 2 vols. (Mexico, 1878).

[6] Gruening, *Mexico and Its Heritage,* pp. 211–28.

[7] For descriptions of hacienda life, see Mme Calderón de la Barca, *Life in Mexico during a Residence of Two Years in That Country* (reprint ed., Mexico: Tolteca, 1952); Gruening, *Mexico and Its Heritage;* Frank Tannenbaum, *The Mexican Agrarian Revolution* (New York: Macmillan Co., 1929); Lesley Byrd Simpson, *Many Mexicos* (Berkeley: University of California Press, 1950); and Eric Wolf, *Sons of the Shaking Earth* (Chicago: University of Chicago Press, 1959).

[8] Tannenbaum, *The Mexican Agrarian Revolution,* pp. 105–106.

[9] Mexico, Accusación fiscal de la Suprema Corte de Justicia, *En la causa instruida a varios reos, por el asalto, robos y asesinatos cometidos la noche del 17 y mañana del 18 de Dic. de 856* (Mexico: Imprenta de A. Boix, 1858), p. 22.

[10] Ibid., p. v.

[11] General Gildardo Magaña, *Emiliano Zapata y el agrarismo en Mexico,* 5 vols. (Mexico: Ruta, 1951), p. 35.

[12] Ibid., p. 39.

[13] Gruening, *Mexico and Its Heritage,* pp. 142–43.

[14] For an excellently researched narrative history, see John Womack, Jr., *Zapata and the Mexican Revolution* (New York: Alfred A. Knopf, 1969).

[15] See Ricardo Pozas, *Juan Perez Jolote: biografía de un Tzotzil* (Mexico: Escuela Nacional de Antropologia e Historia, 1948) for the experiences of a peasant soldier.

[16] See Gruening, *Mexico and Its Heritage,* pp. 465–67; also Womack, *Zapata and the Mexican Revolution.*

2

ON CONFLICT

FORMS OF CONFLICT

Individuals and groups may conflict in a variety of ways. Before discussing conflict in terms of group and social relations, however, it is necessary to provide a framework for organizing and understanding its occurrence. This section will suggest such a framework and illustrate its relevance, although the framework will not be exhaustively used here as an analytic device. The material that follows should be viewed against, rather than within, this framework. Generalizations should be understood as describing village conflicts, even when the village is not specifically mentioned. Unless otherwise specified, discussions describe interpersonal, rather than intrapersonal, conflicts.

Individuals may conflict with one another over particular interests or status claims on a personal basis. They may also conflict as members of groups, in which case the conflict may be between themselves and particular members of the group or generalized between two or more groups.

"Unbound individual conflict" means that individuals act in their own personal behalf and not as members of a larger unit. The unbound group likewise acts in and for itself and not as a subgroup. Unbound individual conflict may be illustrated by the numerous conflicts between women with claims on the same man; groups are not involved here, although small groups or alliances may form around the principals in the conflict. Antagonism between unbound individuals or groups is exemplified in the case of a group of women accused of witchcraft as against the weak group of opponents and critics they collectively or individually generate. These two, small, opposed, informal groupings are specific to the conflict and not part of a larger grouping. If, for example, each of the groups in the witchcraft case had chosen a different *patron* as protector, they could have aligned themselves with a larger grouping and placed their conflict in a larger context. This, however, did not occur.

In contrast to the "unbound" are "bound" individuals or groups. Many individual conflicts have arisen from the alliance of different persons with various opposed factions that have come down from the past. A father-son conflict may thus occasionally be cast in terms of the larger group conflict, as when each is allied to opposing factions. An individual may also be in conflict with both sides of an issue in which he does not wish to become involved because his neutrality is suspect by both sides. This was the case in the relation of members of the study to almost any conflict in the village—in the attempt of both factions in the witchcraft dispute, for example, to read into the slightest gesture an affirmation favoring their own side. The tendency toward binding is very strong. Individuals in conflict seek alliances; groups in conflict tend to see everyone as being either for or against them. There is a tendency to interpret any association as alliance and to regard neutrality as betrayal.

Bound and unbound conflict are not always mutually exclusive. An intermediary case, such as the antagonism between Victoriano and Federico, is a highly personalized affair involving constant citation by each of the other's peculations; but this conflict probably reflects past group affiliations dating back to early village factions, when Victoriano supported Federico's enemy. Old group conflicts may survive and become individual unbound conflicts long after the group context has disappeared. The conflict between Federico and Doña Teresa, for example, stems from the early factions of immigrants and progressives on the one hand and native conservatives on the other.

Unbound individual conflict and low-level unbound group conflict are extremely prevalent—few villagers are not involved in some of these. Their prevalence would seem to suggest an atomistic structure of conflict and an atomistic social structure generally; but to the extent that conflict, or conflicts, may generate groups—so that conflicts become primarily a group affair and only secondarily an affair of their individual members as persons—the conflicts that bind may actually promote a more solid social structure. Assessing the solidarity or atomism of a social system depends not only on the prevalence or absence of conflict, but also on the relation between bound and unbound conflict.

LEVELS OF CONFLICT

Conflict-involved groups exist on various levels; the author distinguishes particularly between conflict-generated groupings and groups whose conflicts have other institutional bases. The numerous temporary and unstable alliances that form among women bearing a mutual hostility toward another woman or group of women is characteristic of informal group organization around a conflict. The *Sociedad Pro-balneario,* a formally organized and registered cooperative created during the Catalino conflict, exemplifies this type as well.

On the other hand, the conflict between a neighborhood—in this case, a neighborhood consisting of small homesites created by separate illegal purchases of an *ejido* parcel—and the rest of the village over this neighborhood's "rights" is a group conflict not initially formed over the conflict itself. Another example of the type of conflict in which the group antedates the conflict itself arises when the various branches of a family in a village are in conflict with one another.

That group-generated and group-involving conflicts differ in character will readily be seen. In general, the group having an institutional basis antecedent to the conflict will be the more stable, effective group. Groups specifically organized around, and generated by, a conflict are unstable because they lack the continuity that would maintain them beyond the immediate vicissitudes of the conflict—e.g., the highly unstable, shifting alliances of women against other women tend to split over friction within the group itself.

The fragility of such groups is to a certain extent countered by formal organization (such as that of the *Sociedad Pro-balneario*), but the strains within the group are nevertheless extreme. The *sociedad* thus tries to "be" the village, asserts that it represents the village in litigation, and sees its opposition as, first, a person, then as a family, and finally as a family with allies and outside supporters. But it requires the presence of common hostility to sustain its unity, and villagers confidently predict that its unity will fragment the moment hostility is abated or removed. Thus, although groupings generated around a conflict tend to form larger units contributing to a more organized social structure, their fragility nevertheless reflects an atomistic base.

Social massing takes place around conflicts in such a way as to form larger groups, and these groups take their place in the social structure along with groups not primarily formed by conflict, but having other institutional bases. These other groups, however, are also susceptible to schism and dissolution from interpersonal conflict, reflecting the general process that ultimately weakens all groups and relations—even those with multiple institutional bases, such as a family and its extended branches or the village itself and its various subgroupings.

Numerous examples can be found of families thus fragmented, or "broken down" from family unit into smaller units. There might be the loss to the family of some individual or segment, or the family might be divided into several factions so that the larger unit is no longer effective in providing cooperative mutual support. The village likewise tends to break down along the lines of its various subgroupings into conflicting-interest groups. Probably all groupings organized around conflict will tend to cut across the lines of groupings organized on other institutional bases.

SIZE OF CONFLICT

It is useful to distinguish and classify conflicts according to magnitude. Conflicts vary greatly in scale, on the basis of a micradic–macradic continuum. At the micradic end there are "two-person" conflicts, or those in which the number engaged is small and the conflict individualized. Larger, or macradic, conflicts begin at any point where personal differentiation yields to a more impersonal group orientation. (The scale might be extended from the intrapersonal conflict through two-person conflict, through the micradic and macradic levels.)

Two generalizations can be made with regard to scale of conflict.

1. Conflicts between individuals tend to grow in scale and to involve increasingly more individuals—family members, friends, or associates—in still other conflicts. There is a kind of outward radiation of micradic conflicts that is at least partly predictable from a knowledge of the network of relations in which an individual is involved at the time of the conflict. Although the spiral from the micradic to the macradic level is neither inevitable nor even especially characteristic, it can happen—in the conflict between the neighborhood and the village, for example. To the neighborhood people, the antagonist becomes an indefinite "they," referring to the larger group, although the latter is not formalized.

2. Macradic conflicts tend to have a micradic base or to become essentially micradic-personal. The basic interpersonal relations characterized here as atomistic are probably reflected in this tendency, so that, on the village level, the formation of a truly macradic agent in conflict with another group or individual would seem unlikely. Even the largest of groupings tend to identify with their most vocal representatives, with the result that the conflict assumes a micradic form, as if it were between the representatives of the group rather than between the groups themselves.

This is true of the Catalino dispute. The focus of Catalino's antagonism toward the opposition varies. At times he has focused on Don Pio; at other times, on Don Federico. The point is that he sees the contest as between himself and one or the other of these two men, or perhaps between himself and a small group of instigators. For its part, the opposition has a vested interest in group identification; that there is a macradic rationale in their position is part of the justification for their position. They insist that each individual is representative of the group and that the group is representative of the village. This case, which will be discussed in detail in chapter 7, illustrates the extent to which forms of conflict can be mixed depending on the moral positions, strategies, and interests of the participants.

STABLE AND UNSTABLE CONFLICTS

Conflicts can also be characterized by their tendency to approach resolution or to remain stabilized over long periods of time. A conflict may be resolved by either the disengagement of the parties involved or by a removal of the cause of conflict. An unstable conflict is one still in motion, tending toward a resolution in either separation or union.

Stabilized conflict is of great importance as a structural feature, because conflicts that endure with few changes over a long period of time contribute lines of opposition that eventually become an informal part of village organization. Much of the recent history of the village can be structurally characterized in terms of stabilized conflict. From about 1924 to the early 1940s, culminating perhaps in the 1950s and then subsiding with the restriction placed on village ceremonial, thirty-five years of village history can be seen in terms of conflicts between factions of progressive immigrants and conservative natives.

Instability can be introduced, of course, when one conflict exacerbates or terminates another. The protracted conflict between the Federico and Pio factions, for example, has been largely (at least temporarily) eclipsed by the Catalino conflict, with the result that the two men are increasingly reconciled as the two "movers" of the anti-Catalino group. Catalino has often pointed out that the village owes much of its unity to its union against him.

In addition to temporal stability, there is also stability in level and size of conflict. A conflict may change in size or type over time and not change its micradic or macradic character, or it may be unstable in this regard, changing in both size and level. One may speak, too, of the presence or absence of stability with respect to issues and personnel. Conflict in the village is more closely tied to interests and persistent antagonisms than to issues. Since a conflict is affected by all previous conflicts among its personnel, alignments are primarily a matter of interests and only secondarily a matter of personnel. The issues themselves have the least relevance and weight.

DIMENSIONS OF CONFLICT RESOLUTION

The first dimension is that of stabilization as against resolution of the conflict; the second defines the formality or informality of its mode of resolution. A conflict may be resolved by such relatively informal means as the intervention of friends or family or by such more formal, institutionalized means as arbitration by a village official or litigation in the higher courts. Finally, the material on conflict may be organized in terms of the level of recourse for its resolution—i.e., the conflict may be voluntarily contained on a lower level of recourse (kept within the village), or it may be brought to the municipal, district, or federal courts or finally to the president of the republic.

3

CONFLICT: GROUP AND SOCIAL RELATIONS

IN-GROUP AND OUT-GROUP RELATIONS

What can be said about village solidarity with respect to internal conflict? Although there is unmistakably an inclination toward factionalism and lower-level conflicts, factions have tended in time (and generally without violence) to work out a relationship, so that their differences have not induced permanent cleavages. Very little of the violence that has occurred in the village is directly attributable to factional dispute. Village solidarity is strong enough to contain factions until some species of reconciliation is possible—until the issue has become outmoded, for example, or until the issue has been transcended by the common experience of the group.

Above all, perhaps, village solidarity is ultimately a matter of belonging; for this is a culture that attaches great value to place of birth, and the sense of being a member and citizen of the village is important. The question of whether an individual is "from" the village brings different responses from those who, like their parents, were born here; those who, though born here, were the children of immigrants; and those who, though immigrants themselves, have been residents for many years. On the whole, assimilation is swift because the village is considered by its residents to be unusually attractive, and most of those who come from elsewhere eventually stay. Some do not, of course, and it is unfortunate that so little is known about them.

Those who stay become village members in some respects but not entirely in others. Some retain connections with their natal village, and many return there to marry. The Arquillos have connections in Buenavista de Cuellar; the Garzelas have family in Puente de Ixtla and Tilzapotla; Blanca and her husband are to be found once a week in their village in Toluca (State of Mexico); and others maintain connections in Chalma and Almolonga (Guerrero). The village is the base, however—especially if one owns at least a homesite, if not an *ejido*. The village even holds an attraction for day workers *(jornaleros)*, who not only own nothing, but are troubled and resentful at not being regarded as thoroughly "of" the village. Nevertheless, the cohesiveness of the village is so attractive that migrant laborers have returned to it after trips to Mexico City and even to the United States.

There are now indications that an expanding work market, coupled with an orientation away from rural life and agricultural labor, will cause increasing numbers of people to leave the village and seek wider alternatives elsewhere. It is doubtful, however, that any gradualized leaving pattern will ever substantially alter the basically irregular, nonsegmentable structure of the village. Factions are organized around an intricate network of alliances, dependencies, and patronages and are not really segmentable parts of the village. Although the village will inevitably lose persons, that it will lose whole groups is doubtful, unless an entire faction becomes identified with one group—if, for example, Catalino's whole family should leave.

Villagers have a strong sense of identity, partly because the village is believed to have a strong character of its own: it is said to be peaceful, civilized, progressive, and "sophisticated" and to exhibit a greater civic spirit than other, comparable villages. Most of the villagers subscribe to this view, evidence to the contrary notwithstanding, and the almost uniform acceptance of this image may affect village relations in time— indeed, may have done so already. The frequent assertions of the village's peaceful nature, for instance, suggest a fundamental belief in the value of conflict resolution by peaceful means rather than by the older *macho* tradition of violence.

Perhaps one of the greatest deterrents to individual violence is the knowledge that a killer will have to leave the village and begin again elsewhere, leaving behind all the advantages that established residence has to offer. He may go to another place where he has a friend or relative, but he will nevertheless be someone *que no es de aqui*—an outsider and nonentity, "not of here" or of anywhere else either since he is unable to return to his original village. Village solidarity, then, is strengthened and reinforced by means of community image, sense of identity, and an awareness of the positive advantages of belonging.

Although the village has no formal internal subdivisions, some neighborhoods are informally called *"colonias"* and given derogatory names. *Colonia de la Rata Muerta*—"Dead Rat Colony"—comprises a group of homesites illegally alienated from the *ejido* of an inveterate alcoholic. The people of this *colonia* were united against the village on the basis of their illegal holdings and their attempt to impede village action to dispossess them. Although they resisted a compromise measure which sought to formalize individual holdings, reduce their size to five hundred meters, and thereby allocate *sitios* to more people, this was eventually accomplished anyway.

Another neighborhood singled out for village scorn consists of a group of houses, belonging to peons in the lower acculturation gradient, around Don Pascual's place. This is the *Colonia Cantaranas* ("singing frogs"), because its inhabitants are fond of singing traditional songs and ballads to guitar accompaniment. This *colonia* is by no means unified, however; it is ridden with bitter internal conflict. A new *colonia* established on the disputed communal land near Don Catalino's *ejido* was conceived in conflict and is an instrument in the Catalino case. Catalino claims the land on the basis of use, and those who collectively represent the village will have to show that the land had been "settled" for a given length of time to have a legitimate claim according to the *Código Agrario.*

Other village neighborhoods are not singled out in this manner. Far from being a basis for the formation of an affable neighborhood group, proximity of dwellings appears to be a good basis for conflict, a common source of quarreling being the real or imagined boundaries of lots. At times a group of this type will be united by kinship ties, however, and this variety of residential grouping will be discussed later.

VILLAGE FACTIONS

In the period immediately following the Revolution, the village was chiefly divided on the basis of immigrants and natives (i.e., families formerly attached to the hacienda). The natives, a very small group, did not claim much of the land to which they were now entitled and some claimed no land at all, possibly because of their acceptance of the traditional peon role, a lingering memory of the old system by which they had been attached to the hacienda, or perhaps because of a fear that the former owners would return. Although differences must have existed among these natives, little is known about this.

The immigrants were people who had uprooted themselves from their land of birth, left their relatives behind, and come without connections to the village in family units, hoping to obtain land. Later arrivals followed relatives to the village, but the latter were by then assimilated into the group that regarded itself as the rightful inheritors of the soil. Natives exhibited some hostility toward incoming groups but did not attempt to exclude them from the village or from community affairs.

Old immigrants report that the natives used to work half-days, which was decidedly not the labor pattern of the hacienda. This may have been owing to a lack of means to cultivate the land or simply a deliberate reduction of effort that had formerly been obligatory. The newcomers, on the other hand, worked a very long, hard day, and their industriousness was resented by the natives, who called them *los hambrientes* ("the hungering ones"). *Los hambrientes,* however, would eventually become *ejidatarios* and would increasingly influence (though remain uninfluenced by) the village. Some of the families of higher status, already somewhat differentiated among the natives, began gradually to associate themselves with the immigrants, and thus arose the first factional division between progressives and traditionalists.

The progressives were led by the Arquillos, the Garzelas (Federico's family), and to a certain extent by Don Pio, who were later joined in secondary leadership by the families of Manuel Gamos and Juana. The progressive campaign from about 1928 to 1930 would result in a redesign of the village in the early 1940s and a liquidation of the more costly village ceremonials in the early 1950s. (The progressives believed that the village should sacrifice expensive ceremonial in the interests of progress—electricity, schools, potable water, and so forth.)

The progressive group exhibited much cohesion, purposefulness, identification with the spirit of change and with the new post-Revolution politics. The conservatives, on the other hand, were divided among themselves and seldom united as a faction, although individuals would occasionally put up a stubborn resistance against progressivism (Doña Teresa, for example, stood up to Don Federico for the band, the bullfights, and the fiestas). Resentment against the progressives and the changes they introduced was accompanied by a certain admiration for their greater sophistication and *cultura* ("culture," cultivation). What rankled was the idea that the progressives, who were not truly "of" the village, had violated the proprieties by interfering in village traditions.

In the 1930s the progressives divided into two bands—one small band joining Pio and supported by conservatives; the other, joining Federico, Catalino, and Abel. (Although several people would attempt to keep the progressive faction intact, the issue of progressive versus conservative would become increasingly obscured by politics.) Don Federico's group, strongly reinforced by a schoolteacher in the late 1930s, would rival Don Pio's hitherto unchallenged *caciquismo*—a more traditional form of political leadership that lasted throughout the 1930s. The struggle between the two factions would ultimately revolve around the competition of their leaders for positions of influence in the sugar cooperative.

Don Pio was the undisputed leader of the village throughout the 1930s and early 1940s. During his nine years as Ejido commissioner, he developed important government contacts and built such a strong group around himself in the village that he was said to be the *cacique* or political leader. Why this changed is not entirely clear—*caciquismo* was dying out, and Pio was himself trying to convert his style of political control and influence into a more modern form of political leadership—but the suddenness of the change startled the village. In an election held in 1938, it was Federico, not Pio, who was nominated as delegate to the sugar cooperative.

A village political leader

Ted Schwartz

Don Pio's demise as absolute *cacique* coincided with "the period of the new schoolteacher." In 1936 a new school director began the village cooperative store, and Pio was among its supporters and officers at a time when he was still in control of the village and his group was relatively united. In 1937—the year that Federico initiated the movement to obtain potable water—a new schoolteacher took over the store's promotion, and Pio attempted to undermine the venture by setting up his own store with the assistance of the owner of the hacienda.

The beginning of the sugar cooperative intensified conflicts. During the election of officers in 1937–38, Federico and Pio competed for the position of field inspector for the area the sugar cooperative served, and each still claims that the other hired gunmen to kill him. In 1938 the village was given the opportunity to buy the hacienda, and Pio not only opposed the purchase but is said to have actively dissuaded the village from backing the group that did buy it. In the mid–1940s Pio and Federico were on opposite sides in the Aleman-Padilla election, Pio backing the "government" party that supposedly lost the election but gained office anyway. Pio was also among those who opposed the replanning of the village.

Pio's political reverses were neither permanent nor ultimately damaging to his career, but they did bring his absolute authority in the village to an end (he retained influence in the village, though his group was much reduced). In later years he would outmaneuver Federico by becoming president of the advisory council of the sugarcane cooperative (the highest position below the presidentially-appointed bureaucracy in the cooperative) and by commanding greater influence with such important people as the manager of the cooperative, the state governor, and local politicians of the official party in Mexico. He would also develop his own rice cooperative group by becoming agent in the village for one of the largest rice-producing monopolists in the state. In this way he would begin to build a clique around himself once again. Pio is now far wealthier than Federico. The latter is today a leader without a faction.

On the basis of the *Sociedad Cooperativa Pro-balneario* and anti-Catalino sentiment, however, even Federico and Pio are reconciled. It is not a warm alliance, but they have set aside their old differences, at least while the Catalino case lasts. The arguments and other aspects of the Catalino case will be reviewed in a later chapter. Here we are concerned only with the fact that the alignment against Catalino has involved increasing numbers of villagers and has created the largest factional grouping, with the greatest solidarity, ever known in the village. This solidarity is often evoked and expressed and has profoundly changed the village's character. Many people believe that if the *sociedad* is victorious, it will split into a dozen factions for control of the resources gained. Be that as it may; for now, the extent of involvement and degree of unity illustrates how a solid, cohesive grouping can be created on the basis of malice, hostility, and interpersonal conflict.

A moderately active progressive at first, Catalino was at one time a counsellor for the sugar cooperative and at another time a salaried employee at the sugar refinery. His three-year campaign against the management of the cooperative, which he considered corrupt, began around 1952. At the beginning he had the support of a number of villages in the area and the nearly total support of the village cane growers, including Don Pio and many who are now Catalino's enemies. Federico, however—by that time a petty official for the cooperative—did not oppose the cooperative and was not among Catalino's followers. Federico was, in fact, the agent of the sugar cooperative who attempted to bribe dissidents. Catalino refused his offer of from 50,000 to 100,000 pesos (estimates vary), and the moral issue caused a breach in their relations.

Federico would himself become unpopular by attempting to enforce certain regulations that were unacceptable to the sugarcane growers (such as the obligation to plant one-third of one's field in cane). Nevertheless, Catalino's support gradually eroded, and, although he and his group made many trips to Mexico City seeking presidential intervention, at the end of three years he confronted the management of the sugar cooperative alone. His defenders diminished in number as management intimidated them with pressures, threats, and a denial of basic rights. Eventually even those who had given court testimony or signed papers swearing to certain "facts" concerning his use and working of the land would swear in behalf of the opposition that they had never authorized his acquisition of the disputed land.

The importance of the Catalino case cannot be overemphasized, as virtually no village happening is untouched by it. The opposition group, united behind what it believes to be a noble cause, has taken on a kind of corporate solidarity—a macradic structuring unusual for the village. It has supported its important officers and evoked initiatives and efforts from its less auspicious officers as well (most of whom are spokesmen for Pio and Federico). They have all taken it very seriously and have thereby gained a reputation of "fighting for the village." If the case has also brought threats of violence—of doing away with Catalino and "settling things once and for all"—not only has no violence occurred, but the village appears, on the contrary, to have accepted a greater number of restraints because of it.

In addition, the village has widely and vigorously explored all the various means of conflict resolution at its disposal, including patronage, cultivation of the bureaucracy, and appeal to the courts. It has engaged many lawyers and has virtually impoverished itself by raising more money among its own numbers than one would have imagined possible. Villagers have joined in many common efforts—repeatedly petitioning in large groups to Mexico City or Puente de Ixtla, for example.

Villagers now, in fact, feel a kind of friendship and tenderness toward one another on the basis of what they regard as their heroic opposition. When one of their numbers was jailed on a marijuana charge, many people visited him in jail and signed a petition testifying to his good character and requesting his release. That he would not be forgotten, that they would "stick together," was constantly reiterated. It is quite possible that this sympathy for a lawbreaker would have been neither felt nor expressed outside the context of the Catalino case.

The "victim" was regarded, however, as a martyr to Catalino's obstinacy, for the police had come to the village in the first place to arrest certain people against whom Catalino had filed a complaint. While these were being searched, the victim had called attention to his intoxication by loudly refusing to be searched. He was searched nevertheless, and when marijuana was found on his person, he was jailed along with the others. Thereafter, no less than forty other persons went to jail to solicit their own arrest on the grounds that all were equally guilty. They even engaged three lawyers to declare their collective responsibility in defiance of the law.

People who have been friendly toward Catalino have been more severely penalized. One man who had only attested that Catalino's son had worked the land for at least the thirteen years of his village residence was refused the signature of the Ejido commissioner on a document that would have certified him as eligible to work in the United States. Shortly thereafter, he testified against Catalino.

Attempts to induce total cleavage, to erode every vestige of Catalino's past support, and to enlist the sympathy of every person not totally committed have been carried to great lengths. Neutrality is not permitted. One man who was for the most part indifferent to the *balneario,* which he saw as a needless expense in the present and a profitless failure should the "people" succeed, was pressured into at least giving no support to Catalino and was thereby acceptable to the opposition party. The more Catalino was isolated, the more it could be made to appear that his problem was nothing more than *egoísmo,* an attempt to expropriate communal property for his own personal advantage.

The structural changes in village factions, then, bespeak a reorganization of lines of conflict, which have in turn generated groups of people representing various interests and orientations in reference to village development. The groups organized around conflict have proved highly unstable; the alignments shift, and the group's internal solidarity depends upon either a real or an ideological orientation. The work, change, and politics orientation that motivated the progressives was perhaps a stronger basis for solidarity than the shared hostility that now unites the *Sociedad Cooperativa Pro-balneario,* which is more like various other small groups generated by hostilities in the village. But the necessity of hostility is implicitly sensed, and hostility is therefore maintained at a level necessary to assure its perpetuation.

The Catalino case has aroused the greatest political participation of women in village history, and women are particularly important with respect to hostility because they are more extremist and vociferous than the men, more ready to express their hatred of Catalino in obscenities. The prodding of Isabel (Victoriano's wife) or Adelina (Federico's mistress) can quickly turn a meeting that began as a calm discussion into an impassioned quarrel. The leaders know this, and these women are therefore called upon to participate in any hearings concerning the case.

Of these leaders, Pio, who does not wish to appear too interested in the affair, absents himself from meetings whenever possible, preferring to confer privately with those who will appear and express his position. Federico, too, leads from the background through a number of easily-excitable young men who could feel power and self-importance in perhaps no other circumstances. One ejido commissioner is weak, indecisive, and incompetent, but he is taken seriously by the anti-Catalino group because he is "fighting for the village." Some people, whose own hopes of gain are negligible, are skeptical of this leadership, but they make up a fringe that will be easily separable from the group once the union of hostility and hope of reward are gone.

The content of the anti-Catalino hostility will be further analyzed in another context and apart from the issues of the case. There it will be seen that Catalino, who is now regarded generally as a stubborn and perennial one-man faction against the village, in many ways serves admirably as a focus of village hostility. There is an attempt in the present conflict to discredit some of the strong moral positions he had taken in the past (refusing the bribe, for instance) and to represent his present activities as consistent with those in the past (that were then thought admirable). Considerably altered feelings are read back into the past, so that many of Catalino's personal characteristics that would otherwise be regarded as exemplary are now inverted to make him the one really suitable repository for village hatred.

THE FAMILY UNIT

First, is the village essentially an accumulation of families whose solidarity and strength of orientation are such that village conflicts may be said to revolve around family interests? Second, to what extent do allegiances—to the village, village factions, the family, or to extended kindreds as they are found locally—exclude or modify conflict?

The structure of our village, which I have characterized as at times loosely atomistic, disunited, and inclined to conflict, is not unlike that of other peasant societies, as Banfield's study in Italy, Lewis' study in Tepoztlán (which is geographically not far from the village), and Foster's discussion of peasant personality have all demonstrated.[1]

Banfield has postulated the family as the basic unit of solidarity, because it exhibits a strong unity of interest and provides a center of orientation for all members of society on the basis of their own individual families. He speaks, too, of "amoral familism," meaning that the prevailing moral code of a society may be broken for the sake of the family. Lewis, concerned with unity and solidarity more than with morality, has spoken of "nuclear familism" in Tepoztlán, meaning that the family can itself be reduced to a minimal unit. (Extended families, characteristic of pre-Conquest, clan-organized societies, are now extremely rare as residence units.)

Only the most quintessential definition of family stability can enable one to formulate a relatively simple ordering of family typology or to compare families in terms of more or less stability. In view of the presence of conflict on all levels, minimal stability will here be defined as that which has endured over time. Conflict level will be characterized in terms of whether a family conflict may or may not result in separation or the cutting off of some part of the family.

The persistence of a family over many years is almost always the result of its having resolved some major, and many recurring, intrafamilial conflicts. Investigation generally reveals a history of conflict in families that today appear free of it. Although only a certain number of families will be found to be in crisis at any given time, over the period of our village's existence, most of its families have experienced crises and have either lost members or sufficiently resolved their differences to remain together. In the pages that follow, then, solidarity will be defined as not the absence of conflict but as the ability either to survive or to transcend conflict. Minimal as this may seem, it is not inconsiderable.

It is a fixed conviction in our village that families commonly do not survive but dissolve through separation, desertion, or divorce, adulteries that become permanent liaisons, conflicts that drive a son or daughter from the home, or antagonisms between the families of a married couple that eventually disrupt the marriage. These are taken so much for granted that if we had not systematically checked the histories of conflict that we have for our families, we would undoubtedly have underestimated the number of intrafamilial conflicts that are resolved and do not break up the family.

The most fragile familial link is between husband and wife; the father is commonly lost in the subfamily consisting of a mother and her children. It is axiomatic in the village that a woman building a family must take into account the possibility that she may lose her husband one way or another and will then have to raise, and later depend upon, what remains of her family. She may lose her husband through desertion, his attachment to another woman, or through his death, natural or violent (for violent death was once quite common). An involvement in some village difficulty may cause him to flee, leaving his family behind.

The greatest solidarity is therefore expected to be found in the subfamily—between a mother and her daughters (a fragile unit because the daughters may marry young and leave the residence group), but more particularly between a mother and her sons. Expecting and even anticipating eventual abandonment and the breakdown of her marriage, a mother will build her future security by binding her sons to her as closely as possible. It is this latter subdivision—the most cohesive, but at the same time the most ideologically- and emotionally-charged substructure of the family unit—that is the locus of nuclear conflict, especially from the point of view of social character. Nuclear conflict seldom leads to an outright rupture of minimal solidarity. To pursue this issue, however, would raise the question of implicit conflicts and require a detailed consideration of the processes of socialization and character formation. Here these themes are developed only insofar as they relate to solidarity and conflict.

Solidarity and conflict are thus very difficult to pin down, and sweeping generalizations are suspect. Lewis reported a kind of negative atomistic structure, highly conflictive and inclined to break down into its smallest units, for Tepoztlán,[2] and this has been widely reported of other peasant societies elsewhere. There exists, however, a voluminous literature debating the objectivity of these reports, and other studies offer a picture of community harmony in peasant villages where individual conflictive confrontations are mediated and muted by a need for the solidarity of group cooperation.[3]

To state negatively that our village is atomistic would allow no basis for objective comparisons with other villages. The fact is that the existing system functions here with relatively little cooperative solidarity and in spite of the conspicuous prevalence of conflict. Obviously, both the residents of the village and the outsider wishing, as we did, to promote community development aspire to higher degrees of community solidarity and (possibly) cooperation. However, with a few insignificant exceptions related to highly specific conflicts, the village characterizes itself as united or disunited depending on the circumstances in reference to which the statement is being made.

In primitive societies, conflict often results in the shearing off of whole sections of a village (usually based on some organization of kinship) and separation along lines of cleavage defined perhaps by clans or lineages.[4] This sort of conflict (involving extended groups having their own organization and internal solidarity, and threatening to plunge the community into schism) is not characteristic of our village, or of peasant societies generally. Thus, Lewis' picture of Tepoztlán—in which all personal interrelation tends to break down to either the individual or to the minimal nuclear family (not extended, or only minimally extended) —represents one of the extreme possibilities of nuclear familism.[5]

There can thus be (1) an atomism of larger kinship groupings (of the kind that characterize Melanesia), but in which the kinship group's internal solidarity tends to absorb the family into a larger in-group; or there can be (2) a fragmentation in which the residence unit is the nuclear family (all relations diminish greatly outside the immediate residence group). There are also societies in which (3) the family itself has so little solidarity that conflict breaks down to the level of individuals. (This is perhaps the ultimate atomism, but internal psychological structure will not be examined here.)

It is in terms of these three levels that we will assess the applicability of the atomism concept to the village. For Banfield, "amoral familism" means only that the family will be a unit against other families in conflict and that the moral code outside the family may be nullified in the interests of the family. Here we speak of conflict between individuals that revolves around particular circumstances, of individual antagonisms not specifically generated by family interests but in which the family becomes involved in the defense or protection of its members. Although the latter variety of conflict is essentially individual in origin, it occupies an intermediate position between individualistic and familial-type atomism.

There can also exist a society in which the family unit is in conflict with nonfamily members at the same time that it is itself in conflict. In this case, family unity may be manifested primarily in relation to other groups. This may be true of our village, where intrafamilial conflict and conflict on all other levels are both highly prevalent. To what extent the family becomes a unit of conflict with nonfamily members, and to what extent it can sustain its unity against internal stresses, is difficult to determine. Crude, quantitative terms based on a count of incidents of conflict and types of family structures may provide some basis for understanding the magnitude of conflict when it is said to be prevalent or characteristic of the village family.

RESIDENCE UNITS.   We are now prepared to examine the family as a residence group—a group that lives together—with regard to degree of proximity and intimacy of contact. Every couple or subfamily (father and children or mother and children) will attempt whenever possible to establish an independent residence unit, because each represents a separate economic unit and attends to its various domestic functions independently of others.

A conflictive community tends to throw an individual back upon the family and to place a premium upon family solidarity. Conflictive families, however, weaken (or reflect the weaknesses of) familial bonds and allow for—even impel—the loss of their members. (Both conditions exist in the village.) Balancing these conditions depends chiefly upon the availability of alternatives to familial functions (such as shelter, security, care, land, work, etc.) and the individual's ability to avail himself of these alternatives. We shall have to view the proportion of compound to independent families as representing not a free choice, bespeaking either family cohesion or fragmentation, but a limited and complex one.

Lewis finds the independent nuclear family as an independent residence unit more prevalent than the extended family as a compound residence unit. He attributes this to the deterioration of clan organization after the Conquest, to the weakening of the function of kinship relations, and to the Tepozteco's love of privacy and independence. Most groups of kin living together are reduced to the nuclear family, and he sees this family as strong and stable. The breakdown and disappearance of the extended family is, in fact, a universal trend among formerly tribal cultures, following rapidly upon their economic integration into, and acculturation to, the expanding urban-industrial-commercial society and its values.

Our village, a post-Revolution community formation, mestizo-Hispanic, with little coherent Indian tradition, and lacking community continuity, should be further along the process of acculturation than Tepoztlán. Tepoztlán had 16 percent compound and 84 percent independent residence units,[6] compared to 38 percent compound and 62 percent independent family, or subfamily, residence units in our village. From Lewis' table in his book, we can establish a ratio of 1/4.4 compound residence to independent family units, compared to a 1/1.6 ratio for our village. These figures reveal the substantially greater prominence of the compound residence unit based on extended families of varying composition in our village.

Before interpreting these facts, some further discussion of the composition of the village's extended family is necessary. We count 177 potentially independent residence units composed either of couples living together (married or not), with and without unmarried children, and subfamilies consisting of a parent and his or her children (in which the parent is considered to be the head of the family and owner of the homesite). A compound residence unit is composed of two or more such potentially independent residence units and is thus a combination of families and subfamilies. If such people as a single dependent parent (e.g., a widow) or an attached sibling or relative were to be counted, the number of compound or extended families would be even higher. A residence unit is not regarded as compound if its components are unrelated by kinship and are only paying rent to live there.

The 177 potentially independent compound residence units consist of 145 couples, one patrifamily, and thirty-one matrifamilies. In the single patrifamily, the father raised his children after his wife's death, and the children, though now married, continue to live with him under his authority. The thirty-one matrifamilies include eight widows who are definitely the heads of their families and twenty-three women who are either divorced, separated, or *madres solteras* (i.e., females fifteen years of age or older, who either never lived with the child's father or lived with him too briefly for it to be considered a free union in the village). The number of

---

TABLE 1

RESIDENCE GROUPS

Potentially Independent Residence Units	177
Couples	145
Matrifamilies	31
Widows	8
Divorced or Separated	23
Patrifamilies	1
Actual Residence Units	117
Couples in Independent Residence	67
Compound Residence Units	45
Subfamilies (same house as unit head)	6
Subfamilies (separate house, same site)	2
Couples (same house as unit head)	30
Couples (separate house, same site)	16
Couples (partitioned-off site)	6

---

matrifamilies is large and, as will be argued later, overwhelmingly influential in shaping the villager's life expectation. Yet the matrifamily is a potentially independent unit—six of the thirty-one are in independent residence.

The 177 potentially independent residence units are grouped into 117 actual residence units, each occupying a homesite. The number of potential units is reduced by 60 with the grouping of 105 potential residence units into 45 compound residence units. We have, then, 45 compound residence units, sixty-seven couples in independent residence, and six subfamilies in independent residence, making up 117 actual units of residence. The compound residence units average 2.33 potential residence units. (If some of the subfamilies seem to have disappeared, it is because they are unit heads counted in the forty-five compound families.)

The extended family as a coresident group is thus surprisingly more prevalent in our village than in Tepoztlán, and its extent far exceeds the field investigator's impression before the tabulation. We were at first inclined to interpret this as denoting a greater degree of family solidarity and cohesiveness than we had reason to expect, and while this may be true in part, weight must also be given to the limitations on expansion in a village whose population has tripled through natural growth and continuing immigration since 1930. Urban land for homesites can be subdivided but not expanded.

Thirty years ago, newcomers could claim both *ejido* land and homesites, but there are many families in the village today who have neither. All unoccupied land is *ejido*. Illegal sales of *ejido* for homesites has increased the number of independent families, but most people must either receive a partitioned bit of their father's site, build another house on the father's site without partition or legal division of the title, or else live in the house of a parent or relative.

Original homesites were fairly large, some measuring more than one thousand meters. Many sites have been sold in whole or in part to others, but if this had been done for the family we should expect a fragmentation of sites to the point where each potentially independent unit would have its own small site and house. This is not the case, however. Space limitations might explain the grouping of family units within a site; but that there are thirty people living in the same house as the unit head causes us to reconsider the strength of the extended family, for there is almost always enough room for the space to be partitioned, or at least for the attached couple to build a separate house.

Our list of compound residential units sharing the same house shows a spread across the entire socioeconomic scale. Almost all of the couples attached to compound residence units are young, though not necessarily newlyweds. Some have lived with their parents for years after marriage, even though prevailing values run counter to this practice. The immigrants from Buenavista de Cuellar, for example, boast that it was customary in their home village for a young man to build a good house before marriage with his father's help and that something better than a thatched hut was expected of him even if he were poor. The Garzelas and Arquillos tend to follow this custom. Others believe that coresidence leads to in-law conflict.

Actually, those families living together in the same house do not provide a surpassing illustration of the stability and cohesion of the extended family. Of the thirty couples who live in the same house with the unit head, sixteen are newly married; more than half of these are free unions that have occurred within the last three years; and five of the other marriages, of somewhat longer duration, are already broken. Only six of the thirty can be called stabilized compound families, and whether their numbers will increase cannot be predicted. Since our list was made, three of the recently married couples have found or built a separate residence (in two cases on the same site as the unit head).

On the basis of our data, then, we can conclude that the relatively high incidence of compound family residence groups reflects primarily a shortage of space and land and the weak economic position of very young married couples and only secondarily the strength of kinship and of the extended family. It is not that this form of residence is attractive, prescribed, or valued; it is chiefly a matter of sharing limited resources. Although six relatively stabilized multifamily households do contain closely knit patrilocal extended families, we think this reflects the weakness of sons.

FAMILY CONFLICTS. To what extent can the stability and cohesion of a family, whether compound or simple, be assessed on the basis of incidents of familial conflict and their result in either resolution or rupture of the group? As the figures and qualifications on residence should indicate, mere statistics cannot measure an issue as complex and elusive as family solidarity.

On the basis of village gossip, court records, and our own experience over three years, I have recorded seventy-nine histories of conflict and seventeen current conflicts within village families—i.e., a major conflict crisis has been recorded for some 96 out of 169 comparable family units. Of these, forty-nine are between husband and wife, most of the rest are between parents and children, and the conflicts seem evenly spread over compound and simple families alike. The data are too partial to warrant statistical testing; my conclusions are based on the occurrence of thirty-two histories of conflict in compound families and twenty-nine in simple families, plus seven current conflicts in compound families and ten in simple families. Ongoing, unresolved conflicts were not considered in my conclusions.

Not all conflict is included in these figures. Although my corpus of village gossip is very extensive, it was not elicited "systematically" but rather by events in the village, and I have missed much gossip since we left. Some of what is lacking is supplied by court records and inquiries, but not all major conflicts get to court. Further, we count peaks of conflict and not the everyday variety, of which few families are free. Thus, while we know of "peak" conflicts for more than half of the village's families, we assume that the number would be much higher if we had more information.

I have recorded seventy-two instances of adultery involving sixty-nine families, and not all of these are included in the figures on conflict. Those that are only alleged to have occurred are omitted if we know nothing about an intensification of conflict that may have led to separation (though I believe that any adultery that has entered into gossip or court records should be considered as bespeaking at least a potential separation of the couple). Within the past three years, there have been nineteen cases of daughters eloping over their parents' opposition. These should probably be counted, since they may lead to the breaking of a family tie, the disruption of the new marriage, or to a reconciliation. Many past conflicts between parent and child over a marriage have not been counted because information was incomplete. All of this suggests, of course, that our figures on major family crises could be much higher than they are.

It is evident, in any case, that the family, whether compound or simple, is neither conflict-free nor conflict-inhibiting; on the contrary, the typical village family must be characterized as unstable and ridden with conflict. Any of the conflicts recorded could lead—indeed, often have led—to separation and loss of family members; but here we must return to our definition of family solidarity as not the absence of conflict but the ability either to survive or to transcend conflict.

We were originally inclined to underestimate this kind of solidarity for two reasons: (1) the villagers themselves regard the family as unstable and distrust it as a basis for security; and (2) village gossip focuses on negative instances—on conflicts, adulteries, separations, and abandonments—and tends to ignore the greater prevalence of family survival. The death of a family member, a flight away from the village to escape from a crime, the unexpected elopement of a seemingly obedient child, the absorption by the recipient family of a child who has married out—all of these may lead to the loss of family members and contribute to the image of the family as unstable and insecure. The frequency of separation is such that even families of higher status and with better chances of survival must ultimately adapt to the possibility of family instability. The family built around maternal authority is one form of adaptation, but the persistence of conflict in this structure will lead us to speak later of patterns of ineffective authoritarianism and equally ineffective, futile rebellion.

It was only by actually counting the conflicts that I was able to note the proportion of families that have survived such vicissitudes, and the residual solidarity is impressive in view of the odds against it. Fragmented families (such as the thirty-one subfamilial matrifamilies in the village), that can persist as independent families, be reabsorbed into larger units, and re-form themselves on the basis of a new spouse, must also be included in the solidarity of which we speak. In fact, all the people and institutions of the village, with all their strengths and weaknesses, should be seen against this background of resiliency and capacity for survival.

The data on these matters cannot be complete. Still, the ninety-six histories of conflict that we recorded give an indication of the proportion of those conflicts that led to separation and those that did not. Of the ninety-six, twenty-five resulted in separation. Of the latter, sixteen were between husband and wife, eight between parents and children, and one between brother and sister. In forty-six cases of conflict other than husband-wife, nine resulted in separation and thirty-seven did not. The remaining cases were still "negotiable" at my departure.

TABLE 2

CONFLICT IN FAMILIES

Total Family Units	169
Major Conflict Crises Recorded	96
Husband-Wife Conflict	49
Parent-Child Conflict	47
Total Conflict Cases	96
Resulted in Separation	25
Husband-Wife Separation	16
Parent-Child Separation	9
Resulted in Reunion	71
Husband-Wife Reunion	34
Parent Child Reunion	37

Note: Conflict crises are about evenly spread in compound and simple families.

Separation, which severs one bond and usually replaces it with another, will itself resolve a conflict, although this replacement is often the locus rather than the result of a conflict. The above figures show that the weakest, most conflictive links within the family are between husband and wife and parent and parent. It should be emphasized, nevertheless, that in any given fifty cases of comparable conflict crisis, sixteen will separate and thirty-four will not (separation that ends in reunion is considered equivalent to nonseparation).

These thirty-four will often persist in spite of continuing conflict, sometimes in spite of legal court separation or open scandal in which both public opinion and tradition call for separation. Women are supposed traditionally to submit, but surprisingly often they do not; and while tradition allows the betrayed man to leave or kill the unfaithful woman, in the majority of cases he does neither. There is only one, doubtful case of a woman having been killed because of an amorous relationship, though the imputed murderer was not living with her.

None of this is as simple as the figures suggest, although they serve well enough to indicate residual solidarity. Some separations are balanced, in a sense, by gains and losses. Marriage, for example— and especially elopement (meaning marriage or free union against the will, or without the knowledge, of the family)—is often regarded as a separation, a loss to the family, and as a failure on the part of the family to hold its members. Where even grudging consent is given and a relation maintained, I do not consider it a separation. Grudging consent does not necessarily mean, however, the end of the struggle to win back the lost member, to maintain control at a distance, or to bring the new unit within the group to compete with the spouse's family.

The fragmented family may gain by the loss or rejection of a member who diminishes its security or productivity. It should be remembered that our figures on separations do not include the nineteen elopements (counting only village girls) that have occurred within the past three years. At their inception, these would all have been regarded as separations and added to our list of conflicts; but the instability of the free unions thus formed is such that in the same length of time almost half of these unions have parted. The girls return to their parents, often with child, in which case they are regarded as "unwed mothers" *(madres solteras),* or they may narrowly have achieved the status of abandoned or separated wives.

Two traditional images govern and reflect the relations between male and female in Mexico. *Macho* and *macha* (true man and ideal woman) will be discussed later; at this point we shall take up *el abandonado* and *la abandonada.*

The Mexican woman expects to be abandoned by a weak, irresponsible, childlike man, who is likely as well to be arbitrarily violent toward her and her children, alcoholic (or nearly), and a philanderer whose adulteries will be a relentless threat to her. Better men have been known to exist and one can always hope, but no woman can discount the near certainty that this is the kind of man she is going to have. She has been conditioned to this image from birth by her mother, from whom she also learns the female defenses of independence and self-reliance on the one hand and token submission and minimal expectation on the other.

Daughters model themselves after their mothers and share their work from childhood. The ten-year-old girl minding her younger siblings seems serious, precociously mature, and already, like her mother, preoccupied with gossip. Very often she feels unloved by her mother, but loyalty, dependence, and the desirability of modeling herself after her mother have been well inculcated. She adopts her mother's attitudes—that other women are essentially prostitutes, that men are irresponsible children, at times violent and to be feared, and that women must resign themselves to suffering through their husband's adulteries and binges for the sake of the children and the endurance of the family (see Appendix 1).

If her mother's experience has not confirmed her expectation, she has seen it confirmed often enough in the village; and there are other bases

A little girl who has assumed the mother-role
Ken Heyman

for such an expectation in any case. Her man may have been among the thirty men killed in the village and all of those killings remembered by her, or he may himself have committed murder and fled to take up a new life elsewhere. (That men who have become migrant laborers might not return is not yet a source of anxiety.) The long years of revolution with its levies and slaughter have also contributed to her attitude.

The male, for his part, thinks of himself as the abandoned one, cruelly and unjustly deserted by a "bad woman" *(mala mujer)*. The mother is, again, far more influential than the father in giving the son his image of the opposite sex and his expectation that he will be abandoned by all women except his mother. Whatever differentials the mother may perceive in the moral status of women, these she transmits to her son, whom she must bind to her. All women are whores, Jezebels, and betrayers; the mother alone will not betray. (This tragic trap is completed as the son learns unconsciously—for it is the most inadmissible knowledge— that she also betrays him, if not in obvious ways, then in ways that are as real psychologically.)

The man is therefore strongly attached to his mother emotionally and strangely bound by her authority. He is certain to distrust women, whom he thinks will betray him or disgrace his manliness by making him a cuckold *(pendejo)*. His songs are full of this theme, and his *macho* behavior is intended to belittle the woman who might otherwise hurt him. He will abandon before being abandoned. In short, he is made into the man whom the woman is conditioned to expect—an unfortunate product of his mother's security system and of traditional sex-role imagery. The situation varies, of course, and so does its outcome. Our family typology will suggest this variation.

A FAMILY TYPOLOGY.   The arrangement of families that best accords with my observations is based on the presence and strength of authority of each parent in relation to one another and to their children. The woman is treated as an effective constant throughout the series, so that the family type is differentiated on the basis of father type.

The scale begins with Type 1 (1+, 1, and 1-), denoting grades of relatively strong fathers, continuously present and influential in the family. Type 2 represents weak fathers who are nevertheless present throughout the family's life. Type 3 represents a woman living with a series of men, each replacing another in the lives of her children, of whom they are the several fathers. Type 4 encompasses families under the care and authority of a woman, usually a widow, who has raised her children through most of their early youth with her husband. Type 5 denotes families of women who have raised their families essentially by themselves, the children being usually the offspring of several men who neither lived with the mother, helped to raise the children, nor contributed much to their support.

Only couples with children were typed. The family types of some older persons were reconstructed, so that the count is somewhat retrospective. All cases involve simple nuclear families or subfamilies.

Once again, the high proportion of Type 1 families surprised us, indicating as it does a greater family stability and male authority than we

TABLE 3

FAMILY TYPOLOGY: FATHER TYPES

Description	Type	Number of Families
Father Present and Influential	1+	8
	1	54
	1–	13
	Total	75 Bicentric
Father Weak but Present	2	32
Serial Fathers	3	6
Father Present Only in Early Family Formation	4	6
Father Never Present	5	20
	Total	64*

*58 Matricentric, excluding Type 4.

had expected. This should be qualified, however. First, the distribution of families among the types was in part imposed by the typology itself and by the criteria of selection. It must be remembered that the criteria were set low and that if a Type 1 classification suggests something about the presence, constancy, or strength of the male in the family, it says nothing about the *quality* of his role in the family or toward his children. Type 1-, for example, could as easily have been classed with Type 2.

Secondly, a quantitative distribution cannot (in the short run, at least) reflect all the various life experiences that these types imply—the social images and expectations that orient behavior and inspire defense, particular life strategies, and security systems. There may be some trend in time toward "modern" families in which the father plays a greater domestic role; when he is more involved in the home he will have a greater influence over his children than he has had under the traditional image-type family of the village. But a check of the age distribution of males among our typed couples shows no trend toward more Type 1 families (i.e., more bicentric than matricentric families) among the younger couples. This is not necessarily true of all families, however; neither does it preclude the development of such a trend among the youngest untyped marriages. We simply do not know how many families might change in the course of their lives—Type 1 becoming Type 2, or, more rarely, Type 2 becoming Type 1.

In spite of these qualifications, there is an indication of greater family solidarity than we had anticipated. The prevalent social image of the village is abundantly reflected, too, however. In at least thirty-two families in which a father is present, the father is rated as weak and possibly irresponsible—fathers exercising less authority over the children than their wives and carrying less weight in their formation in any case. All of the Type 1's together yield a total of seventy-five bicentric-type families; combining Types 2, 3, and 5 (omitting Type 4) gives us fifty-eight matricentric families, in twenty of which there is no male at all but only the mother and the various cultural images of male and *macho* as models for the male child.

Basically, our typology comes down to the essential divisions of bicentrism and matricentrism. Our age distributions indicate that the division of village families between the two has been relatively constant since the Revolution, varying somewhere around a 60/40 ratio. Since we have decided that the more recent, childless families cannot be typed, we really should not look for a trend in age distribution.

INTRAFAMILIAL CONFLICT

THE ABANDONED SPOUSE.   The husband-wife link (in marriage or free union) is the weakest and most conflictive of the familial links, leading to separation in about 30 percent of my recorded cases. Before stating the conflictive issues, however, another matter should be clarified. Writers on the subject see the Mexican peasant family as centered about the abandoned woman deserted by the irresponsible man, and this corresponds to the common social image held by the villagers. It is the reverse view, however—that it is the man who is betrayed and abandoned by a *mala mujer*—that dominates movies, ballads, and the *macho's* view of life. Who actually leaves whom?

Soon after coming to the village, I was struck by the proud independence of its women and by the prevalence of what are called *macha* attitudes among them. From our alcoholic friends, especially, we heard long tearful accounts of how they had been abandoned by women (and by male friends as well), and this would prove, in fact, to be the case. Where we do have information concerning who left whom, we find twenty-three cases of women leaving men, four cases of men leaving women, and only two cases of mutually desired separation. Of the twenty-three cases of women leaving men, twenty are in the court record (a case in the court record is usually in my field notes as well), with a man suing for his wife's return or involving some postseparation settlement.

Women have refused to take back men who have left them and who have then regretted the action, or have taken them back only after a long holdout. We noted, too, that women did not merely passively acquiesce in adultery. They enjoyed its intrigues, the occasional triumphs over other women, the possibility that it might lead to a better spouse, and even the dangerous prestige that may precede the community ridicule that is feared as much as judgment and scorn.

A letter from a woman, found in her own handwriting among the municipal court records of litigation, typifies the resentment of a woman who has left her husband, who has in turn gone to court to try and get her back.

> I will not return to live with my husband. He is badly advised by his sister and certain neighbors to beat and mistreat me. The only time I think of returning is for the sake of the children, who must be suffering. I do not want to go back to him. I want him to move the house off his *sitio,* and then I will return to that house to take care of the children. In addition, he must pay me for the six years I worked for him as a maid.

Another woman left her husband because he never gave her money but spent it all on drink and loose women. (The husband denied this, saying that he had spent his money on billiards and *derrocha*—"throwing it away.") She has also had trouble with her in-laws, feels "anguish" over the life she has led, is tired of living in debt, and wants money only for the childbed *(por la cama).* In both cases the husband was fined, but one of them left the village to avoid paying the twenty pesos a week ordered by the court.

Such cases suggest the striking independence and defiance of women in this village. Women do leave men more than they are abandoned by them, and they do so under varying circumstances—to rejoin their families, to go to their lovers, to live with a man they meet later, or to live and support themselves alone. With or without children, their alternatives are much the same as those confronting a widow.

ISSUES OF HUSBAND-WIFE CONFLICT. Separations often get to court one way or another—we knew of most of those that did and of only three that did not—but not all motivations for separation are reflected in court records. According to the latter, women have cited maltreatment (eight cases) as the most common reason for separation. There were, in addition, four cases of maltreatment and nonmaintenance combined, four cases of women wishing to return to their parents, two cases involving adultery on the husband's part, and one case in which conflict between a couple's respective families led to the couple's separation.

There is, however, a problem here involving contradictory social imagery. I have maintained that the social image of the family upon which villagers base their expectations and life strategies does not depend upon the numerical prevalence of the image-type family. What minimal support such an image requires we do not know; but we do relate the social image of the unstable, insecure, matricentric family of the abandoned woman and the weak, unreliable, philandering man to the strategies that lead women to bind their sons to them and to make their daughters distrustful of men and women alike. (Suspicion of women should hopefully exclude the mother, but it generally includes her as well, even though she may be regarded as preferable to other women.)

Certain adjustments to our view make the image somewhat less contradictory. We believe, for example, that much of a woman's expectation of abandonment comes from her own initial relations with men and apart from that which has been communicated to her by maternal training and social imagery. Here are the "jiltings," brief affairs in which the male's intentions were less serious than the female's; the elopements from which the girl returns the following week; the free unions that fail to meet even the minimum standards of such relationships; and the trail of women with whom *machos* have lived. None of these liaisons are "marriages" in the village sense (which is based on the *intent* of a permanent relation), and one cannot count or even estimate the number of "betrayals" and "abandonments" on the part of either sex in these early stages. No matter who does the leaving, however, the worst expectations of the other are invariably met.

That women abandon men more than they are abandoned is contrary to the community's image of these things; likewise contrary to community image are the frequent cases in which the man neither throws out nor kills an unfaithful wife. Both realities oppose what people believe to be the practice and run counter to the moral code as well, which enjoins women to abide and suffer the worst they may receive from a husband, and men to defend their honor by punishing the wife and the other man. As we shall see, this seldom happens.

The general issues of male-female conflict, then, at least as they are cited in cases of separation, are: (1) maltreatment and nonsupport, (2) inadequate support of the family, (3) outside influences and divided loyalties, as in cases of in-law interference, and (4) adultery and jealousy. All of these issues are common, and though adultery is frequent, it seldom leads to separation and is seldom mentioned as a cause of separation in the court records.

Women make more of a spouse's adultery than do men (though the opposite is supposed to be true), but they do not regard it as a basis for separation unless it leads to nonsupport. Rather, they take it as a threat to the continuance of the family and as a personal humiliation. They will fight the other woman, but the man is not held responsible. There are many conflicts among women over men but relatively few among men over women. Many cases involving allegations of adultery come to court not as separation proceedings, but through a wife's complaints about another woman, through alleged calumnies, or as a result of fights between the women concerned. It is our observation that whatever can be said about another woman will be said and that some women are conspicuously disliked, even though there are no adulteries alleged against them.

Adulteries brought out in the court record always accord with what we have learned from gossip. Others are either admitted or are obvious because of various "illegitimate" children bearing the father's name. (Name notwithstanding, village women play their favorite game of "who is the father" with great skill.) A woman is sometimes suspected of falsely claiming a child by a lover who is more prestigious than her husband. My record lists most of the alleged adulteries known in the village over the past thirty years, and our guess is that the allegations are for the most part (though not invariably) accurate. The list includes more of the relatively stable and prolonged adulterous relations (of which there have been many) than the more evanescent ones; it omits the adulteries that are not known or alleged.

The list contains seventy-two adulteries (i.e., seventy-two adulterous pairs, involving at least one, and, in some cases, two married people). Whether this is much or little the reader will have to decide, as there are no comparative data by which to judge. The seventy-two adulteries involve forty-three men and forty-seven women, with a considerable duplication of men and women among the couples (1.7 average for men, 1.5 average for women), and sixty-nine families. Since all of these adulteries were publicly known, and on the basis of the better-known cases, we believe that most of these families were involved in a crucial conflict. A more detailed analysis of adultery cases is possible, but not rewarding, due to the incompleteness of the data.

Many husband-wife conflicts arise from opposed family pulls or from the competing claims of a couple's respective families. The ubiquitous mother-in-law problem is particularly vexatious in our village. Conflict with a father-in-law is much less common, appearing only occasionally when there is an abnormally close father-daughter relationship (as in the village's only patrisubfamily), in cases where there is reluctance about a civil marriage, or as, for example, in the case of Don Catalino's refusal to forgive his daughter for running away and living with a man against his will (though the union has been a stable one for many years). An unapproved marriage can ramify from parent-child conflict to conflict with the child's spouse to conflict with the parents of the child's spouse. Catalino, however, provides the only case we know in which there was no eventual reconciliation after a marriage over the father's opposition.

A marriage is most often considered unsuitable because of differences in social status between the families concerned, because the parents consider their daughter too young to marry, or because one or the other spouse (the girl especially) is considered to have low morals. The mother's part in forming her son's character makes his participation in a stable and trusting relationship difficult enough. Unless she acquires a daughter-in-law who is submissive to both her son and herself, her attempts to bind her son to her as part of her security system will either discourage or disrupt his marriage. Although she sometimes relies on her daughters for security as well, she places little stock in this. It is rare to find a daughter keeping a mother.

LOCALITY.   Patrilocal or neolocal marriage in the husband's village is the rule and the approved form. Girls are much more likely to marry out of the village than boys; and matrilocal marriages, when they occur at all, usually reflect an absorption of recent immigrants without family to the village. There are thirty-seven patrilocal units; the fourteen matrilocal units reflect (with two exceptions) the coming to the village of a man who had no family of his own here. This absorption of unattached immigrants to the village has been fairly common since the Revolution. Recently, however, the building of *residencias* and of a new housing development has introduced a disturbing contact with unattached "outside" males only temporarily settled in or near the village, who establish unstable relations with unmarried girls in the village.

When people were asked on our attitude-survey interviews whether they would disobey their mothers, they almost without exception answered no.[7] At the same time, a number of women admitted that they had married against their mother's will. Such elopements, as we call them, run counter to community expectations and, of course, affect the "locality" statistics. Although a certain rebelliousness is expected of boys, it is believed that children, and girls especially, should obey their parents. Nevertheless, there were a number of elopements during our three years of contact. In listing them, I did not count the marriages disapproved for males, though these seemed to us much less common. The elopements that we did count were either without the knowledge, or against the expressed will, of the parents. Of the nineteen girls who had eloped, seven had already returned to the village or to their families, five had borne children, and one had induced an abortion.

Most of these unions can be expected to fail. Those still intact are more recent, as indicated by the fact that the five children born of them belong to people already separated. Nine of the nineteen men involved were not from the village (four were brickmasons from Mexico City). Several of the girls were sixteen years of age, and all but one were under nineteen. Those who returned home were taken back by their families; others will be reconciled after their marriage; still others may not return to the village. Elopements and free unions outnumbered the legitimate marriages of the period (although two couples intend to regularize their marriages later). Most such unions come about through elopement and gain acceptance within a year if they survive their initial instability.

FAMILY DISCIPLINE. Discipline, one of the more continuing and stable sources of family conflict, is authoritarian, relatively harsh, and generally in the mother's control, depending upon the family type. Although strict obedience is expected of any child, in practice the system is far more restrictive for girls than for boys. For girls, discipline and restriction are maintained indefinitely; for boys, the system is never as strict and begins to relax markedly in late adolescence.

Villagers believe that evil exists both within the child himself and outside the home and family as well and that a parent who "loves" his child is obligated to discipline physically, severely, and frequently (in some cases almost sadistically), especially when the child is too young to understand explanations or good advice (consejos). Discipline and moral instruction in the home (mainly by the mother, but with the father occasionally administering a severe, and often arbitrary, beating) is therefore intended to quell the evil impulses within the child and at the same time to keep him away from the temptations, corruption, and bad companions to be found in the street.

Keeping bad company, drinking or alcoholism, elopement or marriage against parental wishes, indolence, violence, or any deviation from the moral path—all are taken seriously (as befits good parents) and may lead to parent-child conflict. But such conflicts are most often accepted and stabilized or resolved without a break in relations or co-residence.

The processes of discipline, of moral instruction and guidance, and of socialization of the child as he develops toward adulthood are nevertheless perhaps more than usually conflictive in the village family because of certain discrepancies between the needs of the parents (especially the mother) and the conventions of the general moral code that are supposedly being inculcated. It will be seen later that a larger system is operative here than that which aims explicitly at meeting the demands of general morality and that this larger system tends rather to serve family . security in accordance with implicit maternal strategy.

It will also be shown later that the same vices that the mother appears to deplore are instrumental in binding her son to her. His very weaknesses perpetuate her authority and make him incapable of maintaining a genuinely independent family. She may suffer from his fighting or drinking, but it is to her that he will return for solace or cure. After an unsuccessful elopement and often with child, a girl, too, will return to her mother to endure with her the real or imagined community judgment.

This contradiction between ostensible objectives and the acceptance of contrary results has the effect of undermining the general moral code. The code is further undermined as the growing child experiences the community's assessment of his parents' moral status in relation to the contradiction between the code and their behavior. The male, moreover, will eventually experience the ambivalent attitudes toward *machismo* or the *macho* code, for which there is both explicit disapproval and implicit approval in spite of its overlap with "immorality" and antisocial behavior.

The ambivalent situation described above—though not an ideal type or even numerically the most important situation—is typical of the important social image of the nuclear family serving as an orientation system in its explicit aspects and as a security-strategy response to this orientation in its implicit aspects.

SIBLING CONFLICT.   Conflict between siblings is less common than the forms of intrafamilial conflict already discussed. It seems mild where it does occur, and this may be because the relations between siblings are generally not close. There have been a few marked conflicts, however. In one of these, an older brother inherited all of the family's large holdings. The younger brother, who often worked for him as a field hand in return for his support and little else, resented his inheritance and authority and felt himself to be exploited. His solution was to spend most of his time as a migrant laborer in the United States. In other families having a comparable situation, we find little or no trace of such conflict.

The injunction against subdividing *ejido* parcels as a divided inheritance is one of the few principles of land tenure that is strictly observed and not abrogated by informal illegal practice. Brothers may work an *ejido* together and divide the cash yield, but they do not divide it into portions to work individually. Doña Carmela's three sons share in this way at her insistence that each son receive an equal share of the yield, even though most of the work is done by the youngest (the others work outside the village). While there was some dissatisfaction about this, the conflict was mild, as the brothers hold more or less equal status in the family under the mother's authority. It is more common for an inheriting older brother to assume a position of authority over his younger brothers and unmarried sisters, who may then work for him, but not on an equal basis. This does not necessarily lead to conflict, however, and may, in fact, be beneficial to the noninheritors.

An inheritance by the mother occurs often enough to contribute to the lessening of possible rivalry over inheritance. The considerable number of persons in the village who are now engaged in nonagricultural work in the migrant labor circuit must also be influential in easing or obviating possible sibling conflicts by reducing the pressure and dependence on the family patrimony. Moreover, the situation of a younger sibling under an inheriting older sibling can be compared to the situation between a relatively productive father and his grown sons. The father is not dependent on the work of his sons as he can supplement his own work with the labor of peons, and he may thus be able to help his sons to a better-paying or more prestigious occupation. The noninheriting sons seem usually to accept the situation—to recognize the limitation of family resources and the rights of the eldest son and to accept it as their lot to seek other ways of maintaining themselves.

Above all, perhaps, the orientation away from field labor often more than compensates the noninheriting son for his lack of a share in the parcel. In several families where an older son has gained another trade—such as mechanics, for example—he gladly sees the inheritance pass to a less fortunate younger brother. In one family the fact that the eldest son will inherit is spoken of in terms of his being the least educated. In other families, where no sons have risen above the level of agricultural work, the alternatives involve subordinate field labor for the inheriting brother and general day labor in the village, seeking agricultural work outside the village, or attempting to enter industrial work. In any of these situations, conflict is avoided, or mitigated, by differentiation among siblings and also by acceptance of the system of undivided patrimony.

To say that relations among siblings are not especially close or highly charged is not to say that no jealousy or rivalry exists—for such feelings are evident, especially among youngsters—it is meant to suggest that sibling conflicts seldom reach the crisis pitch described elsewhere in this chapter. The brother-sister relation, for example, is generally positive but not intense in feeling—indifferent rather than conflictive—although siblings do act from time to time in behalf of the integrity and moral status of the family.

In one instance an older brother concerned himself about the moral status of a sister who had eloped. It was said at first that her two brothers would take violent action against the man, but they did not do so. Within two weeks of the couple's return to the village, the disillusioned girl wished to return to her mother's home. Her brothers, however, made her remain with the man in free union "now that she had dishonored herself and everyone knew what she was." This family appeared to be engaged in a process of moral reform, seeking a respectability that it had hitherto conspicuously lacked. The brothers had themselves just eloped with girls but said that they planned to marry them later.

Brothers should, of course, be concerned about the moral status of the family, and it is precisely this concern, insofar as it reflects on all members, that often causes the family to think and act as a unit. Such concern is not limited to the brother-sister relationship, however. In one case, the mother of a Type 3 family (serial fathers) went to a nearby village to live with a lover who had contributed to her support for years, but was forced to return when her two sons, in their late teens, threatened her life.

There are a few instances of a family pressuring a son who has neglected his wife and children for an adulterous relation. It is not unusual for grown children to pressure an errant father into comporting himself decently in public for their mother's sake, though in as many cases such action is left to his wife. Finally, parents may, in pursuit of their own ends, either preserve or disrupt the newly formed families of their children.

KINSHIP BEYOND THE FAMILY GROUP

Kinship plays an important, but not a conspicuous, role in the village in determining its nexus of relations with other places. Outside of the immediate family, kinship tends to be an all-or-nothing affair. A person is or is not a kin depending upon whether he is needed for some reason. Need is more important than degree of collaterality or specific terminological type. The system does not distribute differential functions to each category of kin, however, and expectations of aid, cooperation, hospitality, defense, and so forth have little obligatory force. This is not to say that kinship ties are not valued as resources, providing channels of access to sources of gain, work, influence, prestige, protection, and security, but only to suggest that the results of a given invocation of kinship are uncertain at best and as often disappointing as they may at times be rewarding.

It was observed earlier, in connection with the village's varied composition, that the village was a point of accretion for many people on the move and seeking land after the Revolution. But there had been a good deal of mobility and internal migration in the area even before the Revolution, so that the small group of "natives" remaining from the hacienda period was composed at least by half of people whose families had come from elsewhere to work at the hacienda over a period of one or two generations. The village has continued to grow in this way since the

1920s, gaining more in immigration than it loses through emigration; and the wide dispersal of kin among villages and towns of other states, and into the United States as well, to a large extent determines the network of possible routes of migration.

For each set of kin there was, of course, a first settler. He may have been a true "first," or he may have attached to an acquaintance, a *compadre* ("godfather"), or to an even more indirect relation. It has been seen that newcomers are readily absorbed; invariably they attach to one family and relate to the village through that family. While their permanence once depended upon land, it now depends upon their finding work, a patron, or a wife (i.e., matrilocal absorption of newcomers).

An invoked kinship relation may thus be quite distant—a third cousin, perhaps, or a parent's third cousin, if this relation is even known or recognized—though one naturally seeks a better-known person, relation notwithstanding, if possible. Whether the relation is one of kinship, consanguinity, or affinity is not of great importance. One man contemplated migrating to Tabasco because he has a friend there. Another moved from Texas to Chicago because his father had a friend there whom he personally did not know. This sort of movement contributed to the formation of the village itself.

The village may be seen as made up of a number of originally distinct kindred fragments that have become increasingly interconnected through marriage. Such kindred fragments may be scattered about the village or may comprise one or more compound residence units with a few scattered members. Thus we have one group built around two brothers from Almolonga, Guerrero, and their sons, some of whom have brought wives to our village from the parental village. Similarly, two branches of the now numerous Arquillos are related. Their unit heads are third cousins originally attracted to the village by Don Maximiliano (who was the illegitimate father of Don Catalino's wife). Maximiliano had himself come from another village in Morelos, attracted by a relative in our village. Federico came because of the presence here of his wife's brothers (the Arquillos); and a second uncle of Federico, who was once an important member of the community, had come as an immigrant before the Revolution. Abel later brought his brother's family, but after several years they returned to Guerrero.

Another such group is that of Don Pascual, who, having himself come to the village because of his wife's connections, has received many of her relatives in turn—including her sister's family, her nieces and nephews, and even her more distant relatives and their husbands. The least that he gives them is a place to build a *jacal,* or thatched hut, on his homesite; some he has taken into his own small *jacal.*

In such groups we see that the main functions of kinship include receiving new immigrants and providing shelter, ingress into or sponsorship in the community, temporary support, help in finding work, etc. A relative may provide these things, but that is not to say that kindred fragments in any sense compose a corporate group, or that there is a solidarity among them that precludes, or is especially capable of surviving, conflict.

KIN AND KINDRED FRAGMENTS. The kindred fragments have none of these characteristics. The most cohesive elements of a kindred fragment are to be found in coresidential compound units, and, as has already been explained, it is easy both to overestimate and to underestimate the solidarity of such groups. Don Pascual's relatives are received well but not with the ceremony and special respect accorded friends, *compadres,* influential acquaintances, or prestigious outsiders who represent possible resources against some future exigency. A kinsman may assume greater importance if he also has status, prestige, or influence or if he is a *compadre* as well.

Outside the immediate family, kinship designations do rot provide a distinct or consistent framework for the differentiation of social functions. There is, for example, nothing comparable here to the specific functions of the mother's brother or the father's sister found in many nonbilateral societies. The absence of a clear definition of these functions may be common in bilateral societies such as our village, where this nondifferentiation is quite marked.

Kinship terminology is structurally similar to that used in English, with the exceptions that each position identifying generation and degree of collaterality is expressed by a single term (mother's or father's side ignored) and that sex is differentiated by *o* and *a* endings. Hence: *hermano* and *hermana* (brother and sister), *primo* and *prima* (cousin, masculine and feminine), *tío* and *tía* (uncle and aunt), *sobrino* and *sobrina* (nephew and niece), *hijo* and *hija* (son and daughter), *suegro* and *suegra* (father-in-law and mother-in-law), *cuñado* and *cuñada* (brother-in-law and sister-in-law), *abuelo* and *abuela* (grandfather and grandmother), *nieto* and *nieta* (grandchild, masculine and feminine). The only terms having differentiated roots are *padre* (or *papa*) and *madre* (or *mama*), but these, too, may be regarded as having the same root, with sex differentiated by prefix.

In contrast to the English variant of the "Eskimo" system, which distinguishes the lineal from the collateral relatives of the nuclear family, regardless of whether they are on the father's or mother's side,[8] this terminological reduction carries a certain subjective weight. Given the names of his uncle and aunt, for example, and asked what terms he applies to them, the informant gives the term term—in this case, *tío.* Asked the term for aunt, he replies, "It is the same—*tía.*"

The lineal and collateral are thus not firmly separated in the village. A first cousin is called *primo hermano,* which could mean either a cousin who is the child of a sibling of one's parents or a cousin who is like a brother or sister to one. Second and third cousins, called *primo segundo* and *primo tercero,* are the children of one's parents' first and second cousins; but we know of several instances (how common this may be, we do not know) wherein first cousins call each other *hermano* and wherein an aunt (the mother of such a cousin) may be called *madre.* Further, and probably more commonly, a cousin's husband or wife may be called *cuñado* (brother- or sister-in-law). Another alternative, depending upon how the relation is felt, is to call the cousin's spouse *primo politico* (cousin-in-law). One may likewise speak of a *tío politico.*

These features that blur the line between lineal and collateral relations tend toward the Hawaiian-type system, in which terms identify only sex and generation and in which sex is deemphasized by the application of a single term to each couple and differentiated only secondarily.[9] This is perhaps more than a "tendency"; it may be related to the lack of internal functional differentiation of different classes of kin within the kindred fragment (with its affinal extensions) found in the village.

It may also be related, however precariously, to the general weakness of horizontal (same generation) relations and the greater intensity and structural differentiation of vertical (different generations) relations in the village. I hesitate to emphasize this, because I cannot be certain whether what has been described is unique to our village and its special conditions —to the relatively high number of compound and bilateral residence groups, for example. The horizontal-vertical differentiation is a strong point, in any event. Both the exercise of, and submission to, authority and the expectation of help, support, protection, etc., are vertically oriented. The villager expects more of an uncle and still more of an aunt (as an extension of matricentricity) than he expects of a cousin on the same level, even though the cousin has more wherewithal.

Almost everyone, then, is part of a scattered kindred whose fragments may be found in many different villages, and this distribution of kin is more the result of migration than of "marrying-out." Families decidedly prefer that their children marry within the village, unless such a marriage would diminish their status. Seeking to maintain or to improve status is among the main reasons why men take wives from outside the village.

The Garzelas and Arquillos, for example, have difficulty finding husbands of suitable *categoría* (social acceptability) for their daughters and have recently, and very reluctantly, had to accept a marriage of lower status and *categoría* for one of their girls. Such cross-status marriages are largely the result of a limited choice for people of higher status, who would have to have either frequent contacts over a very broad area or urban contacts to match the range of choice among people of lower status in the village. This factor, among others mentioned earlier, reinforces the inevitable connections between upward and outward mobility.

Kinship ties are in some ways important, then, but are not formally differentiated according to function, except in vertical-horizontal terms. Lineal-collateral distinctions are sometimes made and sometimes not. Kinship relations are, on the whole, not formally cultivated (except in family rituals, in which kinship relations may still not necessarily have the greatest prominence) but passively accepted. Except for its automatic nature, kinship is itself not markedly differentiated from other relations that are regarded as possible resources and is only one of the various resources—including friendships, godparenthood, and relations among patrons, their allies, dependents, and peons—to which individuals have recourse.

FRIENDSHIP AND COMPADRAZGO

FRIENDSHIP. Friendship in the village is a horizontal relation— i.e., it exists among people who are, roughly, peers on any given level. It does not (and, as far as we know, cannot) exist among people who are vertically much separated in status, because this would automatically produce a patronage relation. Such peer friends as may be found in the village are among men rather than among women and are as weak and precarious as other horizontal relations are generally found to be here.

Friendship dependencies are more to be found among men of weaker character. Others maintain their friendships with greater reserve and caution, do not seek reciprocal intensity in the relation, and neither invest too much in it nor expect any particular return from it. Alcoholic and *machismo-oriented* males make much of their friendships, both seeking out their "twins" or buddies *(cuates)* and bewailing their infidelities and betrayals. More productive men spend little time socializing with friends. They usually confine their meetings to a Sunday afternoon chat over a few beers in the village square; they rarely go to one another's houses or even stop by for one another on their way to a meeting or to the *Ayudantia.* Except for formal occasions, they rely on this sort of encounter, which in such a small village will bring people together at least once a week.

In even such a casual assemblage there is a tendency for peers to group together, but little of this assortment of status is deliberate; it is more a matter of habit and of common interests. Only those who represent the "wrong" side in the current Catalino case are excluded; otherwise men are discreet in concealing their animosities and distrust of even their ostensible friends. Men who are deeply antagonistic toward one another join such groups, neither party showing a trace of the kind of conflict that might erupt in vituperation at the next assembly meeting.

Ties that are based on friendship alone and that are not buttressed by kinship and *compadrazgo* (godparenthood) are weak and informal. To ask favors in the name of friendship is by no means to receive them; besides, such requests skirt the edge of the vertical relation and may assume an aspect of patronage. Gossip among and about friends is guarded, but it exists, perhaps only in allusion to what is already common knowledge. The general accuracy of gossip breaks down where close kin are concerned, as people tend to cover up for their close relatives.

They do not, however, cover up for their "friends" (friends in the sense that they are political associates or are at least often in each other's company). Men who have spoken to us of thefts and corruption in the village would protect themselves alone and implicate all the rest. Sooner or later, each of these has given us to understand that the other is not to be trusted, and this is even the case among such long-term associates as Federico, Manuel, and Aniceto, who are also *compadres*. This is not to say that these men do not feel a sort of friendship for each other but only to suggest that they are united above all in collusion. They have been united, serially or together, in acts both good and bad for many years, and their friendship, such as it is, survives everything except a conflict of interests or allegiance to opposed factions.

The *macho* type of friendship is quite different. *Machos* spend a great deal of time together and consider it unmanly to spend time with their families if they are married. When not working, they frequent the bars as drinking companions (this involves at least a third of the adult male population), loiter in the street, sit on the wall of the central square, or idle in the shade of the aqueduct. From time to time, they will go to town for a great or small binge, depending upon their resources. Whoever among them has money will spend it generously on the others. They commonly complain, however, that they have friends only when they have money to buy drinks and that when they lack money, they have to go begging for drinks to cure their own hangovers.

They are extremely sensitive to refusals of their liquor or their company, and many fights, even murders, have resulted from this. When drunk, they range easily from exaggerated affection and declarations of friendship to exaggerated rage and jealousy. Such quarrels break up drinking companionships of the longest duration. There have even been fights over someone's paying too much attention to someone else's buddy.

Such relations are bolstered if the friends become *compadres*, but among them the *compadre* relationship takes on a heightened sentimental tone that is both highly emotional and shallow at the same time, as the following example may suggest. Two young alcoholics were assimilated into the village from a nearby village (one through marriage), were constantly together, and usually drunk. On one occasion, when they lay sleeping in a drunken stupor alongside the road to the village, someone (said to have been passing by on horseback) hacked open the neck of one of them with a machete, exposing but not severing the jugular vein. Throughout the next hour, as we brought them to the hospital in Cuernavaca, they spoke only to each other, still quite drunk and convinced

A *macho*
called *Alacran*

that the wounded man was dying. Again and again they reiterated their friendship, each sentence beginning with the word *compadre.* The victim regretted that he had been struck down without a chance to defend himself; he would not mind dying if he could at least have confronted his assailant (though there was no talk of vengeance). As the victim's muscles were being sewn together, his friend wept.

That there is real feeling in such relationships cannot be doubted, but that there is also theatricality and an unreality in the whole *macho*

At the central washbasin and aqueduct

image is evident. It is less of a genuine social role than a pseudorole learned from the social ghost that continues to haunt songs and movies, the decayed remains of a code, a father for the fatherless. *Macho* relations are fragile and misunderstandings frequent, such as the one that induced Alberto and his friend Ruben to fight each other with machetes while drunk. Ruben was wounded, and Alberto, who has himself been badly wounded in two other such fights, is hurt that his friend no longer speaks to him. He believes it unjust that Ruben blames his tremors on him and claims that the tremors are not the result of his wounds but of "spirits" (*aires*) that entered into him as he lay in the field where Alberto had left him. Such are the vicissitudes of this sort of friendship.

According to a traditional concept (that is somewhat modified for the youngest women), the virtuous woman has no friends but stays at home unless some domestic necessity brings her out. Nevertheless, the washing fountain provides one of the main centers for female contact, gossip, and a kind of brawling that even sober men avoid (women only drink at fiestas). Almost the only stable relations to be found among women are based on kinship or a *comadre* bond. Except for the closest family ties, however, and in spite of social reinforcements, friendships among women tend to be highly unstable, rapidly shifting alliances. Here again, it is the larger issues in the village, such as the present Catalino case, that evoke relatively prolonged relationships among the female partisans. The relations tend, however, to be specific to the issue.

Visiting and socialization not incidental to household duties are considered to be wasteful, indolent, or immoral habits in women. It is believed that such a woman is likely to be having illicit relations with men, with her friends serving as her intermediaries or procurers *(alcahuetes)*. The sentiment against the *callejera*—the woman too frequently out of her house—is still strong. This will be discussed in the section dealing with gossip and conflict among women. At this point, suffice it to say that for women, even the most casual fraternization with men is difficult and that most women rely on their families and allies of the moment for companionship.

COMPADRAZGO. Much has been written about *compadrazgo*, as it plays a major role in all Latin Catholic countries.[10] The institution is much the same in our village as it is in Spain or Italy, but here again there is a blurring of formal structure and a tendency toward secularization, undifferentiated relation overlap, and mutual reinforcement of kinship, friendship, and patronage. I do not offer a detailed study of *compadrazgo* here, although I have data on the most important *compadres* of each family in the village.

Every individual has *padrinos* and *madrinas* who were his sponsors in the sacramental rites of baptism, first communion, confirmation, and marriage, and in the raising of the cross after his death. The parents become the coparents *(compadres, comadres)* of the child's sponsors; the godchild is known as an *abijado* or *abijada*. In theory, the sponsor attends the ceremony, pays for all or part of it, buys the child's costume, the rosary, and the flowers, and thus bears a considerable part of the expense of these ceremonies.

All sacraments require at least one set of sponsors, but often—at a wedding or a raising of the cross—there may be as many as four pairs of *padrinos*. All of the sacraments involve the establishment of *compadre* relations. The most important of these are the *compadres* of the child's baptism, followed by the *compadres* of his first communion. The *padrinos* of one's children at their weddings are less important as *compadre* relations than as *padrinos* in their relation to the new couple.

The parents hope that *compadres* will be second parents to their children, will adopt them in the event of the parents' death, but, more generally, will help them throughout their lives. A *padrino* is expected to help if the child is ill; when the family cannot pay for a cure, the *padrino* is under considerable moral pressure to contribute. In some instances he will bear the expense of a cure; in other instances he may give excuses when pressed and ignore the relation when not pressed, causing it to lapse.

Except for his participation in the first ceremony, however, the godparent is obligated to do none of these things. The most compelling obligation is to accept the invitation; and while there seem to be no consequences for refusing, the person who asked the favor would be greatly hurt and offended if it were refused. To refuse would be called "pride" *(orgullo)* or "humiliating the poor" *(humillando los pobres)*. I know of no one refusing, however reluctantly they may participate, and no one would dare to scrimp on the expense. The *padrino* displays his own status by the flowers, the rosary, the priest's breakfast, or whatever else he must supply. It is only later that the obligation becomes vaguely defined and variously executed.

Compadre relations involve obligations that are also vague and viable in both concept and practice. If the relationship has not lapsed through neglect, the terms *compadre* and *comadre* are used in direct address. When *compadres* are kin, the term *compadre* tends to supplant the kinship term, even as a referent, unless there is some need to specify the relationship. (Except among parents and children, kinship terms are seldom used as terms of address.) Any previous relation—whether of kinship, friendship, or patronage— is considered strengthened by *compadrazgo;* in reality, though, the relations are mutually supporting. *Compadrazgo* tends to have a purely formal persistence beyond the initial ceremony if no previous relation determined that this person be asked.

The more desirable *compadres* are somewhat protected by the inhibitions of those who might ask them. Thus the *penosos* (people who are painfully shy) would like to ask the wealthy or prestigious to be their *compadres,* but they are often deterred by the expectation that they will be considered *igualados* (people who make themselves equal to their betters) or *aprovechados* (people who take advantage of others); or else they anticipate a refusal, which is unlikely. Such people form a reticent group and are in all matters self-disqualifying. At least they have the consolation of seeing themselves as free of these negative traits, and they can resent and criticize those who do what they dare not do.

Many people wanted us for *padrinos* and *compadres.* Some did not dare to ask but others did, and there were people of high and low status in both categories. One family that asked me to be *madrina* later withdrew the request, fearing the criticism of its neighbors, named another *madrina* of its own status, and asked me to be *madrina* in secret. Another couple, whom I had taken to the hospital for a caesarean childbirth, wished to ask us and had reason to do so; but they discussed it with others and finally settled on a horizontal *compadrazgo.* Higher-status families in the village are often called upon for the favor and number the poorest families in the village among their *compadres,* but they are protected from those whose aspiration for status gain is overcome by sensitivity to social criticism.

Such sensitivity is overcome where a stable patronage relation exists, and it is not unusual for a peon or domestic servant to have his employer as *compadre.* The outsider may be puzzled for a time by certain cross-status *compadrazgo* relations—as when servant and mistress refer to one another as *compadre* and *comadre,* or with even greater apparent intimacy as *compadrito* and *comadrita.* Having observed a number of such relations, however, I have found that the basic relation neither becomes less asymmetrical, nor does the fact that the parties reciprocate the same terms of address conceal this asymmetry. One is saying, in effect: "You have accepted some responsibility for my child, and secondarily for me, which goes beyond our ordinary employer-employee relation. I honor and respect you and give allegiance as your dependent." The other acknowledges this relation, the responsibility, the respect, and the dependence.

The cross-status *compadrazgo* is thus integrated with the pattern of patronage. The overlap is not complete, and there is the interpeer *compadrazgo* to consider. Still, seeking a *compadre* of higher status seems to bespeak a desire for the "benevolent patron" and for the security of the dependency inherent in the relation. This sort of *compadre* relation may, however, be as often disappointing as are the other hopes for the benevolent patron. The return to the dependent is highly uncertain, ranging from nothing to most of what was hoped for, but the seeking of higher-status *patrones* and *compadres* continues nevertheless. The village families of higher status may use one another, but, even better, they will have the priest, the doctor, the patrons of the weekend *residencias,* professional people they have cultivated, and regional politicians as their *compadres* when they can.

The asymmetry of the relation is explicit. It is the seeker who receives the favor and who owes gratitude and respect for what is given. There is no thought of a person of higher status asking someone of uncompensated lower status to be his *compadre.* In the cross-status *compadrazgo,* an additional bond of loyalty of the favored dependent to his *patron* somewhat complicates issues between them. One woman complained to us of her employer's treatment of her, calling her *comadre* at the same time that she denigrated her as employer. By contrast, she would refer to her employer's husband, whom she liked, as her *compadrito.*

Thus, the use of the term may lapse altogether, in which case the relation remains only as a recourse under exceptional circumstances. It may also be used formally and automatically, or a bond of affection may be given recognition by the use of the diminutive. The diminutive is much used in the village, mainly as a referent, but also as a term of address.

STRUCTURE OF THE <u>COMPADRAZGO</u> RELATIONSHIP. Even among peers, the *compadrazgo* relationship is recognized as being asymmetrical—one side asking, the other side granting, the favor of being *padrino* and *compadre.* But this very asymmetry is valued and preserved, for one of the cardinal rules affecting the selection of *compadres* is that the favor is not to be returned. A person whom you have asked to be *padrino* to your child, and thus your *compadre,* cannot at another time ask you to be *padrino* to his child, thus returning the favor and canceling the reciprocal, but asymmetrical balance of responsibilities, respect, loyalty, and dependence of which the relation is felt to consist.

The horizontal-vertical relation that is so basic to village organization is once again exemplified in this. The asymmetry of status in *compadrazgo* inclines it somewhat from the horizontal toward the stronger, and preferred, vertical axis; and while the difference may appear slight, villagers regard it as important. It is perhaps in behalf of this status asymmetry among *compadres* that even the poorest in the village will exceed their means in providing the flowers and other components of their contribution to the sacramental ceremony.

Some of the important structural points of this relation should be summarized and emphasized:

1. It is an implicit and almost totally effective rule that one cannot refuse to become a *padrino* or *compadre*.

2. The honor of being asked is far outweighed by the favor, however compulsory, that is given.

3. Although *compadre* and *comadre* are reciprocal as terms of reference or address, the relationship is symmetrical for neither a cross-status nor an interpeer *compadrazgo.*

4. In both cases, but particularly in the latter, it is an explicit rule that when A has asked B to be *padrino* to his child, making A and B *compadres,* B cannot later ask A to be *padrino* to *his* child, reversing the asymmetry of the relation. (How prevalent the *notion* may be, I do not know.)

5. The person who consents to be the *padrino* and *compadre* should continue to give tokens of his responsibility toward the *ahijado,* thus giving the dependent family the assurance that he is their resource.

The discharge of subsequent obligations is optional and, I believe, largely independent of community criticism. Meeting these obligations faithfully is to the *padrino's* credit, but it is usually inconspicuous—evoked in genuine family emergencies and not in status-enhancing display or ceremonial. The optional nature of the donor-*compadre's* subsequent giving may be influenced by the lack of conspicuous status gain. The continuation of the relation depends upon its integration with other relations, such as kinship and patronage, and their current vitality.

KINSHIP, FRIENDSHIP, COMPADRAZGO, AND PATRONAGE

My records indicate that less than 20 percent of our married adults have chosen kin for their most important *compadres.* One might have expected a higher percentage; some informants believe that it is common for brothers, for example, to be *compadres.* Although this is rare, there are some cases in which brothers-in-law are *compadres* (and their wives, who are sister, *comadres*).

The fact is that kinship, friendship, *compadrazgo,* and patronage relations are not sharply differentiated. They all contribute to a single nexus of relationship and should be seen as forming links between individuals and families of single or multiple bonds, occurring singly or in all combinations—e.g., a *compadrazgo*-patronage double bond, a kinship-friendship-patronage triple bond, a kinship single bond, etc.

Friendship bonds are largely horizontal (i.e., among peers). Kinship bonds tend to be functionally stronger vertically (across generations) than horizontally. Patronage ties are inclined toward the vertical (or are, at least, off-horizontal). Finally, the bonds of *compadrazgo* are both horizontal and vertical but are more inclined toward the vertical by the functional asymmetry between *compadres.* The individual's minimal security and, beyond this, his opportunities, contacts, influence, etc., depend upon this network's resources and upon the possibilities he has of using them to his own benefit. The network is comparable in importance to the kinship groups with which anthropologists have often concerned themselves. How such networks work and are structured is less well known.

The social networks of our villagers vary according to the activation potential of their component bonds and the extensiveness and diversity of their resources. Their size varies greatly from one individual and family to another. Some people have few or no kin in the village and do not maintain ties with kin outside the village, or they have few friends, few *compadres,* and few or no stable patronage relations. Others have vast networks of relations that extend to other social levels and communities beyond the village. Higher status generally means a more extensive network, but the variation is great among lower-status families as well, some of which have built extensive networks on kinship and *compadrazgo* and on the cultivation of numerous *patrones*. (Don Pascual, for example, has a very extensive network based on all four bonds, though on a low-status level.)

It will be seen that the rule against duplicating and reversing the *compadrazgo* relation tends to induce network extension, rather than concentration, much as incest prohibitions, for example, affect the network built on kinship alone. The network of relations built on either single or multiple bonds can be compared to ego-centered kindreds as opposed to varied kinship structures. The network based on single bonds differs for each individual, does not constitute a true group, and has no corporate functions.

The analogy between the relational network and the kindred should be pursued further. The kindred consists of all the consanguineal relatives of a given individual and is not a descent group; only full siblings have the same kindred in common. It does not generally function as a group, although parts of it may be assembled on ceremonial occasions. Each villager has some of his kindred living in the village and other kindred fragments in other localities. How extensive this kindred is depends upon a knowledge of its linkages, and since this knowledge is not yet systematically transmitted, the mapping of remembered or known links upon possible links of kinship is highly variable. How kinship bonds can be functionally activated has already been discussed. The kindred is integrated into the individual's relational network, and networks may differ considerably even among full siblings.

In an ego-centered network, by the same token, each individual is bound to "ego" through some combination of the bonds of friendship, kinship, *compadrazgo,* and patronage, and each of these bonds, however reinforced, differs in intensity—i.e., in its readiness to be activated, its present state of activation, or in its latent values as a resource for the person in need. George Foster's important article on this subject most closely corresponds to our own formulation.[11] Foster believes, as we do, that describing the ideal behavior of the several social institutions does not account for actual behavior, and he notes the impossibility of an individual's living up to all the relations in which he is involved in his neighborhood, friendship, kindred, and *compadrazgo.* To form his specific network on the basis of all these relations, the individual selects from among them those which he will maintain on an active basis.

Foster proposes a fundamental model for such social systems, which he calls the "dyadic contract." "Contract" does not seem to me at face value an apt term to use for informal relations, but its use is to distinguish the selective from the ascribed or nonselective. His networks of dyadic contracts are, as I have already pointed out, unique to each individual, noncorporate, and without real group functions. He indicates that such a social system is not adapted to cooperative organization and that, in fact, little cooperation outside of the family is required by Tzintzuntzan work and technology. He describes, too, how these contracts are kept active by a continuing exchange of material goods and tangible services. Foster's system and the one that we have presented would more closely coincide at this point if we add a fifth type of bond to the four already proposed. The fifth, or contractual, bond would, in combination with any of the others, activate the bond and differentiate it from lapsed or inactive bonds.

It should be added, however, that some bonds retain a latent value—especially kinship bonds that are known but unactivated, inactive or potential friendships, and patronage bonds that have become inactive but not conflictive. Lapsed *compadrazgo* bonds are unlikely to be re-activated, except on some new basis, but even these may occasionally be reactivated to meet some special relational need. Latency, then, must be allowed for. Other differences between Foster's system and ours may be the result of differences between our village and Tzintzuntzan.

Foster emphasizes the symmetry of dyadic contracts among people of equal status and particularly the symmetry of *compadrazgo* among peers—i.e., the same goods and services are exchanged, they roughly balance out in the long run, but they must not balance in the short run if the relation is to continue on an active basis. In our village, however, the reciprocal use of the term *compadre* covers, but does not conceal, an explicitly recognized asymmetry between the asker and the giver of the favor of being *padrino*. The *padrino's* continuing expenses and responsibilities are fully recognized, but they are not returnable in kind, as the favor of being *padrino* cannot be reciprocated. The relation between *compadres* may exhibit any degree of intensity or activation; but while it is active, it remains unequal, except insofar as the asker is compensated by the respect and honor accorded the *padrino* of one's child and by the opportunity given him for status enhancement.

If my analysis of the village material is correct, then Foster has either overlooked this structural asymmetry or else the two communities differ in this respect. (It would be interesting if they did, because it would reveal a structural difference comparable to the symmetrical and asymmetrical exchange well known for marriage systems.) That there are important differences between the communities is evident in Foster's assertions that status distinctions are nonfunctional in Tzintzuntzan and that patronage relations, mainly to be found between villagers and outsiders, are rare in the village itself.

Our village, in contrast, is emphatically status-oriented, and even small distinctions are amplifiable. Whereas Foster finds internal patronage relations rare and factionalism absent, we consider patronage to dominate other relations to the extent that maintaining truly horizontal relations is difficult. There is a seeking for *patrones* and a fragmentation of *patronazgo* that would even exceed that which the system now permits. The village system, as we have shown, is in disequilibrium. Its status orientation, its rapid stratification, the prevalence of conflict, and its very reliance upon a diversity of optional bonds in an extended relational network—all reflect this. Apart from these differences, however, Foster's scheme is in general accord with ours. The differences must be resolved by comparative study, which cannot be attempted here.

THE RELATIONAL NETWORK. The villager's relational network contains his immediate resources, his working relations, and his latent or potential support in the various emergencies, threats, and separations that he anticipates, but his use of this network is conditioned by a sense of the insecurity of life and of all relations generally. No one relation, whatever its bonds, is thought to be really secure; all or any part of it could fail at the time of greatest need, although it might prove adequate for lesser needs. We could provide numerous examples of people who assiduously cultivate their relational networks, investing in these relations and hoping for a future return in the form of security and maintenance in old age, even though it is generally regarded as an uncertain gamble, more likely to be repaid in ingratitude and an attempt by others to get the best of the relation. Old-age security and care are believed to reside in the mother-child, and above all in the mother-son, relation.

The few who have no children, however, must rely on the network. Our maid Filomena, for example, was a popular *madrina* and *comadre*. She usually worked and had some money, gave gifts to her relatives and godchildren, loaned money to her friends and *compadres,* and saved none for herself (which was considered foolish by everyone not on the receiving end at the moment). Her only kin in the village were collateral relatives of her late husband. In her twenty-one years in the village she had had almost no contact with her own kindred, whom she had left behind near the Guerrero coast—a separation brought about by distance and a conflict with her mother.

Filomena's relations with her various *compadres* were decidedly unequal. Childless herself, she was always the *madrina,* without the usual balance of having others in this relation to her. People to whom she made gifts and loaned money—even fictive kin, *compadres,* and friends— continually disappointed her when she needed or desired repayment or a return favor. Her best friends, affinal relatives, and *compadres* spoke harshly of her behind her back and criticized her when she became involved in scandal. Embroiled in the witchcraft trial, she was apparently on her own. Yet she is impelled to continue investing in the network. Her main hope lies in a young woman, among her late husband's relatives, who calls her "aunt". Filomena helped to raise this woman, gave her money whenever she had it, refused her nothing, and helped to support her through secondary school. She hopes to live with her when she (Filomena) is no longer able to work; and if this is a reasonable hope, it is by no means a certainty.[12]

The childless widow provides an illuminating but exceptional example of an individual compelled to rely heavily on a network containing no close kin. But the family is no certain resource for maintenance in old age either. At least two old women, *ejidatarias* who had given much to their children and wards, were treated by their families with a neglect that shocked the community. Neither is it unknown for a network of relations to give minimal maintenance to one whom it has exploited and denuded of whatever resources he had possessed. This is the almost institutionalized relation between an alcoholic and those *patrones* who use his land and contribute but minimally to his maintenance thereafter. But such men may also receive partial maintenance, however unwillingly it is given, from those (most often relatives) who have received nothing from him.

An individual's network may lose members through conflict; indeed, there is a considerable turnover of relations that are activated, lapsed, or latent at various times of his life. A man's friendship bonds are unstable (varying according to the types of friendships discussed earlier), while a woman's friendship bonds change with every new antagonism and alliance. The network may make an individual more independent of a particular conflict or separation. At the same time, however, the overlapping networks of different individuals, and the diversity of relations these include, also involve an individual in conflicts that may not otherwise have touched him, or may place him in a position of conflicting alliances.

No relation is proof against conflict. In conflict, even very close relations may lapse or become antagonisms. *Compadres* may cease to use the term with one another (though they may continue to use it as a referent), and the same is true of kin. Men are normally discreet and guarded but will still sooner or later offer damaging information about their friends, relatives, and *compadres,* thus revealing the antagonisms that seem to lie hidden in all such relations. This is also done as a kind of moral defense—an assertion of the superiority of one's own moral status over that of the rest of the community. In open conflict, this goes even further. Here the term of kinship or of *compadrazgo* is not dropped but is given even greater emphasis in reference, as if to say, "This man is my brother-in-law, *compadre,* and long-term friend, but I am forced to say this of him nevertheless"—the idea being to lend credence to the accusation and, hopefully, to ennoble the accuser.

The Catalino case provides a dramatic illustration of how a network can shrink in conflict; but there have been other instances in the past—such as the factional conflict centering around Federico and Pio, for example—when many people were forced to realign their networks. Many networks will continue to reflect these earlier assortments years later. It is striking how many of Catalino's antagonists were formerly close associates who called him friend, relative, or *compadre.* They continue to do so today—he, with irony; they, in the manner described above. It might be said that the network has remained the same but that many of the links have been reversed; but it is more to the point to say that almost all the people Catalino might once have relied upon have failed him.

This failing to some extent antedates the present dispute over the land and water rights. It began during the later years of his struggle against the management of the sugar cooperative, when many of his friends and supporters were either bought off or intimidated away from him. The present alignment is instructive. In general, it is the bulk of the most nearly horizontal relations that have become antagonistic. His wife and children remain with him, along with a very few who had formerly been in a position of dependent alliance to him as their *patron.*

But few people, especially in Catalino's weakened position, can depend upon a single *patron.* Catalino's brother-in-law and *compadre* Federico was one of the prime movers of the opposition. Federico's wife (who is Catalino's sister) continued to give her brother passive support but would not oppose her husband publicly. Catalino's second or third cousin and *compadre* Abel Arquillos continued to support him weakly but was restrained by fears for his own safety and by anxiety over the threat that he would himself be as isolated as Catalino, just as cut off from many who formed part of his own relational network. As we left the field, Abel had somehow accomplished the delicate feat of supporting Catalino as his witness while still maintaining outwardly friendly relations with Federico and others who are among Federico's close friends and *compadres.* But still others had cut him off, and those remaining did not trust him. The relation had become superficial.

Catalino's sons managed to retain their relations with old friends in the Youth Club and on the basketball team. His eldest son, charged with *egoísmo* by some other young men with whom he worked in the United States, was almost totally isolated for a year, until he became a foreman in California and the others related to him as dependents. Catalino's wife, too, was almost totally isolated. Women were much harsher than men in their offensive against her; but this meant little change for her, except in the casual encounters she might have with women at the washing fountain, as she had never formed idle relations with other women. She had always been the object of much envy and antagonism, in any case, and was, I believe, quite capable of supporting it with or without the hurt that her husband experienced.

For his part, in the last resort, Catalino relied for protection and support upon his own *patrones,* which is, as we have seen, characteristic of this society. He was sustained against his opponents mainly by a lawyer-politician from Mexico City who had a weekend residence in the village, and he also received some, but much less, help from Don Maximiliano, his wife's illegitimate father, who was now a national senator living in Mexico City. (Maximiliano has always done very little for them when he might have done much. Even when asked to fix certain irregularities in his grandson's military service papers, he responded only after long and humiliating petitioning.) These and a few other of Catalino's bureaucratic connections, plus his own abilities at litigation, were all that stood between him and the unconditional success of his opponents. Yet with the lawyer's help, he was still more than just holding his own after more than four years of controversy and conflict; and in spite of the seeming depth of the present hostility, a settlement of the case might still restore a part of his former network to him.

Numerous other cases can be cited to illustrate the village's social structure as it has been characterized here with respect to its susceptibility to conflict and its minimal capacity to survive most of its conflicts by stabilizing them, reconciling them, or by enabling the fragments of a separation either to persist as such or to form new units. Even the Catalino case, which is one of the most drastic conflicts ever to occur in the village, has produced some new alliances and led to the reconciliation of some old conflicts. The seemingly high degree of solidarity exhibited by the group in opposition to Catalino is, however, as fragile as all other social groupings. Many predict its fragmentation should the case be resolved, and its split into factions should the anti-Catalino group succeed in gaining the desired rights to build a bathing resort cooperative. All past cooperative ventures have either broken down or been transmuted into a minimally cooperative residue run by governmental authorities.

The villager's social network meets ordinary needs that are neither extreme nor blocked by conflict, but it is an unreliable instrument, offering no guarantee of security. Its greatest asset lies in its multiplicity of bonds; but the hopes of the individual always rest upon the family— particularly the mother-child kernel—and upon the "benevolent patron".

---

[1] For a consideration of the definition of peasant, see Jack M. Potter, May N. Diaz, and George M. Foster, eds., *Peasant Society: A Reader* (Boston: Little, Brown & Co., 1967) and Eric R. Wolf, "Types of Latin American Peasantry: A Preliminary Discussion," *American Anthropologist* 57 (1955): 452–71; see also Edward Banfield, *The Moral Basis of a Backward Society* (Glencoe, Ill.: Free Press, 1959) and Oscar Lewis, *Life*

in a Mexican Village: Tepoztlán Restudied (Urbana, Ill.: University of Illinois Press, 1951).

[2] Lewis, *Life in a Mexican Village*, p. 61.

[3] Robert Redfield, *Peasant Society and Culture: An Anthropological Approach to Civilization* (Chicago: University of Chicago Press, 1956).

[4] Lola Romanucci Schwartz, "Conflits fonciers a Mokerang, village Matankor des iles de l'Amirauté," *L'homme* 6, no. 2 (1966): 32–52.

[5] Lewis, *Life in a Mexican Village*, chap. 14, pp. 321–24.

[6] Oscar Lewis, *Tepoztlán: Village in Mexico.* (New York: Holt, Rinehart & Winston, 1960), p. 60.

[7] Erich Fromm and Michael Maccoby, *Social Character in a Mexican Village*, p. 239.

[8] George Peter Murdock, *Social Structure* (New York: Macmillan Co., 1949).

[9] Ibid.

[10] For a comparative historical review of *compadrazgo*, see Sidney Mintz and Eric Wolf, "An Analysis of Ritual Co-parenthood (Compadrazgo)," *Southwestern Journal of Anthropology* 6, no. 4 (1950): 341–68.

[11] George Foster, "The Dyadic Contract: A Model for the Social Structure of a Mexican Peasant Village," *American Anthropologist* 63, no. 6 (December 1961): 1173–91.

[12] See Appendix 1.

4

CONFLICT
AND MORALITY

RELATIONSHIP BETWEEN CONFLICT AND MORALITY

To villagers, involvement means conflict, and morality consists principally in avoiding, rather than in doing, a thing. For once in conflict, disengagement is difficult. Grievances multiply, and villagers pride themselves on being unrelenting and unforgiving. Although such positive traits as charity, forgiveness, and reasonableness are extolled in conversation and counsel, morality is essentially a matter of negative proscription—of not murdering; not maligning, defaming, or spreading gossip; not fighting or quarreling; not entering into public affairs or the affairs of others.

Thus conflict-avoiding strategy is, in effect, summed up in the important phrases *evitar dificultades* ("to avoid difficulties") and *de no meterse* ("not to put oneself into things"). To do the opposite—as in the case of the *pleitoso* or *revoltoso* ("troublemaker") or of the person who is *metiche* ("always putting himself into things that do not concern him")— is regarded as either a defect of character or as general immorality; for, properly speaking, nothing should concern one. Whoever places himself in a position of prominence will inevitably involve himself in conflict with others, subject himself to criticism, and invite a suspicion of immorality.

The principle of avoidance is, however, neither whole nor consistent. Although the general moral code counsels an extreme avoidance of involvement, group membership and the various ties of the relational network impel involvement. Whereas the general moral code advises one *de no meterse*—not to put oneself into things—the code of manliness exhorts one *de no rajarse*—not to yield or give in.[1] The careful person will avoid difficulties; nevertheless, those who take the lead in village affairs *do* put themselves forward; and most of those who are variously involved in conflict have not heeded the warning.

There is no countervailing moral precept that carries the force and conviction of the principle of avoidance. Expressions of family solidarity or of kin ties are mild by comparison. People who take office commonly declare themselves foolish for doing so and always speak of withdrawing. Others regard themselves as superior for successfully avoiding involvement, although they are also subject to criticism for "holding themselves apart" out of pride or pretention.

EGOÍSMO. Other types of immorality commensurate with not avoiding difficulties and putting oneself into things are *egoísmo, categoría,* and *envidia* (considerably less feeling is attached to theft, adultery, violence, or murder, though, among these, theft of property arouses the greatest concern). Villagers believe that *egoísmo* is a dominant natural characteristic of all men, but especially of Mexicans, and that it is immoral and a bad character trait however universal it may be. An *egoísta* is one who pursues self-interest to the detriment of the common interest of the group or who derives personal benefit from group resources.

It has been pointed out elsewhere that the *patron,* who often establishes his ability to dispense patronage by profiting from community resources personally, may legitimize his position and mitigate its aura of immorality by sharing some of the personal benefits he derives. By paying a rebate to the community in the form of strategically located patronage, he can overcome the stigma of *egoísmo* and even become a benevolent *patron.* This may be illustrated by the difference between Federico, who is considered to be *egoísta* to a high degree and is widely condemned for it, and Pio, who manages things in such a way that he is regarded as a benevolent *patron*. Catalino's opponents charge him with *egoísmo* on the grand scale on the grounds that he has personally expropriated part of the village's communal land. This did not become a matter of strong protest until it became evident that the commercialization of this property as a public bathing resort would cause his personal benefit to be very great, and then his *egoísmo* became colossal. Catalino is a *patron* to a very few dependents, and all the rest are outraged because they feel excluded.

Egoísmo involves a kind of stubbornness that neither consideration of community or public interest nor even corruption can affect. During the period when the entire village was being rebuilt and streets laid out, for example, a great number of people had to accept adjustments of their homesites and, at times, considerable dislocation. Most people accepted this, but four or five others opposed the plan, refusing to accept a movement that would be personally disadvantageous, compensation not-withstanding. Pedro, whose house was in the exact middle of the new main road, refused to move his house, and the village was nearly resolved to move it by force when he was shot by visiting gamblers from Guerrero and his death obviated the use of force. Of all the cases of threatened violence that never came to violence, only one man successfully held out against the village. Don Pio refused to move his store to accommodate the plan to enlarge the main road that passes by the aqueduct, and the store remains in the main street to this day.

Catalino has this kind of stubbornness in abundance, but the cases of Catalino and Pio illustrate a point: namely, that a man who is stubborn, but in other ways beloved, will transcend the label of *terco* ("stubborn") and admiringly be called *mula,* an affectionate way of saying that a man has a certain manly obstinacy. In spite of hard feelings, a successful *pleitoso* ("squabbler") may one day be referred to with deference as a great *pleitista* ("great fighter"). Thus, Don Victoriano, who is one of Catalino's adversaries, tells us that Catalino is a *pleitista* second to none. "With ten men like him," said Victoriano, "I could take Mexico City." Needless to say, this attitude is not unique to Mexico.

CATEGORÍA. The immorality of *egoísmo* is compounded when coupled with *orgullo* (pride) and *categoría* (pretention to a status that has nothing to do with socioeconomic position). *Categoría* is far more resented than plain *egoísmo,* which involves no such intrinsic differentiation. The greater feeling attached to *egoísmo-cum-categoría* derives from resentment of the rigid class-caste status differentiation of the older colonial and hacienda societies. Here again, public feeling toward Federico and Catalino differs from the feeling toward Pio and others like him who avoid the taint of *categoría* and remain accessible—"of the people"—even when this, too, is a pose. (The daughters of Federico and Catalino are often referred to, derisively and resentfully, as *las categorías*, which means that they are criticized for aloofness.) Thus, the opposite of *egoísmo* is to be *"por el pueblo,"* for the people and the village. Pio succeeds, and Federico consistently fails, in taking this position. Outsiders are evaluated as being "for" or "against" the *pueblo*, as are the owners of the *residencias* and all external agents who come in contact with the village.

ENVIDIA.   Assertions of status place an individual in a position of status competition, and the term *envidia* encompasses this general competition with its possibilities of ill-will, malice, and action by others to reduce the upstart's status, or at least to cancel his gains. *Envidia* has often been described as part of the social milieu of atomistic conflict for Mexican and other small, or peasant, communities. Although our villagers believe that *envidia* is universal and inevitable, our own observations have convinced us that it is not true that *envidia* follows upon any or all success. Economic success, especially, brings respect and overcomes much that would otherwise detract from a person's general status. It is only when success is tainted by unmitigated *egoísmo, orgullo,* and *categoría* that it becomes the object of *envidia*. One also finds that a considerable status differential brought about by an individual's success evokes less *envidia* than cases of smaller status differentials.

The village is rife with petty resentments and petty *envidia,* the most miniscule differentiations evoking pride (in invidious comparison with others), resentment, and malice. Lupita, one of the poorest women in the village, despised by others, can say that she at least has beans to eat and can look down on her neighbors who gather the wild herbs and mushrooms of the fields. Lupita could also derogate her sister's greater cleanliness as *orgullo,* while someone can look down on *her* because she has no shoes. Such comparisons do more than merely place each individual in his socioeconomic niche; they represent a situation of attack and defense of status marked by vehemence, pettiness, malice, and resentment.

Small differences among neighbors particularly excite these reactions. Lupita, for example, does not normally compare herself to Don Salvador, resent the fact that he has a good house, or that he farms thirty *tareas* of land; instead, she focuses on her poorer neighbor's diet. Invidious comparisons are made within fairly narrow status domains, and the superior position is always assumed to carry at least some trace of *categoría*.

To eat cultivated food gives one an edge over those who eat uncultivated wild foods. To be dark of skin puts one at a disadvantage with one who is light of skin, unless the disadvantage is partly overcome by wealth. To be *huarachudo* (shod in *huaraches*) gives at least an element of *categoría* over one's barefoot neighbor, but the term *huarachudo* itself mocks the pretention of the person in *huaraches* from the position of the *calzado* (one with shoes). Thus, *egoísmo* sets one in conflict with others, but the conflict can be prevented, and hostility disarmed, through the eschewal of pretention to *categoría*. A *patrón* who makes claims to *categoría* must pretend that he is making them on behalf of the people.

Large status differences, then, are not the primary foci of *envidia* and conflict, but very small status differences evoke a multitude of conflicts and resentments, attempts to puncture pretentions and to deflate claims to *categoría* while asserting one's own claims at the same time. Status context provides one of the main sources of generalized macradic conflict.

The major components of the general status system are socio-economic status, political status, categorical status, and moral status. Categorical status includes the presence or absence of "culture" in its popular sense, such aspects of "cultivation" as more than rudimentary literacy and pretentions to "higher" manners or morality; and racial and ethnic affinities. The section that follows will consider village notions about race, *cultura*, and *categoría*.

CATEGORÍA AND RACE

Although *categoría* is in some forms openly admired, on the whole it is regarded as undemocratic—a lingering residue of notions of aristocracy and status from the feudal society of the past—and is resented. It may be looked upon as reactionary, or it may be considered advanced with respect to acculturation. But it is almost always considered pretentious and, in men, even effeminate.

The person of *categoría* is thought to be good-looking, neither too mestizo nor too Indian. He has a family background that differentiates him, however slightly, from the rest, as his people, though they may have been very poor, were not ordinary peons. He is literate, perhaps self-taught, has intellectual pretentions, and is a good speaker. He has a modern-type house (rather than merely a good one), nice clothing, and certain kinds of consumer goods—though the latter are less important as these will be increasingly possessed by those who lack the other attributes of *categoría*.

Categorical status is not simply an aspect of socioeconomic status and does not depend upon wealth. Those who have it, especially in its most inalienable forms (such as race), can feel pride and a certain superiority, though they are among the poorest of the poor. The wealthy person who lacks it is ridiculed both by those who have it and those who do not. Categorical status is respected and resented at the same time, but it gives much gratification to those—like the Garzelas and Arquillos families—who have it, whether they are rich or not.

Categoría brings confidence. Diametrically opposed is the self-disparagement and self-disqualification so marked in the attitudes of many of the poorer people of the village, especially those who are ethnically Indian. Attitudes toward race are extremely important in the village, and the word *raza* is commonly used with reference to the older horizons of Spanish versus Indian, conqueror and conquered. The indigenous race is sometimes spoken of proudly—especially in patriotic celebrations when it is oratorically assumed that everyone has some Indian blood of which he is, or should be, proud. This is also a middle class intellectual pretention, a vestige of the Revolution of 1810, although the outcry against the Spanish conqueror would be reevoked one hundred years later. Although a certain pride in racial identification does exist, it is in many ways the antithesis of how most villagers feel about Indianness.

Skin color is the paramount topic of discussion upon the birth of a baby. A child who is lighter-skinned than his parents is greeted with delight, and if he has light or curly hair or blue eyes—however unappealing he may be in other respects—it is believed that he is beautiful and superior, that the world will favor him, and that his life will be easier. If the baby is as dark or darker than his parents, the disappointment will be accepted with regretful resignation. Families who have no reason to expect otherwise exhibit the same negative feelings (with apologies to me) about darkness of skin and Indianness generally.

Race is of great concern among the Arquillos and Garzelas. They call themselves mestizo (in both cases, Indianness is stronger on the wife's side), and Catalino says that his mother was decidedly mestizo. He is himself, however, considered by the village to be as white as Federico and Abel. Although their children vary in color, they are all among the lighter-skinned of the village. People who consider them handsome act as if even their physical appearance were deliberate and are ambivalently admiring and resentful.

Abel Arquillos' son married a girl, partly of Italian descent, of a "good family" of their home village of Buenavista de Cuellar; and while the Arquillos rejoiced that he had married "up," her family condemned the marriage and has refused either to forgive or to see her. Even though the boy is relatively high in *categoría* and is barely distinguishable as a mestizo, she had married "down." There was great concern over the birth of their first child, and, though the family loves the baby, there was unconcealed disappointment that the child was as dark as his father rather than as light as his mother. Typically, Abel's mestiza mother was the most vociferous in calling this to attention. Playfully biting the child's genitals, she said, "You see, he will be dark. This is where you can tell."

There is equal concern over the engagement of Federico's daughter, who is white in appearance though her mother is mestiza, to one of the darkest men in the village. Although he is handsome, this darkness is believed to spoil his looks, and though the marriage was opposed by her family on multiple grounds for years, villagers never doubted the real reason—indeed, they often spoke of it openly: "Pity that a girl of *categoría* should marry someone like that, but that is what happens when a girl is *pasada*" (i.e., past the age of marriage, as Maria was considered to be at the age of twenty-three).

For another example, Doña Rosa's daughter had an illegitimate child by one of the sons of Anselmo Arquillos (Abel's brother), and, as Rosa's family ranges from *mestizo-moreno* to *mestizo-claro*, they were delighted with the child, who has light skin and soft curly hair. Although he is not attractive otherwise, the child is regarded as such a great acquisition to the family that there is little regret that his father has refused to marry and become part of the family. They have gone so far in pride as to decline the Arquillos family's offers of compensation.

As in most European cultures, race is spoken of in terms of blood—e.g., whites are white because they have clean blood; Indians are dark because they have dirty, contaminated blood. This is why whites become ill on an Indian diet. Indian blood makes Indians and mestizos stronger and able to ingest rough, unpalatable, and even contaminated food without getting sick. The idea that there is something unclean and intrinsically inferior about dark skin and "dark blood" is very common in spite of attempts to create a proud *indigenismo*.

This may be seen in a conversation we had with Doña Eufemia, one of the village midwives, whose alcoholic son, Macario, we had attempted, but failed, to rehabilitate. There were times when Macario showed somewhat more intelligence and self-confidence than most of the other inveterate alcoholics, and I remarked to his mother on one occasion that, as he had good qualities, it was a pity that he could not overcome this vice. She agreed, saying that he had to have some good qualities because there was some white blood in her family and that Macario's character reflected this strain. Her other sons did not reflect this strain, as they were dull and plodding *puros Indios* ("Indian through and through"). The good that is in Macario is the result of this drop of white blood; it is the bad Indian blood that is ruining him.

This explanation was followed by a story about a little blond daughter Eufemia claims to have borne, who as a small child was the victim of a *mal de ojo* ("evil eye") from a white woman on a train. "Give her to me," the woman had joked. According to Eufemia, the white woman felt that such a lovely child should not belong to an "ugly Indian," and from that day on, "Believe it, she would not eat and slowly wasted away to her death. I was not allowed to keep her." Such tragic self-disparagement is very common.

Many qualities are attributed to Indian blood, and some are attributed specifically to a mixture of bloods. On one occasion, Rodolfo—who has blue eyes and is considered goodlooking, though effeminate (which he is)—refused to continue riding in my car when I had picked up Catalino and his wife. He explained later that because he has Indian blood, he is capable of great hatred which he will not forget until the day he dies and that that's the way Indians are (under almost any other circumstances, he neither feels nor refers to himself as an Indian). This idea that Indian blood is violent, capable of great feeling and passionate hatred, is expressed not without pride; indeed, pride itself, strong, unyielding, and unadaptive, is supposed to be another attribute of Indianness.

It is in justification of violence, particularly, that this sort of pride is cited. Jesús Zorros once told me that he had quit the employ of a wealthy doctor in indignation over what he believed to be injustice and bad treatment. "That is the way I am," he said, "because I am mestizo. That is what the mixture of blood does. It gets hot, it boils. We cannot tolerate an injustice." Jesús, like Rodolfo, realizes that he is oversensitive but feels that this is something in the blood that cannot be helped.

Stupidity is another attribute commonly assigned to Indian blood. *Indio* is often used as a synonym for stupid, backward, stubborn, and intractable (negative traits that are in some contexts admixed with pride). There are many stories that ridicule the stupidity of the Indian, but there are others in which his stupidity is only apparent and in which the person who imagines that he is triumphing over the stupid Indian is actually himself being taken in.

Thus, Indianness is the antithesis of *categoría,* while the various attributes of being white or Spanish are among its essential features. There is no easier means to *categorical* status than being born with light skin. Such racial attitudes are common in many parts of the world where there has been a long relationship between the conquerors of one race and the conquered of another or the domination of one racial group by another, even when the dominated are the more numerous.

In the village, the racial picture is complicated by the presence of some families having an African strain, descended from early black hacienda workers brought from Veracruz. These people, it seems to me, feel even more inferior and self-disparaging than others, though there is a somewhat greater compensatory drive and less acceptance of inferiority in some of them. They are said in the village to have "black blood," but, aside from the general disparagement of black skin, they do not seem to be otherwise penalized. More prestigious people say that the Anclillos, for example, are lazy and alcoholic and that this is why they failed to take advantage of the early land partition as initial village families and hacienda workers. The Anclillos have some pride in being native to the village, and the family has lately begun to grow in status through the activities of one of its younger men.

The dark-skinned, more Indian people of the village do not identify with blacks as they have encountered them elsewhere in Mexico or in the United States. Their main awareness of blacks comes from their mutual association as migrant laborers in the United States, where they sometimes have friendly relations; and while they are aware of racial discrimination in a general way, they say that it does not exist in Mexico. Racism, as we know it, is not a policy in Mexico, but racial attitudes, as we have demonstrated, do exist. Certainly, there is an ideal of color matching in marriage. Failure to match skin color makes a marriage "down," and a good many advantages are required to offset this. *Mestizaje* is accepted and continuing, nevertheless, although as Santiago Ramirez, a Mexican psychoanalyst, has suggested, there may be some continuing association of *mestizaje* with bastardy.[2]

Attitudes toward race and skin color probably have their greatest effect upon character formation in the child, because they condition the child's early reception by adults and thus affect his self-confidence and initiative, his individual expectations, adult possibilities, and the motivations behind social mobility. The child who has a lighter skin is more likely to be favored, treated deferentially, and considered for a higher education by his parents, because they will have greater career hopes for him.

It is possible that skin color was of greater importance, even in these psychological and social respects, a generation ago. Certainly there are more possibilities at present for mobility across racial lines and their gradations. Education is now more generally available above the lowest social strata, and political influence, at least on local and state levels, is frequently in the hands of the mestizo. The Revolution provided new social opportunities for the mestizo and Indian, but older attitudes persist strongly in determining status, and particularly categorical status.

Degree of acculturation away from Indian and other traditional forms growing out of the colonial culture is still to a considerable extent correlated with skin color, though this is probably on the decline. It is nevertheless probable that Indian types and whites occupy opposite ends of the acculturation gradient in our village, which covers the full range from those considered pure Indian to those considered white.

The rating is based on what members of the community considered these people to be rather than on our own assessments, and we think that it is probably valid, though there are borderline cases that are arguable in terms of *claro* and *moreno*. The distinction between C and D, for example, is particularly dubious with respect to cultural or acculturative considerations; for correlational purposes, we would fuse C, D, and E. Degree of acculturation might be signaled by the way a girl has her hair cut or styled, by a man's possessing a suit jacket, by reading habits, or just by literacy as against nonliteracy. These qualities decidedly enter into status, prestige, and influence, although they are, like skin color, secondary to wealth.

TABLE 4

RACIAL COMPOSITION OF THE VILLAGE*

A.	White	46
B.	*Mestizo Claro* (light mestizo)	129
C.	*Mestizo Moreno* (dark mestizo)	205
D.	*Mestizo Negroide*	12
E.	*Indigena*	15
F.	Unclassified	3

*Distribution for the population over sixteen years of age.

All deficiencies and faults, both social and personal, are commonly attributed to lack of "culture" *(falta de cultura)*, which is believed—even by those who would characterize themselves as lacking in culture—to account for most of the problems confronting the village and Mexico as a whole. There is a certain similarity of content and tone among references to *falta de cultura* and to Indianness as a racial type. Notions of race and of ethnic culture are bound in an anthropological sense—i.e., one becomes involved in questions of *Indianismo, Hispanicismo,* and *Pochismo* (the question of Mexican-American subcultural groupings).[3] In the popular sense, however, *cultura* refers exclusively to the culture of the formerly dominant group.

As in the most preliterate cultures in contact with a prestigious and powerful culture, literacy is regarded as an almost magical endowment. Most of the villagers have learned not only to write their names but to produce a signature so elaborately drawn and highly personalized that it is difficult to imitate. Many who can do no more than this regard themselves as basically literate. The most highly literate people, however, read books and reflect their literacy in their speech—in sophistication of vocabulary, for example, or the ability to turn a phrase in Spanish—and this talent elicits both admiration and envy tinged with resentment and distrust. Federico and Catalino are "men of words". They have read much and can speak with a persuasiveness and elegance that, under certain conditions, moves their auditors far more than the outsider might imagine.

Acculturation precipitates achievement for all who can purchase its accoutrements, but its aspect of *categoría* may deter families that seek upward mobility along the lines of economic rank. These may allow themselves a cautious and tenuous tasting of the outward signs of *categoría* as they move toward unquestionable higher status, but to exhibit any outward manifestations of *categoría* before their economic status has been recognized by all would expose them to ridicule for presuming above their rank. Many of the younger people, however, wear urban clothing, have urban or foreign manners, and more modern types of houses long before they attain an economic status that would once have entitled them to these manifestations of *categoría,* because these things are taken as their most immediate and easily attainable route to status.

On the whole, though, it is still felt that an affectation of *cultura* is pretentious and that a person who affects urbane speech, for example, is putting himself forward, making himself vulnerable, and making a claim that he will in some way have to justify. Such people are particularly susceptible to criticism and malicious gossip; they will be relentlessly singled out for their flaws and immoralities and for the inconsistencies between their life conditions and status aspirations. Lighter-skinned families that have always lived in an aura of permissiveness and greater expectation may expand in *categoría* before their individual economic conditions entitle them to assume the outward forms of advanced acculturation status, so that they may have better houses, modern appliances, furniture, and clothing, and better education for their children without experiencing serious internal difficulty. Other families, however, will hold back, amassing their wealth and eschewing claims to advanced categorical status, feeling secure and even superior, but always ambivalently so.

MORAL STATUS

Moral status is set forth here as a purely formal instrument, as a component of general status. While socioeconomic status, especially—i.e., economic success and its results—takes primacy over the other types of status among men, moral status is nevertheless of great importance and is one of the main preoccupations of community life.

Moral status has its own components, and different groups are concerned with different aspects of it. There is a particularly sharp differentiation between the moral concerns of men and women, for instance. Women are greatly preoccupied with the constant assignment and reassignment, attack and defense of the moral status of one another. But moral status means more to women than to men, because for women, other status components are largely "given" by marriage or by family status, whereas moral status is directly attached to their own personal behavior. A married woman derives her socioeconomic status by and large from her husband, but her moral status depends upon her own behavior and defense of her "moral record," or reputation. Because their moral status is evaluated in terms of the other women in the village more than on the basis of general moral standards, women are self-appointed keepers of each other's moral records.

For men, moral status is less important than the other components of general status. As in many "Latin" countries having an extreme formulation of the double standard of morality, particularly of sexual morality, both men and women are supposed to be highly concerned with the morality of woman but not of men. While the moral concern of women is taken for granted, it is expected, believed, and said that men guard the moral status of their wives, fiancées, sisters, daughters, and sometimes their mothers, notwithstanding their own moral conduct toward other women. Thus, in one case a brother was enraged by his sister's elopement even though he had obtained the woman with whom he lived in the same manner.

Men are supposed to guard the fidelity of their wives jealously and are expected to react drastically, even violently, to any damage to the moral status of the women in their family. *"Mujer mala, matarla o dejarla"* ("a bad woman, kill her or leave her") was often reiterated in the course of our interview. Our own observations generally confirm this male concern for the moral status of women, though only a few cases meet these expectations exactly. The most general difference in observed behavior lies in the intensity of response.

It is highly unusual for a man to leave or to kill a woman for an alleged or proved infidelity. Although the murder of one woman and two men since 1927 might come under this heading, on the whole the woman will be beaten at most. That men are morally concerned about the behavior of their women exerts some restraining influence upon the women, while recruitment by men of partners in their own "immoral" affairs (immoral for the women involved) spurs women to consider defiance. Unattached or unsupervised women elicit some male concern, but not all of it, and are under less restraint, except for that exerted by the female community. A balance is reached that sets the level of "immoral" incidents.

There are a considerable number of cases, well-known in the community, in which men have not responded to, or have acquiesced in, the immorality of a wife, daughter, or sister. The village's most professional prostitute was positively encouraged into her career in the interests of her sister, brothers, brother-in-law, and later her husband. The latter, an alcoholic, took her "engagements" as infidelities but did not respond with violence even when jeered by other men. He left her once or twice but always returned. Typically, it was she who finally left him, tired of his condemnations at the same time that he stole her money to buy drink.

Motives of self-interest and exploitation have obviously entered into a number of other such cases of acquiescence or promotion of immorality. Where a man does respond to a woman's moral lapse, however, he is inclined to hold the woman responsible if his fiancée, wife, mother, or even younger girls are involved. Men and women are nearly unanimous in holding the woman responsible, and it is uncommon for action to be taken against the outside male, though there are a few instances of both violence and litigation for damages.

There are some contexts in which moral status is important for men—in the political realm, for example—but these are far from effectively deterring immoral behavior. A man may have a despicable moral record by village standards and suffer no direct consequences from this other than knowing that his record is public. He may, in fact, enjoy a high general status in spite of his low moral status. The sexual differentiation in moral responsibility and the relative independence of moral and other status components contribute to undermining the behavior-determining effectiveness of the moral code.

Male and female tactics differ in the morality contest. The man is discreet and careful about gossip and calumny; not that he does not indulge in these, but he does not engage in the open brawling that characterizes competition for moral status among women. Moral status is not likely to be the subject of open conversation among men. An attack on another's moral status will be publicly made in a political contest; otherwise it will be made in virtual secrecy. Gossip is considered effeminate in a male, and the two young men considered most effeminate on other counts do gossip a great deal among the older married women.

Women are far more concerned than men with the sexual aspect of moral status: this is the area of a woman's attack and defense of moral status, and it parallels her struggle with other women over men and other interests. Men, married or not, are considered mostly exempt from moral evaluation in this regard. Male adultery and philandering are both expected and highly prevalent, and while this does not make them moral, they are simply accepted as a prevalent immorality. "What can you expect of men?" the attitude runs. "This is their nature, the way they are—pigs, *chingones, cabrones*" ("fornicators, billy goats"); or as one long-suffering wife said, "It is that ugly part of them and of their natures, and we are both [i.e., both sexes] its victim. What can one do?" This seeming disapproval conceals, as we shall see, however, a certain amount of hidden approval.

With the few exceptions of women who enter into male or community affairs, women direct their struggle and conflict almost exclusively against one another. Even when two or more women struggle over the same man (perhaps the husband of one), the man is often bypassed as an incidental. That he has strayed is the fault of the evil woman who tempted him, and the women fly, not at him, but at one another or at one another's reputations. In direct conflict or not, however, women compete in terms of their relative moral status, with the result that each bad mark against another's record is carefully preserved and cited at appropriate times with much zest, fighting spirit, and malicious enjoyment.

USES OF WITCHCRAFT

Like many other bachelors *(solteros)*, Eusebio fears certain women of the village with whom he has, or has had, sexual rapport. Some women, he told me, can cause a man to do their bidding by simply putting something into his food. Once, sensing that one of them was up to something, he scarcely ate for a week. After Filomena was declared a witch by her neighbors, two young men fell ill (which proved beyond a doubt, a neighbor told me, that they had had relations with her).

Such a woman can not only make a man do as she wishes, she can also destroy his perception. This is known as making a man *tonto* ("dull," "unperceptive") so that he will not be aware that she is trifling with others. How else could he tolerate her infidelities calmly, even though he is a *buey* ("ox") or *pendejo* ("cuckold"). Thus, Cristina made her husband *tonto* so that she could pursue her affair with Don Pio; Alejandra did the same to her husband, Jesús Zorros, when she cavorted with the son of Don Pascual. Many instances of this can be cited, for it is very common. It is at least a way of excusing a man for failing to become violent or vengeful, as he should.

Thus, too, the abandoned woman can punish. Several married people have told us without hesitation that the husbands have been given illnesses by the "punishment and hatred" of the abandoned first wife. Don Pascual, an extreme example, was subject to numerous illnesses and chronic insomnia for many years because his first wife and her family had inflicted an invisible hole in his back. He could sleep only when his present wife closed up the hole with her hand, and he was cured only after several years of treatment by his sister-in-law in another village. One young man, who finally died of leprosy, had been bewitched by a woman whom he had abandoned and refused to marry because he was the only son who "remained faithful" to his mother. For a long time, his sister Mirella told us, he vomited worms and small monstrous beings.

Abandoned women are not always satisfied so easily and will often afflict a family. That Cristina's mother-in-law lost one of her legs was blamed on an abandoned woman, and the woman (or women) who caused Don Valentin's *mal malo*—the disease, not unlike epilepsy, brought about by witchcraft—also gave his seven-year-old niece the same *ataques*. "But one does not tell so small a child that she is bewitched *(embrujada),*" explained Antonia, her mother. "I tell her that her attacks are caused by an eclipse of the moon." In the case of Valentin and his sister Antonio the witch is unknown, but the same structure is assumed. A man is not without recourse, however. For fifty pesos he can buy a paper whose words will protect him. It is called *"la santa nomina,"* and though in form it resembles a Catholic invocation, it pleads that the Holy Name will protect this person whose name is given from *"todo ataque de maleficio"* ("all attacks of evil").

The wronged wife can also take revenge against an evil temptress. Doña Carmela, for example, had, unknown to no one, been having an affair with Cristina's father. It remained only for Cristina to "fall upon them" in the fields one day, drinking tequila and eating sardines ("Oh, *la grande vida,* don't you know," added his wife, telling me of it). Cristina and her mother went to a *curandero* ("healer") at a spiritualist center in Emiliano Zapata and paid the man five hundred pesos to strike Carmela with an incurable disease (he wanted one thousand pesos, but they struck a bargain). Eventually Carmela did become ill—her body swelled and her legs were covered with sores—and she went to the same *curandero* to be cured. His cure did not work, however, and Carmela complained that for this she had paid one hundred pesos. The *curandero,* pretending not to have known her name before, said, "But if you are Carmela, how can I cure you for one hundred pesos when I have been paid five hundred pesos to kill you?" This *curandero's* fame grew, for everyone had been satisfied —Carmela with the supreme logic of the information; Cristina and her mother, because they had had results.

A small bit of tattered cloth is enough to make a *muñeco* ("doll"), the instrument of malefaction. Lucio's mother moved to our village primarily because of the *curanderos* hereabout that might cure him of his illnesses. She was told during the course of an ineffective cure that someone had made a *muñeco* and that Lucio's pains would not disappear until it was found and burned. One day a *muñeco* was found in the fields; Lucio took it home and burned it (three days of burning were required to destroy it, so loaded was it with evil), and suddenly he recovered, just as the *curandero* had predicted. Many women whom Lucio had abandoned may have wanted to do this to him.

Such powers are not confined to the living. There are also ghosts who will not rest until one has satisfied certain obligations toward them, and only then will an individual or a member of his family be free of witchcraft. One day a *curandero* told Don Pascual that a dead man wished him to sell his (the deceased's) tools to buy candles for the Virgin with some of the money. Pascual, who is known in the village as a "collector" of "lost" tools did this, and his child, who had been subject to *ataques,* improved.

Doña Teresa often feels bewitched by the ghost of her mother, with whom, during the latter's lifetime, she had had a long and bitter conflict climaxed by Teresa's giving her mother a sound beating (the mother gave birth to a child fathered by Teresa's fiancé). Teresa usually suffers from headaches and strange pains, but this is her *mal malo,* and she knows the difference. There is a small house built around the resting place of Teresa's mother in the village's simple cemetery, and there, from time to time, Teresa spends hours in meditation.

A CASE OF WITCHCRAFT. The witchcraft case described in the following pages took place while we were in the village and involved persons with whom we had been especially intimate. The case is interesting because it suggests what is involved in *embrujamiento* ("witchcraft"), including the coveting of work, temporary alliances among women, hatred over *desprecio* ("scorn"), and the compounding of past grievances on the part of the accuser, the counteraccuser, and their various allies as well.

A house that once belonged to the Mexican painter Diego Rivera is located on the edge of the *Colonia Cantaranas,* one of the poorest *colonias* of the village. Don Pascual had long been caretaker of the house, and, though he said he had not been paid for two years, he longed to keep the job. It was difficult for him to accept the fact that the owner had decided to keep Filomena, who had been our maid in that house, as caretaker.

The arrangement pleased Filomena because it meant that she had a place to live, an income, and odd jobs for Chucho Garzelas, her new "husband." Of the two buildings, the smaller housed Alejandra and her young husband Jesús Zorros (who helped Filomena as caretaker), as well as Amanda, a new addition to the village, and her several small children (Filomena had always been adept at subemploying). Soon, however, Chucho left Filomena to rejoin his legal wife (fulfilling the village's worst expectations), and the three women consoled one another (for even Alejandra feels that she holds her husband only by a "knowledge" of "certain things").

Guadalupe, allied with Don Pascual from the start and now his *comadre*, bitterly resented Filomena, who had treated her with inconceivable contempt during our stay. One evening when Guadalupe went to relieve herself at the facilities in our enclosed grounds (as she later told the justice of the peace when she was called as a witness) she saw a sight so shocking that she ran to tell her sister Asunción. In the living room of the smaller building she had seen Alejandra in the nude, staring at the ceiling, and muttering incomprehensibly. Many candles were lit, she was reading from a book, and Filomena, Amanda, and Leticia were with her. Asunción advised Guadalupe to forget it, *"de no meterse."* It was well known that Alejandra knew the witchcraft of repossessing a man whose affections have wandered. She was probably just helping Filomena to get Chucho back, keeping her own hold on Jesús, and helping Amanda to snag a man named Antonio. Leticia was probably trying to get Cristina's husband back. (It is not irrelevant that Leticia is thought to be a "natural witch" in spite of herself. It is often remarked about the village that she once caused and stopped a hailstorm.)

Guadalupe was willing to forget it until one day the following week, when, coming to pick *guavas* from our trees (with our permission), Filomena threw a rock at her as usual, and Guadalupe, feeling scorned to the limits of possibility, became infuriated. Now Pascual became deeply concerned, fearing that Alejandra, who had been "surprised" in an amorous embrace with his son, would harm his son. Pascual therefore accused these women of witchcraft to the justice of the peace; and at this point another witness, a nephew of Pascual, appeared, claiming that he had blown out the candles. He did not say this before the justice of the peace but merely voiced it about the village. When called upon to testify, he left town.

The four accused "witches" denied that any such ceremony had taken place and became very upset—indeed, quite ill at the time—though the situation would grow much worse. Leticia's husband beat her soundly, for (as he explained to me) a man cannot allow his wife to make a *tarugo* ("stupid fool") of him and that if she continued these witching games he would have to beat her again (though this was primarily an assertion of his manliness). He then went to Asunción to get the facts; Asunción blamed Guadalupe, and Guadalupe assured him that she had not seen Leticia there—someone else must have implicated her in the *chisme* ("gossip"). For her part, Leticia whined that she had only gone to the house that night to borrow money from Filomena, who always had it to lend (true, the villagers explained, because she always stole from us). Leticia's attempts at disassociation worked rather well at the outset, and the gossips were not too hard on her. All felt the agony of betrayal of a *compadre*.

The case became a *cause célèbre* in the village. "And I know it is all true," said Doña Mirella, who had many an old score to settle with Filomena. (Filomena always refers to Mirella as "that woman who took my husband," or "the unwed mother," or, worst of all, as the girl and her mother who occasionally had "the same men.") "I'd like to see those women burned at the stake," Mirella said, "with green wood." Other villagers were less extreme, but they all call witchcraft *"esas porquerías"* ("unclean things") and consider it a very serious matter.

Many who had been Filomena's friends were quick to denounce her as a fool for becoming involved with a man, wished to make it clear that they had never "really" been friends, and said that she was now "the lowest of the low." Amanda did not have this problem, as everyone looked down on her anyway. She was new in the village, had arrived without a husband, but with several children and in such extreme poverty that she had had to beg to bury her dead baby. Filomena, who is a strange mixture of cruelty and charity, had given her a place to live and food to eat and had even helped her along with Antonio. Alejandra had never had friends in the village but had always kept to her *colonia* and her relatives (Pascual and his wife) and was known to have books of black magic, including *El libro de San Cipriano.*

Not all men held themselves aloof from discussion of the case. Epimenio, for example, added to the *chisme* ("gossip") the fact that he knew the power of this book because the priest had made him burn his own copy if he wished to continue to receive communion or go to confession. "And that," Santos would add, "should give you an idea of just how powerful it is. All this black magic is nothing compared to *El libro de San Cipriano.*" Everyone took serious note of this "scientific" postscript to the case.

Pascual waited for Filomena to leave the village, because the glacial stares and lukewarm greetings that she received from friends made life difficult for her, and, in addition, her new employer had not paid her for several months. Filomena, however, was stubborn. When Alejandra and Amanda began having visions (Alejandra saw a fanged woman; Amanda, huge black spiders crowding her into a corner), she laughed at them and came immediately to me, certain that this was of importance to what I was studying and that I should know about it. (Filomena acquired a certain detachment through her association with me and the knowledge of what I was trying to learn. She pondered the problem of why they had "cracked" and she had not, supposed that she was just "stronger" than they, and was grateful for that.)

Alejandra and Jesús then moved to a room Filomena had taken in another house, because Alejandra had become too ill to face her neighbors. Assured that I had my notebook with me, Filomena took me to see her. Weeping wretchedly, Alejandra told me about her visions—how she felt a breath on her neck when she tried to sleep at night and how a fanged woman would then pull her hair and tie her feet. She said that she had a diarrhea like *"bava de nopal"*—"saliva" of the Indian prickly pear tree (Filomena nudged me to write this down as it was important in *embrujamientos*)—and explained that her illness really dated to an earlier time when Guadalupe had put a spell on her.

(Several years earlier Pascual had taken Alejandra to a nearby village where his sister-in-law told her she was bewitched. At the spiritualist center at Emiliano Zapata, however, she was told that she was not bewitched but was suffering from a fall she had had several years earlier and that she must have Pascual rub her belly to get well. During the "treatments" Pascual and his son had both propositioned her and counseled her to leave Jesús. In a biblical manner of speech characteristic of Alejandra, she had replied to Pascual, "No, in these waters you will not cleanse yourself.")

That the witches were having a run of bad luck gave the villagers a happy sense of cosmic justice. Soon the witches were given *apodos* ("nicknames") by their accusers—Filomena, *"La Podrida"* ("the rotten one"); Alejandra, *"La Chorriente"* ("the gusher," because of her diarrhea);

and Amanda, *"La Bomba,"* which villagers later changed to *"La Boa"* ("the serpent"), the title of a popular song with an indelicate *doble sentido* (see Appendix 2).

Finally the "witches" began to disassociate themselves from one another, each claiming that the others had had unclean living habits and that their intimacy had been a trial. Filomena told me that Alejandra did possess those books and that Alejandra had, in fact, been helping her to get Chucho back. She, Filomena, was not a witch, however. She had spent many pesos (as if it were worth every cent of the expense) going to the very best centers in Mexico City, because Chucho's wife was, and had been, practicing black magic against her. Much good it does to light candles to saints when everyone knows that the Devil is much stronger than God! Chucho's wife had been praying to *El Rey de Los Reyes* ("the King of Kings").

For Filomena, Chucho's legal wife represented the real conflict and Alejandra's magic, child's play. Filomena had now bought *La Oración de la Muerte* ("prayer of death"), a prayer to Jesus to give the purchaser victory over another person and to deprive that person of peace forever. Chucho, believing himself bewitched and threatening to come with his gang and kill her, became very ill with *el mal malo,* staggering about conspicuously, claiming amnesia, and, in general, doing Filomena much harm.

When Pascual brought the case to the municipal court, however, no witnesses were mentioned, and for lack of witnesses, the court case never materialized. (Pascual's nephew had returned to the village and told Filomena that he was prepared to affirm or deny in court that he had blown out the candles, depending upon whether she would pay him at least one hundred pesos.)

Alejandra regained her health by going to a famous *curandero* in Mexico City (though she assured me that it was a "true miracle"). Amanda is now united *(juntada)* with Antonio, which is as good as married in our village and environs. Filomena left the village to work in Mexico City, and when all the bases for antagonism were removed, the talk of witchcraft died down as well. Neither Filomena nor Alejandra will be labeled as witches unless there is another score to settle someday or some reason why this episode should be recalled. The villagers are not purposelessly vindictive, but the uses of sorcery are many.

Witchcraft as a form of conflict has here been seen as an expression of the struggle of women over men, of women for the preservation of their families, and as a (probably ineffective) sanction for familial stability. Witchcraft and accusations of witchcraft occur most often where family instability is greatest. The women most often suspected, as in the foregoing case, are those of Indian type, at the lower end of the acculturation gradient, who are either sexually active themselves or whose sexually-active husbands cause them to be sexually and socially defensive. Witchcraft, along with gossip and the contest for moral status, adds to the atmosphere of interpersonal malice and conflict.

THE MORAL RECORD

One may speak almost literally of the "moral record," a phrase suggested by the village expression *"a no manchar sus papeles"* ("not to soil one's papers"). It is so nearly palpable that one might almost imagine each person in the village possessing a book in which he keeps moral tabs on everyone else, both for actions concerning himself and as much as he knows of the moral history of others. In this imaginary book he accumulates his list of grievances, *agravios, desprecios,* and insults in indelible ink and his past credits and debts of gratitude in dim, disappearing ink. The record of grievances persists and multiplies; debts of gratitude, on the other hand, do not accumulate but are dependent, where they exist at all, upon recurrent activation.

Villagers agree with this view of themselves. *"Así somos,"* they say: we are ingrates; we never forget a wrong or an insult; we are sensitive and hot-blooded, and we know how to hate. And this is true: friendship is short, hatred is long. Formal, skillfully exercised patronage alone maintains the loyalty of its dependents, and even patronage requires a continual activation of loyalties, together with a sensitivity toward minimums and thresholds. This keeping of a moral record gives the strongest evidence of the importance of the moral precepts so often violated.

If a man suffers no important reprisals for political immorality, for example, his actions are nevertheless all recorded in the tenacious memory of the community. This record may not strike him down, but it may jab at his pretentions; or, if it does not lower him in some absolute sense, it at least establishes the general level against which all men rationalize their moral status. Women are greatly preoccupied with this general level, and some of the most virtuous women (by village standards) are among the most active and vicious keepers of the record. It is important not only to keep the record but also to disseminate the information on which it is based, for each act of dissemination affects the overall relative moral status of each member of the village.

POLITICAL MORALITY

COMPROMISED PEOPLE IN UNDERMINED ROLES. Villagers believe that village leaders are equally corrupt. Even those who are asked to take political office protest that this will invite a suspicion of self-interest. The only way to avoid suspicion is *"de no meterse,"* and those who put themselves forward in spite of this caveat are always assumed to be lining their own pockets. If they are not taking from the public treasury, it is assumed that they are being "bought off." We were often struck by the constant allegation or suspicion that someone is being bought; even a proffered drink may be construed as bribery.

There have been many absurd allegations that Catalino, for example, "buys" the important people who visit the village from Mexico City by giving them fruits from his orchard or avocados, or that he (who is obviously bankrupt) has bought the services of the *licenciado* who represents him. "Bought" always means buying a person, paying him off, getting him to do something immoral, or receiving some kind of patronage or service in return for cash payment. Although suspicions are exaggerated to the edge of paranoia, people are, in fact, "bought," and "purchases" of acquiescence are quite common in the village.

It is alleged—and probable—that the owner of the hacienda bought the acquiescence of Federico and Victoriano so that he might have allies in his actions to change the site of the village's kindergarten. Whether an actual cash payment was involved is not the point; he may merely have excited their hopes of some gain in patronage and special privilege from him and used their influence to make villagers sympathetic with his plight of having a kindergarten outside his gate. He is even said to have "bought" the priest (by paying for six months of Mass in advance) to persuade the villagers to build another church outside the hacienda.

Buying off opposition is a commonplace tactic of the sugar cooperative and amounts, in fact, to a village game. Someone will initiate an
apparent campaign of protest against corruption in the sugar cooperative
for the sole purpose of naming his price. Whether he does this cynically or
with partial self-deception is of no importance. Victoriano, for example, is
currently outraged over the failure of his campaign against the cooperative.
He had been urging people not to plant cane, had not planted it himself
for a year, and was finally told by the cooperative to name his price. He
asked for, and was promised, a truck, returned to cane planting, but never
received the truck. His son told us this story as an example of the
treachery and hypocrisy of the cooperative management.

Federico and Pio are also said to have received cash payoffs from the
cooperative. That Catalino Arquillos refused to be bought off and cease his
activities against the cooperative when all of his followers had been bought
off at much lesser prices is always spoken of with incredulity, as if there
were something sinister behind it. On several occasions it has actually been
cited to us as proof of his unreasonable, incomprehensible stubbornness.

Occasionally one sees something like admiration for this act of
refusal, but it is more often cited to make other points. Manuel says, for
example, that Catalino did not act against the sugar cooperative until he
had lost his job and that he refused the bribe because he had expected
more money (a mere 50,000 or 100,000 pesos did not interest him). We
have no reason to believe this, although not too long ago another such
resister actually became a leader, in this case the cooperative manager.
Manuel was one of his followers, and, like all the rest, he omits an
explanation of his own role, neglecting to mention whether he accepted a
payment at the time he dropped from the ranks of Catalino's followers.
Acceptance, however, is not held prominently in awareness.

Political authority as such is discredited. All past or possible leaders,
office holders, even minor functionaries are compromised by their records.
The roles themselves may be said to be undermined and their authority
diminished regardless of who plays them (Don Pio alone seems to inspire
confidence). The system involves, then, compromised people occupying
undermined roles that carry only discredited authority.

Corruption is not confined solely to the political leadership. It exists
on all levels and affects every office or formalized position, from the
Ayudante Municipal (highest political administration in the village) to the

kindergarten teacher. On higher and lower levels, corruption is serious.

The kindergarten teacher, for example, and others as well, have from time to time raised money for the school, but villagers complain that the results of these fund-raising drives are never apparent. Both the kindergarten and the school lack even brooms and school supplies, though money is periodically allocated for these purposes by the village, the state, and the federal government. In one instance, the kindergarten teacher held a raffle to raise money for toys and supplies for the kindergarten. She sold many tickets (we sold several hundred pesos worth for her among our friends) but later complained that many who had bought tickets had not paid, but had only pledged to pay for them later. She raised some 300 pesos, we knew, to raffle an alarm clock worth maybe 60 or 80 pesos. But the clock disappeared while in her possession, the raffle was repeatedly postponed on the grounds that more tickets had to be sold and money collected, and finally the raffle was forgotten (not precisely forgotten, but those who remembered it either said nothing or spoke of it only among themselves). Both the money and the clock remained in "someone's" possession.

Much of the money that is raised by dances, supposedly for the maternity clinic, the school, the Youth Club, or the Center of Rural Welfare, remains in the hands of those who monopolize the presentation of these affairs. (Dances were held for the maternity clinic rent while our study was paying the rent.) Octavio collected rental fees from private parties for the use of a phonograph bought by the study for the Youth Club. The Youth Club itself has an income from admissions to watch television and from the dances as well. Only some of this money goes for the purpose for which it was intended, however; some of it is undoubtedly kept by the administrators.

A number of people are involved in running the dances. For a long time Octavio was in charge of music and the "hall"; the *Ayudante Municipal* and the then promoter of the Center of Rural Welfare were in charge of ticket sales; Epimenio and a few others tended to the sale of beer. All of these were said to be pocketing much of the money that was raised and turning over only a small sum to the village. Epimenio invariably declared that no profit had been made on a given evening because many people had taken beer without paying for it. Although the others in charge might demand a public reckoning, no public reckoning was ever given, and this "nonpayment" amounted to a good many cases of beer. It was "well-known" that Epimenio was keeping much of this money (it was observed on many occasions that beer had to be paid for before it was given), even though some of it might have been lost through an occasional credit. The same was true of tickets.

Again, the administration of the maternity clinic was involved in allocating serum for vaccination and other medicines that are supposedly distributed free throughout the state from the Department of Health of the Mexican Federal Government. But virtually everyone in the village believes that these medicines are not given free, that they are sold, and that the nurse and the "promoter" for the center have sold them in the village of the nurse's family. One way or another, the serum was not distributed properly, and the most feeble alibis were given for its absence. A scandal in a nearby city revealed that the administrators of the medical supply department of the state branch of the health department, who were supposed to administer free medicines to villages and hospitals in the state, had not only been selling these medicines illegally but had been trafficking in narcotics as well. They were dismissed, but not before they had done a profitable business for many years.

UNICEF officials who visited the village told us that powdered milk had been sent here, but we noted that it had not arrived. Nevertheless, Doña Teresa's daughters and sisters were photographed in the village for publicity purposes for the United Nations Organization of Infant Health and Care. The pictures were printed in UNICEF brochures stating specifically that these children were recipients of the milk (that had not arrived) and implying that their healthy looks were owing to the UNICEF powdered milk campaign. The milk does appear, for sale, at certain drugstores in a nearby city.

Señorita Garzelas (who did not know whether to be amused or indignant, proud or angry) told us that the Center of Rural Welfare had used a photograph of her father's house, which he had built himself many years ago, to demonstrate how it was improving village housing in rural areas. Such happenings are notorious, are generally believed by all the people of the village, and strongly influence their expectations of the behavior of people in office.

COLLUSIVE PARTICIPATION. While I am not able to offer documentary proof of these many grafts and public pilferings, the point is that corruption in public office exists on all levels, from the very top to the very bottom. Innumerable other examples could be given—of committee members who have taken public funds, or of the many people employed by the study (to work on projects with the Boy's Club, for example) who have taken seed or feed or have otherwise taken private advantage of public funds. Villagers believe that everyone does this sort of thing (Don Pio excepted), and Federico offers a perfect example of a man who has for many years served the village to his own advantage.

One wonders how such a system can work at all, because the administration does have some real functions, a certain amount of progress does take place, and the system is not overthrown. The answer, at least in part, is that there is a kind of passive acquiescence and, more than that, an almost active, collusive participation by most people throughout the system.

Most community participation is of a voluntary nature. Even where laws and sanctions exist, there is a reluctance to invoke them. In spite of much talk at meetings and discussions threatening the use of coercive sanctions, they are seldom evoked and are generally ineffective when they are invoked. On one occasion, for example, Don Pepe was brought to the municipal court and charged with taking more than one thousand pesos of the cooperative store's funds. The settlement agreed upon involved his repaying the money to the village, and on this note the case was dismissed. But Pepe made no attempt to repay the money, no further litigation ensued, and he is today an accepted member of the community. Although no one has forgotten, the fact is that the most vociferous of the aggrieved have themselves committed similar crimes against the community. Manuel, Federico, Anecito, and Victoriano, to name a few, are as notoriously guilty as Pepe himself.

The point to be noted is the general lack of opposition and protest. In every case of this sort, the money involved belongs to a large group of people, and it might be expected that some would seek retaliation or reparation. But protests are few, and those that do occur generally find little support and die out as disruptive attempts of the moment on the part of some individual troublemaker (a community definition). This collective collusion goes a long way toward explaining the election and reelection of corrupt office holders who are well-known for crimes against the very office to which they are reelected, as well as the election and reelection of weak, irresponsible, but controllable and nondisruptive candidates. In litigation, it is reflected in the general absence of witnesses against the accused and in the absence of vengeance, even against murderers of kin.

It is a puzzling phenomenon, this mass collusion in the maintenance of a system. It imitates the outward appearances, but not the actuality, of responsible democratic government, for the individual who takes private advantage of a public trust rationalizes that everyone does what he does, which is true. This is not his defense, however; his defense is denial, and his security lies in the knowledge that the village will not pursue inquiry or public accusation very far. One would think that a system as corrupt as this, which is nevertheless maintained somehow and whose forms are still approved and seemingly valued, would require a great deal of rationalization to reconcile the discrepancies between real and ideal behavior. Yet this is not the case. To a certain extent, individual responsibility is submerged in the notion that everyone will steal given the opportunity. An individual most often regards this as true even of himself.

Behavior thus rationalized is not, however, rationalized away. It is neither denied nor treated with indifference. It is a matter of common discussion and protest in the village, but it rarely "goes public"; rather, it is discussed in small groups outside public meetings and on occasions when people are called upon for further action. It may be said, in fact, to rationalize nonparticipation and withdrawal from responsibility. Thus, many people who refuse to pay the taxes, contributions, and labor required of them by the village will cite, when solicited, allegations of past misuses of public funds.

At a time when the village was trying to raise money to pay for the transportation of some milk goats that the study had paid for, one heard again and again about the "chickens of three years ago," what had happened to them, and who had privately sold them and kept all the proceeds. I have asked: "If the village knew about this dishonest transaction and knew who was responsible, why was nothing done at the time? Why were these people not prosecuted? Why were they not forced to give an accounting or to return the money?" To this, there was no reply, as nothing was done; protest had taken the form of disgruntled muttering and a reaffirmation of general skepticism. At one meeting that I witnessed, there was an oblique reference to the education committee's misuse of money in the sale of these chickens. But the speaker backed down quickly when the person referred to rose and said: "That concerns me. The money was not misused; it was absorbed by school expenses. And it all happened three years ago anyway." That ended the discussion.

Such protests seldom go beyond allegations, and allegations are invariably denied. People who told us of the sins, crimes, misdemeanors, and delinquencies of others in the village did not (with perhaps one exception) speak of themselves or admit their own failings. Each officer of the cooperative store, for example, attributes its failure to the mishandling of funds by its officers, implicating all of the others and excluding himself, although all become equally implicated once all have testified.

An informal maintenance of forms is vital to the village's morale, to its sense of being a village, of being part of a kind of political system, and of being included in something that offers some hope for the future and some security for the present. Community decisions must be made, and there is a progress orientation that is part of the national postrevolutionary heritage. A certain number of public works is required, and to activate the heavy, corrupt bureaucracy that lies above the village in behalf of such public works requires years of petition, litigation, lobbying, fund raising, and so forth.

All this requires leadership and occasional meetings of the village as a corporate group to express and ratify group decisions. It requires a village government to exercise authority in the allocation of land, water rights, living sites, and public utilities. It requires an apparatus for the resolution of conflict. The orientation toward education, which is strong in the village, requires that at least part of the village occasionally concern itself with its school. The Center of Rural Welfare, in spite of its obvious deficiencies, also requires active participation by some (though there are times when the life of this organization is reduced to the appearance-maintaining activities of its paid promoter).

Even though few offices may actually be active, there is still a need for leadership and for even the mere holding of office, of participation in the maintenance of institutional forms. Democracy is believed to involve a turnover of personnel; no one person (even Don Pio, who has general approbation) should hold the same office too many times or too sequentially. Don Pio's nine-year tenure as president of the *Comisariado Ejidal* is considered a bad thing because it smacks of *caciquismo,* whose taint Pio himself would avoid. The modern political leader wants to maintain the forms of elective office and discard the image of the *cacique* who ruled by force, patronage, and influence.

The notion persists that village affairs are a communal concern, that the nucleus of village government is a communal organization of *ejidatarios,* and that many people should be involved in village government. Add to this the notion that all men are equal in their defects, however variable in their virtues, and one sees why the village continues to rotate through office people against whom it has accumulated a lengthy record of allegations and grievances. There is some concern, however, that the younger elements of the village become involved and that they begin their first exercise of public office with an untainted record *("que tengan papeles todavía no manchados").*

Those who hold office serve the public by maintaining various facades: the false fronts of a village democracy, of a national democracy, and of a functioning *agrarismo.* All contribute to these socially-important appearances, and they contribute in the hope that these forms will someday be made real. In view of the general skepticism and awareness of the hollowness of forms, one might think that no involvement remains with the forms themselves. But this, as will be shown, is not quite true.

The quality of this service that everyone owes may be illustrated by the following episode. During a period of leftist student agitation on behalf of the Cuban Revolution and Castro, when such actions as the teachers' strike and the dynamiting of the statue of Aleman at the university were criticized, the office of the president called for a massive demonstration of loyalty and support of the "Mexican Revolution and its leadership." Party organizers went to all villages and municipalities; buses and trucks were hired; and as many men as possible were gathered from a radius of well over a hundred miles around Mexico City.

In the village, each "delegate" received free transportation to and from Mexico City and ten pesos for the day; above all, perhaps, there was the allure of an excursion to the big city. Sixty men from our village went, and the next day the newspapers carried pictures of thousands upon thousands of people gathered in Mexico City's *Zocalo* to hear a speech by the president. The white straw hats of the *campesinos* were conspicuous in the crowd, and the press insisted that this showed the peasant's overwhelming support of a government interested in his well-being.

The members of the village expedition took a different tone upon their return. Alfonso, for example, said, "Yes, I went. There was the president speaking to us from his balcony, and we know that he really turns his back on us and [gesturing] puts the money in his pocket." Why, then, did he go? "Why not?" he replied. "The money is provided, we are asked to go," he shrugged, "and there were soldiers with guns and bayonets all around us. What could we have done there, then?" (The soldiers were stationed around the *Zocalo* in Mexico City. No one was forced to go from the village.)

Thus, in so many ways, the facades are maintained. They serve not only as appearances to conceal a contradictory reality but hopefully, also, as a framework for a new actuality. This is not to suggest that this hope is among the primary motivations behind the maintenance of forms. The problem of the real functioning of the system must be explored further.

REAL LEADERSHIP.   Apart from those men who are placed in positions for the purpose of maintaining those positions in the institutional structure and who really do lead or serve in a relatively active way, the village achieves most of its modest progress by means of a system of petitioning that integrates the village with the bureaucracy above. This system requires the services of skilled petitioners, intermediaries, men of words, men gifted in the patient, obsequious cultivation of those above them on behalf of the village. The village's real leadership and initiative is in the hands of a very few such men—Pio, Federico, Octavio, and Gabriel occupying the top four positions, with a great many others variably occupying the fifth position.

These men exercise the village's real leadership whether they happen to be in office or not. Leadership is thus actually independent of formal office, and this is one reason why the village's progress or its level of function or malfunction is little affected by who happens to hold office at any given time. Decisions are made by the same people, regardless of who holds the top offices. Only one of the younger men, who aspires to something more than placid office occupancy, is far more active and influential when he is in office. Out of office, he tends to recede into the background; but he remains influential all the same, and his influence, like that of the other top men, will probably grow until it becomes relatively independent of his actual office positions.

There are roughly three types of office holders: experts in petitioning and cultivating outsiders, mediators between the village and people of wealth or influence of the village, and mediators between the village and the higher bureaucracy. Whatever may be said about their peculations—for they do extract their own rewards—they mediate successfully on the village's behalf and can say of the *Ayudantía*, the school, the basketball court, the postal service, or of some improvement in the road or transportation: "I was largely instrumental in obtaining that for the village. I made many trips to men of influence and led the village beyond its own inertia to take the minimal actions necessary to this achievement."

Federico, Pio, Octavio, and a few others do not exaggerate such claims, however much they may line their own pockets in the process (this will be charged against them, whether it is true or not). Such men must be creative. They must be able to transcend the limitations, obstacles, and deadweights of the bureaucracy with its multiplicity of doors, offices, contacts, and channels. They must search for and cultivate all potentially benevolent *patrones,* create new benevolent *patrones* whenever possible, convince a potential *patron* that he is benevolent, and serve as intermediaries between the benevolent *patron* and the petitioning peon. They must establish swift rapport with the outsider approaching the village and explore his possibilities—always probing for their own benefit, of course, always looking for a job for themselves or members of their families, or a contact or other personal benefit—at the same time that they try to discover whether through this person they can reestablish their mediating role for the village. And they are extraordinarily successful; the village is recognized as outstanding in the region for this, for through the activities of a very few people, the village maintains a large network of outside relations and resources.

Village leaders have succeeded in the very difficult task of extending their influence beyond this village to a network of villages. This is especially true of Federico and Pio, and, during the period of his struggle against the sugar cooperative, it was true of Catalino as well. It was our village that inaugurated and organized the local network that later received potable water and electricity. Our village has also been outstandingly influential in the development of local centers of rural welfare, and for a time, families of other, sometimes larger villages sent their children here to attend school. For its size, the village is involved to an unusual degree with outside agencies, including federal agencies and most of the organizations for community development. This density of contact noted before is due to, and maintained by, the few men repeatedly mentioned in these pages. Even Victoriano, who is less of a leader than a braggart and bluff, has maintained a number of contacts for the village with outsiders and the state's governors.

Village leaders have been successful in extending their leadership because they not only initiate projects for the network but also follow-up the petitioning. All of the villages around this one engage in petitioning— i.e., attracting the outsider, inviting him to banquets, and flattering him, though the results very often scarcely suffice to pay for the *mole* traditionally served on such occasions. The president, the state governor, the director of the sugar cooperative, and the politically-ambitious wealthy men of the area are all cultivated in this way. Village representatives, however, are skilled in the follow-up—in tedious office-sitting, in reminding over long periods of time, in reinforcing pressures, petitions, and appeals, and in flattery. Few people in the village have this gift, but Don Federico has it in abundance, as we were to see repeatedly during the period of our stay.

The Cuernavaca millionaire who donated the money for the bridge and for road improvements, the governor of the state, and the director of the sugar cooperative were all feted and petitioned during our stay in the village. They are greeted by the band and by the pretty girls of the village; a solemn procession then ambles slowly through the streets before the car of the distinguished visitor and his entourage. There are school performances or band performances, invariably with fireworks, and there is finally a sumptuous meal with much drinking and toasting and many long, flattering speeches. (Victoriano, who excels at flowery, obsequious speeches, is often used on these occasions.)

Seating arrangements are carefully planned so that Federico will often be in a position to talk with the guest of honor; almost everyone else (including Pio and Octavio) sits at a distance and remains silent throughout the proceedings. This long conversation, the involving of the visitor, the delicate preparations, and the follow-up as well are often left to Federico. Although Catalino's skill in these matters exceeds Federico's, his present position excludes him from participation in such doings. Catalino was, however, the speaker for the village until about 1957. He made an eloquent speech of greeting when the study had its first contact and conference with the village elders and had been urgently pressed to do so by people who are now his bitter enemies.

There were some significant differences in the receptions given to various important people during our stay. The villagers felt so remote from the governor, for example, that Federico and his wife waited on the guests' table, the villagers asked me and Dr. Ted Schwartz to represent them at that table, and Pio did not appear until the lunch was over. At the site of the disputed land, the men approached the governor very cautiously to plead for his help in their struggle against Catalino. The supplication was brief and quickly over (and, we are now certain, unheard and unheeded). The governor's wife, surrounded by the women at this point, became very embarrassed by a quarrel that erupted between the wives of Catalino and Victoriano.

Surrounded by three of his *pistoleros* ("bodyguards," "gunmen"), the director of the sugar cooperative was banqueted in the enclosure of Pio's home. Very few men of the village were present, but I had been invited along with three girls who were to join the table after the meal. Pio, who was seated next to the director, gave me his seat so that we could converse. The villagers sighed and smiled with pleasure, and while the director was pleased with everything that day, he nevertheless kept none of his promises concerning what he would give the village.

The aspiring *politico* who had built the bridge was treated respectfully, almost obsequiously, but this was a more symmetrical situation as he was a petitioner himself. He wished to enter state politics, wanted the support of the villages, and had come through on promises he had made to other villages. In this case, almost all of the "active" men of the village were seated at the long table at which he was given the place of honor.

PERSUADERS AND PATRONES. Village leaders tend to attain eminence on the basis of four factors, all extremely rare in our village and its environs and not mutually exclusive: (1) an ability to meet people of higher status, (2) an ability to speak persuasively and well on public occasions, (3) a tendency to maintain a certain formality amid general informality, and (4) leadership based on patronage.

The first two factors form the most powerful base of Federico's position and elicit an admiration for Catalino that survives even the greatest hatred toward him. Most of the village's potential leaders feel hopelessly inferior to Federico and Catalino in their use of language, believing that *el castellano* ("Castilian") is part of their inherent *categoría*, their Spanish racial heritage. We were told that Pio, who is an awkward, tense, painfully shy speaker, used to stay near Catalino at village meetings when they were both young men and an older generation was in control. Now one of the most powerful figures in the area and Catalino's enemy, he owns a book on public speaking, which he claims to have read and which he keeps to remind himself of the heights that he would very much like to attain.

A strong concern about form and procedure is not characteristic of this environment; nevertheless a small number of people do care and are characterologically structured to maintain the minimum formality required to keep the lower layers of the bureaucracy intact. Octavio is an admirable example of this, as he can advance formal proceedings and agenda over any amount of bickering and bantering and sees to it that resolutions and actions are all properly worded and signed and put into the right channels.

The community leader whose greatest strength lies in his position as *patron* is of great importance, in spite of the paucity of those who qualify. Here, particularly, is Pio, with Federico rising in the ranks. The combination of patronage, local political leadership, and higher political aspiration is a transformation of old-style *caciquismo* and is distinguishable from other, more rationalized bases of leadership. Pio's leadership depends primarily on patronage, and here some observations should be made about the relationship between patronage and corruption.

Pio is *patron* on his own level and in his own locality and on higher levels of patronage as well. He is a leader of the Type 1 and Type 4 categories at the same time. That he has personally benefited greatly through his activities as *patron* and political leader is, on the whole, not resented because his record is considered to be cleaner than most. His exceptional regard is based not entirely upon personal qualities but also upon his dual role as leader and *patron,* which enables him to be the benevolent *patron* on the local level (a condition that he, in particular, has developed highly).

The importance of the image of the benevolent *patron* from whom all blessings flow has already been discussed, and it was remarked at that time that villagers react differently to Pio, Federico, Octavio, and other leaders on the basis of a concept of *egoísmo.* A man who takes from public resources for his own benefit is said to be *egoísta* and is bitterly resented, however general the practice may be. At the same time, however, it is taken for granted that anyone who gets ahead and rises to the level of *patron* does so to a very considerable extent by this means, particularly if the position is not inherited. Many people have achieved this position through the rapid stratification that followed the Revolution in Mexico, but however they have achieved it, it is assumed that some cost to the community and to the people in general has been involved.

But the onerous aura of *egoísmo* can be mitigated by the proper exercise of patronage, which means by becoming a benevolent *patron.* Anywhere in the structure, the attitude of petitioners toward those above them will be governed by whether their petitions are occasionally, and in some personal manner, granted. On the local level, Pio pays off some measure of what he has taken from the public. He turns a certain amount back to the public by allocating a portion of it to community projects or for individual needs. He may sponsor a religious festival or perhaps a special Mass. The point is that only a certain portion need be thus distributed for him to satisfy the minimum requirements of the benevolent *patron.* I believe that he exceeds the minimum requirements and that this is probably connected with his ambition to elevate his status as *patron.*

As he rises, the minimum payment that exempts him from being an *aprovechado* (one who "profits"), and *egoísta* rises correspondingly. As he has risen higher, he has had to do increasingly more as *patron,* and the amplification of his possibilities aids him in this; for as he becomes more involved in the higher bureaucracy, he can distribute the favors of his higher offices rather than his own wealth. He can favor the petitions of his local constituency over those of his general constituency. From small favors, such as making his truck or small loans available to his dependents, to larger ones—such as intervening in the affairs of the sugar cooperative, obtaining the use of its earth-moving equipment for road work in the village, intervening in a court case or with the governor—he can "pay off" a larger sum and not from his personal assets.

This turning of a certain percentage back into public use and of a differential allocation function on the part of the political leader *cum* benevolent *patron* characterizes, in my view, the entire system on all levels. A certain amount is channeled into private aggrandizement and a certain amount is turned back to public works. If the appearances of progress are maintained, and if the dispensation of favor and the return to the public of its own wealth to some extent exceeds the minimum, the man is not severely resented.

Even the notoriously corrupt director of the sugar cooperative, who bled the whole area for a decade, is remembered favorably (at least compared to his successor). He is said to have been *"uno que sabía tratar con la gente,"* which means that he granted access and could be reached, an important attribute of the benevolent *patron.* Perhaps he also did enough in the way of small personal or community favors to gain something of the image of the benevolent *patron,* inhibited or prevented from doing more by his corrupt followers and surroundings. He did not, however, leave more than the minimum that he had to leave, and that which he did distribute was offset by a debt of ninety million pesos that he also left behind.

The balance between venality and progress, the conditions that determine the proportion of rebate to the public weal, the perception of minimal levels in that which impels progress toward raising these levels, the maintaining of appearances—these are all interesting problems. A road is built, let us say, not with the five million pesos budgeted for it but with two million pesos with the rest in kickbacks, and the road is not fifteen centimeters thick as planned but only five centimeters. Perhaps this mere appearance of a road that serves in some marginal fashion can be converted in another year through another building program with more rebates and perhaps a slightly higher proportion going into the road itself. Thus is progress made. Corruption remains almost universal, and potential resentment of it is sapped off by its very practitioners assuming the guise of the benevolent *patron.*

[1] Dr. David Riesman suggested the term "countermorality" in private correspondence, 1961, and this codal inconsistency may be thought of as such.

[2] Santiago Ramirez, *El Mexicano; la psicología de sus motivaciones,* Asociacion Psicoanalitica Mexicana Monografias Psicoanaliticas (Mexico: Pax, 1958).

[3] Julio de la Fuente, *Cambios socio-culturales en Mexico* (Mexico: Escuela Nacional de Antropologia e Historia, 1948).

5

MORALITY
AND VIOLENCE

VIOLENCE AND MURDER

One might expect that violence and conflict would be closely related and pursuing a vicious circle in a community exhibiting much of both and that their high incidence would lead to disruption and instability in the community. Surprisingly, this was not the case in our village, where conflict and violence tend to be separate, limited, and gradually diminishing conditions. Although major conflict has continued over the years as issues have changed, violence and conflict have not fed upon one another; each event has been kept isolated by a number of implicit social devices and by the ambiguities of the moral code itself.

Although our villagers and neighboring villagers as well characterize the village as peaceful and all the surrounding villages as murderous in comparison, we have conservatively estimated the murder rate at 178 per 100,000 people—i.e., an average of .94 murders per year for an average population of 525 over the past thirty-four years. It must be kept in mind that from 1927 to 1960, the period covered by our statistics on murder, the population increased from an estimated 250 to 800 persons (525 being midway between these points). (An average population of 400 over this period is more likely, and this would give an average murder rate of 235 per 100,000 people.)

My list, which I believe to be nearly complete, of all the homicides that have occurred in the village since its inception, or its vicinity (if our villagers were victims) shows thirty-two people killed. Of seventy-seven incidents of violence short of killing (of which we have a record from 1923 to 1960), fifty cases involved nonlethal assault with weapons and with serious consequences that might in most cases have resulted in a killing, and twenty-seven cases of fighting with less serious consequences. The list of violence is undoubtedly far less complete than the murder list. My sources were the court records, village gossip, and systematic inquiries with informants. The three overlap and together fill out my knowledge of the circumstances of murder and violence.

That the village regards itself as peaceful reflects its post revolutionary experience (1924–30) more than its earlier history. As of 1961, there had been no murder in the village since 1956 (although there had been dramatic killings in four of the neighboring villages), and there has clearly been a marked decline in the number of killings since 1927. Dividing the thirty-four years of which we have a record into two halves of seventeen years, reveals twenty-two killings in the first seventeen years (up to and including 1944) and eleven killings in the second—i.e., twice as many killings in the first than in the second half of a period in which the population more than tripled.

Taking the average population during the first seventeen years as 400 (although it was probably less) with 1.2 killings per year, and the average population during the second seventeen years as 660 with .63 killings per year, it is clear that while the population tripled (and allowing for the population increase) the rate of killings per 100,000 dropped from 300 to 95. This average rate is high by comparison with world figures and may be even more marked considering that the last killing took place in 1956. But that there has been a decline shows strongly, in spite of a relapse in 1948 when there were five independent murders.

This pattern accords with figures for the state, as well as with other studies of violence in Mexican villages. The studies by Paul Friedrich and

June Nash, however, generally report rising murder rates, with a high incidence of motivated and also of political killings.[1] In this report, I will offer evidence that for our village, which is mestizo in contrast to the Tarascan and Mayan villages referred to in the Friedrich and Nash studies, the murder rate is declining and that the great majority of murders can be described as unmotivated—i.e., mostly unrelated to stable or persistent conflicts.

TRENDS IN VIOLENCE.   Serious violence is also on the decline, though the rate of decline is probably less than that of murder. But trends in violence are difficult to evaluate. While the murder record is complete, or nearly so, acts of violence have been recorded or not on the basis of their severity. For this reason, we shall consider only those fifty cases in which assaults with weapons resulted in serious wounds that might have led to death. Of these fifty, nineteen occurred in the first half of the period covered by our record; thirty-one, in the second half. When allowance is made for population increase, the rate for the two halves appears nearly constant.

This constancy, however, actually indicates a decline in violence, for, in addition to population growth, cases of moderate violence have been entered into the court record more often in recent years, so that the number of cases counted for the first half is much less complete than the number entered for the second half. In spite of this more complete recording, moreover, there has been an even sharper decline in the last five or six years, there being only two cases of serious violence during the past six years compared to twelve in the previous six, and sixteen cases in the six years before that.

To have assembled genuinely comparative data for neighboring villages would have required similar fieldwork experience in these villages —court records alone are relatively useless without the village background —and this was not done. We do not know, then, precisely how peaceful or nonviolent our village is in relation to others. But since our rates are very high, and if the social reputation of these villages is to be believed, the rates in other villages must be substantially higher. It is said, in addition, that the State of Morelos is a paradise of peace and order compared to the adjoining State of Guerrero, where men are said to kill "without considera-tion." By comparison, men of our village are said to be cowards—but we shall consider social imagery later. At this point, murder and violence should be examined more closely.

First of all, all killing and most serious violence are male activities. The thirty-two murders of our record were all committed by men, and thirty of the thirty-two victims were men. The seventy-seven cases of violence involved seventy-nine men and nine women among the aggressors and eighty men and eight women among the victims (though the distinction between aggressor and victim is often slight).

It is generally believed that Doña Teresa was behind two of the killings—i.e., that she paid to have men killed against whom she had some grievance. As has already been indicated, however, people are commonly believed to be "bought," and in the case of an apparently unmotivated murder, villagers and relatives of the victim will suspect that the killer was paid by someone known to have held a grudge against the deceased. This is seldom proved and is, in fact, often suspected in anticipation of a murder that does not occur.

Another indirect chain links the murder of a man who was then *ayudante* ("mayor") and Doña Benita's husband to Don Pio, who was his political opponent. In this case, the victim was killed by a peon who worked for Carmela's husband, and the latter is said to have paid the peon on behalf of Filomeno. In any case, both the peon and his employer left the village for good. In still another case, Abel Arquillos' young son killed a young man said to have been hired by Don Salvador to kill *him*. It will be recalled that during the height of their political opposition to one another, Federico and Pio each claimed that the other had hired peons to kill him. Pio's family quite seriously believes that Catalino has hired men to kill him but that the men have not yet made their move.

It is also said in the village that one Chucho, a dependent of Pio's, offered to kill Catalino's son, who was then involved in the Catalino dispute along with his father. This is not difficult to believe, as Chucho, an extreme *macho* type addicted to alcohol and marijuana, claims to have killed men on some of his solo binges in other towns. Whether all or any of these allegations are true one has no way of knowing. Some are imagined; some are accusations designed to becloud the intentions of others. The circumstances of the cases involving her name make the accusations against Doña Teresa at least plausible, and it is not unlike the Pio group to disguise projections as suspicions. But these are only conjectures.

ALCOHOLISM AND VIOLENCE

That men are more involved in violence and killing reflects not only the divergent codes of behavior discussed earlier but also the exclusive right of men to nonceremonial drinking and drunkenness (women drink moderately and only at fiestas). The tie-in between aggressive violent behavior and alcoholism is nearly complete, in my opinion—that is, the aggressor is almost always either a heavy drinker or an alcoholic and is in most cases intoxicated when the aggression is committed. This would be difficult to prove from the record directly, as information on intoxication is not always known or given. Intoxication is definitely mentioned in eight of the thirty-two killings and is ruled out in none of the others. It is mentioned in seventeen cases of violence and would seem probable in thirty-five others as well, with the rest unknown but not precluded.

Experience leads us to believe that the coincidence of violence with some degree of intoxication is much higher. We have listed seventy-eight people whom we know to have been aggressors in violence. This list includes the names of eleven women, only one of whom has a history of alcoholism (Doña Teresa is the only female ex-alcoholic) and sixty-seven men, only two of whom are neither alcoholics nor heavy drinkers: these are Roque (Pio's brother), who does not drink, and Mirando, who is an ex-alcoholic. (Another, about whom we are uncertain, is probably a heavy drinker.) Twenty-two from this list are also to be found on my list of heavy drinkers and alcoholics.

Forty-two of the seventy-eight who committed acts of violence are no longer in the village; some have died, but many have simply left the village permanently. Unfortunately, these names of the latter could not be traced systematically. Some of them may have been transients—people who had not been in the village long and who, having few ties, left after a fight in which they had injured another and feared possible arrest or vengeance. The belief that punishment or vengeance can occur, though it seldom does, tends to rid the village (though not the region) of most of those who commit violence, in any case, and this is one reason why so few are actually punished—some of those who stay have protectors, and the others do not remain in the village to await arrest. Court records for both murder and violence repeatedly end with the notation that the culprit is *"en fuga"* ("in flight").

We cannot know about those who leave, but unless there is an extraordinary selection of those who stay or return, the proportion of two nondrinkers to twenty-two drinkers or alcoholics lends weight to the argument that most violence involves either temporary or chronic intoxication. This is not to say, of course, that all members of the heavy drinker and alcoholic subgroups are violent or homicidal but only that the violent and the killers are often from among these groups. On our list of twenty-seven alcoholics now living in the village (who are intoxicated as much and as · often as possible, rarely working a week without missing days for drunkenness), thirteen, or about half, are on the violent list, and a few alcoholics not on the violent list are potentially violent. As one would expect, nine out of twenty-nine on the list of heavy drinkers, a smaller proportion, are also to be found on the list of the violent. Here one finds chronic, weekly intoxication but with more control, such persons getting drunk on weekends and holidays but not during the working week or at every opportunity.

The magnitude of the problem may be suggested by the following figures. Of 165 men over twenty years of age in the village, 29, or 17.6 percent, are on the list of alcoholics, while 27, or 16.3 percent, are on the heavy drinker list. The total of 56 men on both lists thus constitutes 34 percent of the men over twenty years of age, and, as mentioned, all but two of the men still living in the village who have a record of violent aggression come from this 34 percent. To this, we may add that the two lists—of drinkers and of the violent—were compiled independently, from independent criteria. Of the 22 on the violent list, 9 are found among the alcoholics and 13 among the heavy drinkers.

This indicates a more or less similar draw from the lists of alcoholics and heavy drinkers, and, in this respect, the two classes are not clearly differentiated. In a related matter, however, the two are differentiated— the heavy drinkers showing much less drop in productivity and control (productivity estimated by decrease in land use; control, by the interference of intoxication in the work week). Thus, of the *ejidatarios* who number among the two classes of drinkers, ten of the heavy drinkers work all of the land they are allotted, as against only four of the twenty-nine alcoholics, while only one heavy drinker rents out part of his land, as opposed to ten alcoholics who rent all or part of their land to others. We thus tentatively conclude that incidence of violence is related more to frequent and complete intoxication than to the patterns of drinking that our two classes distinguish.

ALCOHOLISM AND MURDER. There is little direct evidence to support our belief that most of the murders occurred with at least the killer in a state of drunkenness. Although intoxication is cited in the court records in only eight of the thirty-two cases, the records are unreliable, as many of the murders were not investigated, the killer having fled the village to escape capture or vengeance. At least seven of those who left we know to have been at least heavy drinkers and violent men. Only three remain in the village, all men of high status whose crimes are now many years in the past.

A few more facts will suffice to indicate the various conditions of murder and violence. Twenty-seven of the killings were committed with firearms, two with knives, three by unknown means. In the cases of violence not resulting in death, firearms were used eighteen times, machetes twelve, knives eleven, rocks four, and fists four times. In most instances, then, killing came from the use of firearms. Machete fights usually produced grave, but not mortal, wounds.

Four killings took place in the streets of the village, six in bars, three in the fields, two in private houses, the rest unknown. For violence, we find thirteen incidents in the streets, nineteen in bars, two in the fields, five in private houses, and the rest unknown. As the mothers of the village so often warn their children, the streets are dangerous. While the bars are known for their frequent fights, only a few of these are considered serious enough for our violent list.

FLIGHT, PROTECTION, AND REHABILITATION

Most cases of murder and violence escape punishment by law or vengeance. Usually the worst consequence to the offender is that he must leave the village, and in this way the village has lost at least forty-five of those whose names occur in cases of violence. Only three who have killed remain in the village, but some who come to the village have killed or injured elsewhere.

Filomena's husband, for example, came to the village from Guerrero after he had drunkenly killed a man at a dance. He left his land and animals behind, joined his relatives, and would later be joined by Filomena. But he was later killed by a son of Maximiliano, who was also drunk, and the latter, though protected by village leaders, left for another village where he had relatives. There he killed another man and fled back to the village, where he was neither molested by the law nor by relatives of his first victim but was finally murdered by an *ejidatario*. The *ejidatario*, in turn, left his *ejido*, his wife, and relatives and went to live elsewhere. There he soon took another woman and began again, but without land. Only one man from the village, an uncle of Don Pio, actually died in prison. Two of Pio's uncles had killed men in the village and had otherwise been repeatedly involved in violence. After the second murder, however, one was captured, declared insane, and finally died in the penitentiary in Cuernavaca.

Pio protected his brother Roque in what was one of the most clearly motivated and premeditated murders in village history. When Roque's wife, whom he beat beyond the limits that even a good wife is expected to endure, left him and returned to her father, her father complained, and, in 1936, Roque ambushed him in the fields with a rifle. After his father-in-law's death, he left the village long enough for the case to be closed (with his family's influence) with the usual notation that the alleged assailant was *"en fuga."*

Since then, Roque has run his corn mill, become a progressive and productive farmer, and is among the most respected men in the village. He rarely mixes with villagers in the streets, except during religious processions of which he is in charge. He is always armed; when he goes to the fields he takes his pistol, and usually his rifle as well, on the grounds that he might see some game. His family has feared the vengeance of the sons or other relatives of his victim, but these have never made a hostile gesture toward him. It should be noted in passing that Roque is one of the few who never drinks (because his mother does not allow it).

In 1937, Anselmo, who suspected his wife of having lovers, beat her so severely and frequently that on one such occasion she took refuge in the house of a village leader who had once been mayor and who was at that time president of the Ejido Committee. Believing that this man must be her lover, Anselmo went to his house and shot him in the back while he was eating. Whether the status of the deceased demanded greater action or whether the victim's family financed it, Anselmo was the only murderer ever pursued. He spent five or six years in the penitentiary and was deprived of his *ejido parcela*—the most extreme punishment to our knowledge. Having survived the penitentiary, however, he returned to the village where he was treated with respect and even deference, as if the village or its movers repented his punishment. Awarded a *parcela* that had been vacated by others and restored to his full status, over the subsequent years he has been offered, but has refused, all of the various offices of the village government.

Alfonso, twice elected mayor, is a heavy drinker who has been repeatedly involved in court actions and was once convicted of manslaughter for killing a former mistress (though he denied his guilt, claiming that they had only quarreled because she had other lovers). He is said to have come to her house drunk, and, finding the door closed, fired his gun through a closed shutter behind which she was listening. The body was discovered a day later, and he was arrested, still in the village and unaware that he had killed anyone, though one witness said that the shooting had been direct, that the bullethole in the shutter was an old one, and that they had been quarreling over Alfonso's jealousy. In any event, Alfonso was sent to the penitentiary for two years, but he did not lose his *ejido*. He was later brought to court again for entering the house of a woman who no longer wanted to be his mistress, armed, drunk, and threatening. Afterwards, however, he was named village justice of the peace and served a year in the office.

Although he used to be *enamorado* (in a floating "enamoured" state) and is still considered quarrelsome, at times violent, Alfonso is well-liked and respected in the village. He is warm, pleasant, and loyal, usually bantering with his friends, and is a phenomenally hard worker in spite of his weekend drinking. At fifty-two, he is still very much the *macho* in speech and behavior but is mainly involved at present, aside from work and family, in leading the anti-Catalino group. Actually, he leads no one and is not aware that he is a follower. He has always belonged to Don Pio's group and has held the appropriate antagonisms as opponents have shifted in time.

To know Alfonso well, however, is to know that he fears violence and is much attracted at this stage of his life to his land and family. He is productive but conservative in the sense that he does not attempt to expand the resources he was allotted, and though his status is moderate, the house that he built is among the village's best. For him, the major deterrent against violence is the knowledge that if he kills he must leave.

Violence gets to court more often than murder, because in cases of less serious violence the accused does not necessarily leave the village, or he leaves it only temporarily, depending in part upon how much protection he feels he has. (One *macho* felt confident that because of Pio's protection no one would be able to hurt or jail him. This did help, but, more than that, people feared retaliation to charges brought against him.) Those who are brought to court and convicted are fined. The jail is seldom used, and then only until the fine is paid; paying someone's way out of jail is a function of the network. Very many (the number cannot be precisely estimated) incidents of violence, however, neither get to court nor go beyond the village level to the municipal court, where punishment may be meted out. They lead instead either to private grudges or to estrangement and reconciliation.

It frequently happens in court that two men who have hacked one another with machetes in a drunken fight will say that it was all a mistake, profess their friendship, and refuse to press charges. They may both be fined, however, and even the poorest will pay fines, even if it means borrowing, in lieu of accepting a jail sentence. Whether cases are brought before the authorities, even where neither party wishes it, depends upon the obligation that village authorities feel to report incidents of violence. This varies but seems to be on the increase, because the village authority feels that he is himself culpable if he does not report cases as required by the law. Although no official has been punished, there are reprimands on the record for unreported or incompletely reported cases. As this practice becomes more effective, the handling of violence is increasingly taken out of the village and brought into contact with a formal legal code.

ROLE OF THE AVENGER. In the discussion of political structure it was pointed out that a reluctance to use force tends to make the operation of local governmental impositions—e.g., the paying of taxes—largely a voluntary matter. This contrasts interestingly with the seemingly authoritarian philosophy governing the discipline of children within the family. It will be recalled that discipline and corporal punishment are deemed more applicable to the younger child; as he gains in understanding, corporal punishment is supposed to give way to vaguely sanctioned *consejos* ("advice").

The moral force of the community against killing and violence is roughly equivalent to the force of such *consejos,* which look rather disapprovingly upon those things which people really "shouldn't do" but which, after all, are only to be expected from human nature. Villagers regard Mexicans—especially Indians, mestizos, rural people, illiterates, etc. —as particularly susceptible to such things, and in this respect the "human nature" so often cited becomes coextensive with cultural and acculturational boundaries. Violence is expected, not of everyone perhaps, but at least of some people according to their nature (just as it is expected of the child and the youth when beatings have given way to *consejos*), and there is an uneasiness about the use of punishment and force, unless it arises from a momentary swell of anger or indignation or a momentary sense of the obligation to be indignant.

The main sanction against those who have killed or seriously injured others is the necessity of flight. One flees the law in the knowledge that pursuit is unlikely if much trouble, danger, or expense is involved. One flees as well the vengeance of kin or friends of the victim, but this flight is often more symbolic than pragmatic—that is, it may release others from the reluctant necessity of resorting to law or taking vengeance.

In some cases the fugitive is living in a not too distant village and his whereabouts are known, but there is only one case in which such a person was apprehended by the law. Apart from the law, the fugitive often acts as if he fears vengeance, yet none of those who have killed or wounded others in our village has ever suffered vengeance. Many, of course, did not remain to test it out, but others were accessible to kin and possible avengers of the victim. Although avenging a slain kin is approved of and even obligatory, and although people often speak vindictively, vengeance has, in fact, never occurred.

When Maximiliano's son killed Filomena's husband and she wished to avenge his death, she went to the authorities in the municipal seat (after the local justice of the peace and mayor had hedged about acting) and was told that she would have to pay the expenses of the pursuit and arrest. Her husband had many relatives in the village, including some cousins with whom he had lived. But the murderer later returned to the village and was killed by someone else, not in vengeance.

Protection, too, is more symbolic than effective against an intent to avenge. It may ease a killer's fears, but it is not what really prevents vengeance. Twenty-two men who have injured others remain unmolested in the village. Some fled and later returned, but none has suffered reprisal. Villagers who speak of the "hot blood" and vindictiveness of their people are surprised when it is pointed out to them that no instance of vengeance can be found in the village itself (we do know about what amounts to blood feuds in two neighboring villages said to be Indian rather than mestizo). They are likewise surprised to see that the list of killings somewhat contradicts their notion of peacefulness. Lack of vindictiveness is often taken as a sign of the superior pacifism of our villagers, but the same behavior may be called "peaceful" or "cowardly," and this subject will be discussed later.

In 1927 a group of our villagers went out unarmed to undam a stream that was unfairly diverting water into a nearby village from the fields. Two of our men were killed and others gravely injured by men who were well-known to the men of our village. A legal complaint was made in the municipal court, but since the offending village was of another municipality, our villagers received no satisfaction. They did not, however, attempt to take revenge themselves. As early as 1927, in other words, when the new community was still in the process of formation, villagers took only legal action in return for violence in a dispute that was vital to their interests. By contrast, a similar dispute between the offending village and another village disturbed the valley for years and finally required the intervention of troops and the state government.

Fighting often occurs in bars, for it is a custom of the *macho* type to visit other towns to drink, look for prostitutes, and possibly to pick fights *"a ver quién me conocía"* ("to see who knew me"). For another instructive incident, a man nicknamed *El Calor* ("heat"), originally from Guerrero but then living two kilometers from our village, had a bad reputation and appears in the court records for fighting in the village. Once, when he came into the village in 1948, a man in a group of our village men shouted, *"Aquí viene El Calor, le vamos a dar en la madre"* ("Here comes El Calor, we'll let him have it!"). *El Calor* fired into the group, killing a man, then returned to his village, followed by about twenty men, where he took refuge in a house. The men surrounded the house, "waiting for him to come out" (as they put it). He did not come out, however; but it began to rain, and, as night was approaching, they decided to go home and resume their pursuit the next day. But there was no further pursuit, and *El Calor* did not return to the village.

MOTIVATION AND PREMEDITATION

Motivation and premeditation are difficult factors to establish, for, as might be expected, the records are most incomplete on these matters. The "typical" murder—typical insofar as it reflects the social image of such events—involves jealousy, anger, and intoxication, although in its "pure" form it may be motiveless, the grotesque result of a drunken quarrel over nothing. There is a Mexican joke to this effect. A group of men begin drinking together in a bar. After a few drinks they call each other "friend". After a few more they call each other *compadre.* Another round and they have become "brothers," embracing one another with protestations of affection. After more drinking one says to another, *"Yo soy tu mero papa"* ("I am your very father"), and then there is a killing.

Some killings conform closely to the model, but the model must be expanded to include the whole nether region of the *macho* ethic. *El Calor,* who exists in the *macho* world exclusively, was "called," threatened, challenged with a *mentada de madre* (a general class of insults to the mother). To say that you are someone's father when you are not is a commonly used *mentada* that recurs several times in the court record as a prelude to violence. To call someone *"hijo de la chingada"* is to say that he is the son of a woman who has been violated. (The meaning is more complex, but the reader is referred to Octavio Paz and Santiago Ramirez for further discussion.)[2] In one quarrel that led to the near fatal stabbing of Doña Teresa, her antagonist, drunk, compounded the insult by calling her an *"hija negra de las siete mil chingadas"* ("black daughter of seven thousand 'abused' women"). There are many variations in which the *macho* and *macha* are proficient. It is both the insult which the *macho* may not brook and also that which comes most readily to his lips when he is offended.

Other motivations might include a drink refused, an attempt to leave an all-night drunken gambling session, or a bit of joking or teasing, which usually composes much of the exchange among men of this type, suddenly taken seriously. At times a genuine issue enters into a quarrel, as when Adolfo and another man fought in Doña Teresa's bar over their views on a current land dispute in which neither was directly involved. There are instances of all of these. Eight of those who killed and left the village and one who remains are all clearly *macho* types, and what we know about the others suggests that they might also be so assigned. All such men are dangerous, and most of the killings and acts of violence are attributable to them. In the most completely *macho* types, violence is an automatic response almost beyond their control.

Himself a *macho* to the last detail, Lucio differed from many of the other thoroughgoing *machos* in exhibiting traces of an aspiration to some of the higher, antique reaches of the *macho* code in which touches of chivalry and the troubador still survive—*"justanciosos,"* villagers call them ("jousters," from *justa,* referring to tournaments). Lucio's moods led him to an introspection rare among his type. His self-image demanded pretensions to a code of ethics that contained such rules as not using obscene language, not seducing or accepting the wife of a friend, and not killing except as provided by the code.

Like others who in some ways tried to adopt his rigid social form, which had such clear antisocial potentialities for the community of his choice, he served as a *comandante* (village "peace officer") and told me proudly that he had been selected because he feared no man, armed or unarmed. Most importantly, he had found a community in which he wanted to remain, in which his mother and brothers had settled, and in which he was striving to earn respect. But there were a few heavy drinking bouts, and in one of these he and two others raped a prostitute who had been imported to work in Doña Justina's cantina. Justina brought charges and insisted that he be arrested. He was forced to return to his natal village (from which he had had to flee years before for another incident), and so he lost what he most wanted in spite of his resolution.

Most men in the subgroup from which a high proportion of violence arises are less divided within themselves. A few could possibly kill or commit violence without intoxication, but most are very different in their sober and drunken states. Sober, they often seem withdrawn, depressed, sullen, and isolated. Drunk, they are sociable, euphoric, and generous, but, as the joke suggests, intoxication beyond this point brings back the irritability, a loss of euphoria, and a touchiness about insult or the withdrawal of others away from them. The amiability itself takes on aggressive and dangerous overtones.

Insofar as murder and violence are typical in the above sense, they indicate even less grievance-based conflict than might be supposed—i.e., in many cases there is no specific grievance antedating the violent incident. Moreover, there are fewer results of violence, with respect to conflict, than might be expected (here I speak only of our village, where murder and violence seem not to extend themselves through vengeance and feud). One murder was a species of vengeance but not for a previous murder. Around 1937 a baker seduced a young girl (with her consent, it is said), and her family had him killed and burned. Three other homicides are said to have been paid for by others with grievances, but these are unprovable allegations.

Except for one doubtful case, we know of no murders or acts of violence that have led to retaliation in kind. Instead, further conflict tends to be suppressed, or kept from open aggression, by the assailant's leaving the village or by the assailant, his family or relatives maintaining a wary distance from the most likely possible avengers. Against the general norm of nonintense relationship described earlier, this distance need not even be conspicuous.

Where there has been violence, there may or may not be a later reconciliation. The greatest danger that the violence may ramify is in the period immediately following the incident, and this may be avoided by the assailant's real or token flight, as well as by certain ineffective or token actions by the community against the expected avengers. The inertia of the responsible officers of the community and municipality allows for this sort of settlement by allowing sufficient time for the *"llamarada de petate"* ("straw fire," connoting a rapid subsiding of passion, enthusiasm, or interest) phenomenon to operate.

VIOLENCE VERSUS CONFLICT

Prevalence of violence is not closely tied, then, to prevalence of conflict, and the test of solidarity proposed earlier is corroborated in the community's capacity to contain, eliminate, or limit, with a minimum of resulting conflict, even the high incidence of killing and violence that it has experienced. There is, moreover, an evident trend toward reduction of these incidents, and the community has had at least some part in this.

It has been said that murder and violence are largely male concerns. But the male population is itself internally differentiated, with a very high proportion of homicide and violence coming from the *macho* subgroup, which largely, though not entirely, coincides with the subgroups defined as alcoholics and heavy drinkers. No woman has ever killed in the village, and only two of the thirty-two people killed were women. Women do appear more markedly on the list of violence, where eleven of them are to be found. There is no intoxication involved, however, as there are now no alcoholics or heavy drinkers among the women. The most violent, and the only former alcoholic, among them is Doña Teresa, whose bar has been the scene of much violence for about thirty years.

Doña Teresa is a spinster with an adopted daughter whom she beats often and to extremes of severity. Her violent encounters with others are the most extreme of any woman in the village, and she is a *macha* if there ever was one. Hers is the oldest bar in the village and the only one that was, and is, not a center of prostitution. She is also an *ejidataria* who was formerly active in community and church affairs. She used to manage the band (almost all of whose members are alcoholics), was patroness of all major village fiestas, and was particularly interested in bullfighting—and not because all such activities were occasions for drinking at her bar.

She has had lovers because her wealth made her desirable, but as she says, "I would never let a man saddle me. What for?" But she shot and almost killed one of her early lovers for having an affair with her mother, and in a conflict with another woman, she bashed the woman in the mouth with a rock, breaking her teeth. During disputes over irrigation rights, she took her gun to the fields and threatened to use it in defense of her rights.

All of the other instances of violence among women involve fights, almost invariably over men but not with men, and although severe beatings are sometimes administered, these cases should on the whole be classed among the more purely verbal battles, in which, however, the verbal component of the morality contest is even more destructive than the physical violence that is only occasionally involved. If vindictiveness (in the sense of retaliation in kind for violence) is deficient in men, it is in no way deficient among women.

Jealousy over men and defense and attack of moral status are the issues in almost all female violence and conflict, though they are much less commonly the basis of violence among men. The "typical" form of male killing and violence does not have its counterpart among women. Moral and social status are not issues among men as they are among women, although conflict, and even violence, over political status does appear in the male realm. The two domains of conflict are almost wholly separate, except insofar as women must adapt to the disruptions of the family caused by male violence.

A few women of the *macha* type (loosely defined) do goad men into more *macho* positions or define male pacifism as cowardice, and it has been noted that the men who control factional tactics sometimes manipulate the violence, hostility, and vindictiveness in some of these women as political resources. Witchcraft, too, may be regarded as a mutual form of violence, retaliation, and control variably subscribed to by some women as witches or users of witchcraft and by some men as victims or users of cures and countermagic.

BASES OF TRENDS

In seeking an explanation for the trend toward a reduction in the rates of killing and violence, the latter should be considered not in terms of their temporal distribution but in terms of a social process; for the properties of the community change with each incident of killing or violence, and this in turn affects the future rate of such incidents. It has been seen, for instance, that in many cases the killer or aggressor is eliminated from the village with a minimum of conflict-perpetuating involvement on the part of others, while, at the same time, others have come to the village who have committed violence or murder elsewhere. If there were a balance in the number of outgoing and incoming aggressors, there would be no change in the rates of violence. Inequalities in the circulation of such aggressors must therefore exist.

It should be remembered, too, that most of the present inhabitants of the village are immigrants: of 410 people over sixteen years of age in 1961, only 118 (or about 28 percent) were born in the village (less than half of these had at least one parent born in the village), whereas 151 were born in the State of Guerrero. The initial influx into the village was spread over seven or eight years after 1924 and was heaviest from 1928 to 1930, and there was also a considerable turnover of population.

The village was more or less formed and relatively stabilized soon after 1930, when virtually all of the land had been divided into individual parcels. It consisted at that time of a small group of original families intermarried with immigrants, a group of immigrants who had received most of the fifty-two land parcels, and a group of nonlandholders derived from the two preceding groups plus the continuing immigration of peons and day workers. Some of the latter acquired house sites when they were still available and became relatively stable residents, though without a parcel for cultivation, their stake in the village was less than that of the *ejidatarios*. But from their own ranks and from continuing immigration as well came many with neither parcel nor house site, and the status of the latter group is particularly unstable.

If the main sanction against serious violence and murder is that the aggressor must leave the village and begin again elsewhere, we would expect the aggressors to come mostly from the ranks of the most unstable, but all of the above groups and segments are represented on the murder and violence lists. Five of those killed were *ejidatarios;* the three killers who remain in the village with apparently unimpaired general status are from among these; and still other *ejidatarios* and their heirs, from both native and immigrant families, are among the decidedly violent. Thus, if there is a predominance on the lists of those who have lesser stakes (land or house site) in the village, this is only to be expected from their relative proportions in the village. The potentially murderous or violent are not selected on this basis.

The argument that they are to a very considerable extent drawn from among men who are frequently or habitually intoxicated suggests a possible characterological factor, which we consider to be beyond the scope of this presentation. It is more to the point that the "typical" situation or context of murder and violence is a probable extension of a character-type prone to intoxication and violence and of a *machismo-*centered subculture comprising the remnants of the male version of an earlier cultural horizon. That this subgroup and subculture represent a lag in the acculturative process in which the village is involved is very important. The violent who exile themselves from the village and otherwise eliminate one another are not being replaced at the same rate. The institutions that produce such individuals are being altered, and the continuities of their subculture are being broken. These changes will be discussed here only in their most immediate connection with village solidarity, conflict, and violence.

Some cases of village homicide and violence involved aggressors who were visitors from nearby villages or transients; one homicide involved itinerant gamblers who were playing in the village, and while these men killed only once in each place, their supply is probably not so small that they cannot keep replacing one another in the village. Their contact in the village, however, is with their peers; in the whole region, with members of their own subgroup, and this limitation of contact of the potentially violent or murderous mainly to each other suggests that they tend to eliminate each other.

There may also be selective or other social mechanisms that make it likely that those who return from temporary exile, or those who stay because they have connections and are well protected, will not contribute further to the rate of serious violence, but the cases to which this applies are too few and diverse to argue the point. Suffice it to say that the murderous and violent *are* being eliminated from the village, and this must account in part for the downward trend we have noted.

We know of three men who have killed elsewhere, two of whom immigrated to the village thereafter. One of them was killed in the village; another has left at least temporarily; the third has been involved in serious violence and verges on alcoholism but seems accepted and respected as this "goes" for peons. Even if a few are unknown, however, it is most unlikely that there are more than fifty to balance those who have in one way or another been eliminated.

It would be useful if we could also say whether the alcoholics and heavy drinkers are being replaced among the young. Their numbers remain high but, like the murder and violence rates, must be declining from higher past levels. There are nearly as many men under the age of forty as over the age of forty on the lists of alcoholics and heavy drinkers, but in terms of the overall age distribution for the village, there are proportionally more alcoholics among the older than among the younger men. From what we were able to learn of them, many of those eliminated from the village through murder and violence (both as aggressors and victims) would otherwise be on our alcoholism and heavy drinker lists, and most of these would have been among the older men.

That the rates of murder and violence in the community are high but diminishing may therefore be attributed to several factors. These include a social and characterological difference of provenience between those who participate in public conflict and those who are violent, a mechanism that alerts the community to the possibility of violence and its avoidance, and mechanisms that limit violence and its possible reverberation into further conflict and violence. An examination of conflict and violence thus teaches us something about social solidarity, which may be said to lie not in the absence of violence but in the community's capacity to control, diminish, or limit, with a minimum of derivative violence or conflict, even the high incidence of potentially disruptive killing and violence that it has experienced.

VILLAGE SELF-IMAGE

Villagers, and people of other villages as well, regard our village as more peaceful, less violent, and somewhat more "cultured" and progressive than the surrounding villages of the region and see no inconsistency between this image and the high incidence of violence and murder. For one thing, their memory is selective in favor of the social image. They are surprised at the amount of homicide they can recall when pressed to do so, as many cases had been forgotten until they were recalled to memory by my notes from the court records. For another thing, people tend to remember particular cases on the bases of their relational networks. Each informant has a particular selection of cases that he can recall without reminders, and although the total case record could be recovered by finding the links in a number of such selections, the person's individual case awareness is much smaller.

The notion of *"no es de aquí"* ("he is not of this place") enters importantly into this selection. A person is "from" the place where he was born, but this defines only one point on a larger scale of "belonging." It might be said, for example, that someone who was born in the village was not "from here" because his parents, or perhaps only his father, had come from elsewhere. Especially in collective reference to a family, all or some of whose children were born in the village, it may be said that "they are not from here."

There are circumstantial degrees of "being from here." An immigrant may acquire "belongingness" by being an *ejidatario,* having a homesite, cultivating land, or by length of residence, but the natives whose parents were born in the village may easily dismiss all the rest as *fuereños* ("outsiders"). For the small minority of natives who take this position, almost all of the violence and murder since 1928 have taken place socially outside the village. The social image does not depend on these natives, however, for they have a bad reputation themselves and would not be considered "cultured" or peaceful taken by themselves. The most stable immigrants are those whose characteristics most closely coincide with the social image. Asked where they are from, they will name their natal village; but when they say that our village is peaceful and progressive, they are speaking of themselves and what they have accomplished in this respect.

The discussion of village factions in an earlier chapter described the emergence of a "progressive" faction composed largely of immigrant *ejidatarios.* There must have been selective processes that had the effect of differentiating the character of the immigrants from the natives, for there is general consensus on what these differences were (though some natives evaluate them in their own favor). The families attached to the hacienda were supposed to have been lazy and to have adopted the work habits of the immigrants only reluctantly. Many were said to have been heavy drinkers or alcoholics; they liked gambling (especially cards), fiestas, rodeos, and bullfights. Some were said to be so unenterprising, fearful, self-disqualifying, and inured to peonage that, though they had first choice, they either claimed no land at all or much less than they might have for fear that the hacienda owners might someday be restored to power.

The community was reorganized as an *Ejido* in 1924 and remained for several years in the control of the natives who had been with the hacienda before the Revolution. It was a small and weak community compared to others at the time, and its leadership was said to have been inept and nonprogressive. In a water dispute with a neighboring village, the community suffered two deaths and several serious woundings. At about the same time it lost a large part of what was originally to have been the village *Ejido* to the *Ejido* of the nearby municipal seat (the village is even now the smallest in the municipality).

Balancing such losses with corresponding gains depends upon the manipulation of political influence and bribery, and the skill of some of the immigrants in these matters would make our village preeminent among its neighbors after 1930. It was the immigrants, or leaders among them, with some allies from the original group, who wished to bring stability and peace to their new village. The pacification cannot be wholly attributed to them and there is nothing about the process that is unique to the village, but it is likely that the village was (and still is) somewhat in advance of its neighbors in the general trend of acculturation toward urban, commercial, and industrial values and patterns.

The men who led the new element in the village had a definite program which they put into effect gradually, and this helped to remove some of the conditions conducive to violence and to break some of the continuities of the violence-prone subculture. They succeeded in suppressing card playing in the village, for example, and later closed a bar that was the source of much conflict and violence because its owner employed imported professional prostitutes (including his daughter, his wife, and his wife's sister). Except that it was implemented by community legal action, how they accomplished this I do not know. But it would be wrong to see in these measures a moral puritanism comparable to the American or northern European varieties. Here they sought to moderate vice rather than to condemn it, for each of the leaders stands, or has stood, in a morally compromised position in both private and public affairs.

In their campaigns against the major village fiestas, bullfights, and rodeos, their objective was to oppose the economic drain of the levies for such events and also to limit the amount of drinking and violence that notoriously accompanies them (the bars profited greatly, as the village played host to its neighbors). They succeeded in persuading the village to reduce the festivals considerably and also succeeded in eliminating the bullring, the symbolic center of the *machismo* subculture. (The imagery of the latter had been based on the cowboy and the gunfighter, but those who now molded themselves to the image were farmers and field hands who depended upon the bullring to support their pretensions.) All trace of the old bullring was obliterated when the warehouse of the rice-growers' cooperative was built on the site, and although most of the neighboring villages still put on the traditional festivals and *jaripeos* (rural-style bull-fight combined with rodeo), the last *jaripeo* took place here in 1952.

Thus, by devoting greater attention to the school, to public works, and to certain kinds of cultural activities, particularly in the thirties and forties, the immigrant progressives helped both to create and to actualize the village's image. Strongly oriented toward social mobility, political influence, stability, and security, they demonstrated repeatedly that they had no taste for violence, and it was they who developed the various devices that helped to eliminate the violent and murderous from the village. Having no disposition to expose themselves to danger, they lived discreetly, excluded violence from their factional and political disputes, and preferred dissimulation of their feelings toward one another to the "manly" challenge of the *macho* code.

Partly as a result of this influence, *machismo* was still further devaluated, until by the late 1940s, when the second generation was approaching adulthood, a distinct alternative ethic had been introduced (largely embodied in the Youth Club, whose imported sporting activities especially command prestige). Today the two paths are widely separate among young men. Few young men have the hope and stake in the land that their immigrant parents had; nevertheless, whether in sports, new diversions, work outside the village, education, or new bases for social mobility, they leave the new *macho* far behind. The latter, who feels inferior to the other young men, is considered "lost" to his vices and appears more as a defective or weakling than as a representative of the *machismo* subculture. The subculture, in fact, shrivels around him, affording him not even the cultural rationale, survival that it was, that sufficed his predecessors.

This chapter, then, has attempted to indicate some of the bases underlying the high levels of murder and violence in the village, to square the village's self-concept of pacifism with this violence, and to indicate some of the bases for the present trend toward lower rates of murder and violence. With no attempt to predict the future of such trends, I have noted those characteristics and changes in the village that might have differentiated it to some extent from others, putting it somewhat in advance of neighboring villages. Advancement is assumed, not on the basis of comparable data on murder and violence in other villages—as no comparable study exists (even Lewis' data on Tepoztlán are incommensurate with our own)—but because there is consensus among the villages about the relative pacifism of our village and also because our village is advanced in certain other traits that relate to violence.

Apart from this differentiation, our village participates with others in the region in a general kind of progress. Since the thirties, for example, there have been repeated campaigns by both state and federal government for "depistolization". Village militias have been disarmed and disbanded, and even recently state and federal police have made raids on the village to seize all unlicensed arms, with the result that only a few illegally-owned arms are still to be found in the village. People with influence can obtain permits, but this still contrasts with the day when every man had a firearm.

---

[1] Paul Friedrich, "Assumptions underlying Tarascan Political Homicide," *Psychiatry* 25, no. 4 (1962): 315-27; June Nash, "Death as a Way of Life: The Increasing Resort to Homicide in a Maya Indian Community," *American Anthropologist* 69, no. 4 (1967): 455-70.

[2] Octavio Paz, *El laberinto de la soledad* (Mexico: Fondo de Cultura Económica, 1959); Santiago Ramirez, *El Mexicano, la psicología de sus motivaciones.* (Monografías Psicoanalíticas: Asociacion Psicoanalitica Mexicana.) Mexico: Pax, 1958.

6

MORALITY
AND THE CHURCH

MORAL CODES AND CHURCH MORALITY

The religion practiced by our village is neither coextensive with the beliefs and practices approved by the Roman Catholic church nor do the moral dicta of the church wholly coincide with the village's general moral code, although they do provide a standard of moral reference within it. The moral code deviates from the explicit, formal morality approved by the church in attributing less importance to murder and adultery, for example, and more importance to, say, theft of private property.

It is remarkable that the general moral code remains effective at all as a standard of reference and moral evaluation, since so much behavior—including violence, adulteries, free unions, and failure by those who profess Catholicism to meet even the minimum ritual requirements of the church—commonly deviates from it. People know that the church is concerned with such things but do not feel its condemnation in a personal way, except as it is generally voiced against sinners in sermons.

Many people who call themselves Catholics rarely attend church. A rough check on church attendance shows that of 410 persons sixteen years of age or older, 94 attended church frequently, 64 with moderate frequency, 108 infrequently, and 144 rarely or never. (Frequently means that the person generally goes to mass; moderate frequency, that he goes to mass occasionally; infrequently, that he attends holiday and special masses irregularly.) Women predominate among the frequent churchgoers, this having more to do with their concern about moral status than with their greater religiosity.

The most prominent men of the village are more active in church affairs than other men. Pio and his brother Roque, for example, who have been alternating the only *mayordomia* between them for years, are responsible in general for the village's participation in religious ceremonies, festivals, and processions (Pio sees to it that funds are raised for a new church door or finds a *patron* to donate it). But unlike other towns and villages,[1] there is only one *mayordomo* here and no one competes with him. Others take functions upon themselves: Manuel organizes the annual pilgrimage to Amecameca, a nearby shrine of *El Santo del Sacromonte* ("Saint of the Sacred Mountain"), and Roque invariably organizes the Christmas *posadas* (candlelight processions on each of the nine days before Christmas).

Below the level of the general moral code, there is common acceptance, or at least no strong public disapproval, of much that the church would consider sinful. Most of these men who are active in church affairs, for example, are also known for activities that flagrantly violate church morality. That they have mistresses, however, or that the organizer of a religious function lives in free union with his latest wife, is known and simply accepted. Public opinion is less tolerant of women in similar positions, but, though their lowered moral status is made apparent on certain occasions, on most occasions it is not, and they are not excluded from religious roles from which they do not exclude themselves.

Adelina, for instance, has a decidedly low moral status, as she has been involved in numerous scandals, had had earlier affairs with men, and has an illegitimate child. She has been Federico's mistress for more than sixteen years—she and her children constitute, in effect, a second family for him—and is also a *macha* type who has engaged in a number of fights, both verbal and physical. In spite of all this and of her relatively low socioeconomic status, however, she is very active in public affairs of all sorts and is particularly known for leading the singing in all religious processions.

Adelina and Federico's legitimate wife differ greatly in moral status, but, of the two, Adelina is better liked, more generally respected, and certainly less resented than Federico's wife, who pretends to much *categoría* and regards herself as the ideal woman and wife (her very morality is a form of *categoría*). Yet Adelina, for all her acceptance and recognized religious functions, accepts her own inferior moral status and the morality that condemns her as well. That one who is aware of the church's disapproval neither rejects it, feels overwhelmed, nor even strongly guilty about it is typical. Adelina accepts the fact that her life has turned out as it has, even though it is not as she may have wished it to be.

Her moral status is only occasionally made visible. When she goes to Cuernavaca with Federico and her children, for example, she and the children walk fifty feet or so ahead of him on their way through the village to the bus stop. No one is deceived by this, but it is a concession to the general morality and to Federico's wife. At a village feast to honor and petition a wealthy visitor, Adelina (and another woman who was a legitimate wife) entered inconspicuously by a rear gate, explaining to me that because of her status she should not enter public gatherings boldly. Having made this token concession, however, she then took her place in the front of the group of women gathered around the table of honor. Other women would be even more sensitive to a lowered moral status and would behave accordingly.

The immediate aftermath of a moral lapse is much harder to take than the long-term consequences of a lowered moral status. Both effects, however, depend on public opinion, primarily that of the village women; they are not derived directly from the church. In general, everyone accepts a level of conduct much lower than that defined by the general moral code, and while the infracode level of general morality coincides with the expected moral level of life, there are vertical gradations. One lives above the infracode level at the risk of being resented as proud or pretentious of *categoría* (one woman calls her sister proud because the latter keeps herself cleaner than she thinks reasonable for women of their low social status).

On the acceptable infracode level, free union is approved, though its lower moral status is not forgotten. Public disapproval, recognition, or approval of a free union depends on its duration, on the wife's fidelity, and on the quality of the family thus formed. It is less approved if it involves the breakup of a marriage or another union, but it can still gain respectability in time.

Because her lover was never free to live with her, Adelina's case falls below the level of free union. Even if he had broken with his other family to live with her, she might have gained the infracode level of moral respectability. Instead, however, she remained his mistress and saw him increasingly reconciled to his family (there is a similar distinction between the abandoned illegitimate wife and the *madre soltera*). Adelina's low moral status was somewhat ameliorated by the continuance of her relation with Federico over many years and by her responsible raising of their children, to whom he gave his name and support. But even the long-established free union remains lower than the church-sanctioned marriage, and while the infirmity of its moral status is not constantly in evidence, it is characteristically revealed in critical situations. As will be seen, separation in a free union of even long duration often involves both protestations that no marriage had existed and legal procedures that assume that a marriage had existed.

Church morality has its effect by being a part of the general moral code; its effect is partly independent of the influence of the church itself. Aside from its role in the establishment of moral standards, the church and its representatives are not active moral agents in the village. The priest has, in fact, little contact with village moral life. Instead, he and the church act on the local level like the villagers themselves, as part of a greater moral system, and in most ways do not actively or effectively contravert the infracode level of morality.

The priest, who lived two kilometers away at the church of the municipal seat and who served several other villages as well, came to the village on Sundays and ceremonial occasions. Though we knew only this one young priest well, the people of the village have known many and are open in their dislike and total rejection of interfering priests. This priest was well-liked, for he did not constantly press them for money or intrude into their personal affairs. He knew that many of them were unmarried (43.5 percent of our couples were not married in church, compared with 25 percent for Tepoztlán)[2] and that this was a legitimate matter of church concern, but he does not pressure, censure, or interfere in particular cases and makes only general references in his sermons.

The priest does not interfere in village conflicts, and no one would think of consulting him in their resolution. Surprisingly to people who know northern Catholicism, he does not intervene in family conflict either, even though this, unlike political morality, is believed to be within his moral realm. Still more surprisingly, it is doubtful that it would occur to anyone who is in "moral difficulties" to consult a priest.

Parents do attend to the religious status of their children, however. There are none to our knowledge who are not baptized themselves and who have not baptized their children as well. Catechism classes were filled with children of both sexes, the classes taught by visiting lay sisters, assisted by women of the Catholic Action group (who particularly represent the higher-status families, such as the Arquillos and the Garzelas), who attempt to inculcate the church's moral code.

Their effort has been modernized; except in the home and in general religious functions, few adults in the village have had a comparable religious education. The new approach is concerned not with individual morality but with the great forces of "evil"—thus, church sermons often take up anti-Semitic, anti-Protestant, and anti-Communist themes. On one occasion the sisters who teach the catechism attended our weekly showing of documentary films in the *Ayudantía.* One film, about a museum of natural history, mentioned evolution and showed fossils of dinosaurs. The sisters denounced the film and told people to stay away, but few did, though many told us about it. The film continued to be popular, in fact, for more than a year of weekly showings.

Thus, the church has been, and tries to remain, a source of moral precepts and ideological orientation; but as a direct, active agent affecting conflict and immorality, it is negligible. Even confession is largely absent from the village's sphere of morality. The priest tells us that very few people attend mass regularly, attend confession, or take communion; these have become primarily matters of special ritual occasions. Before a family participates in some sacrament, such as a marriage, those most immediately involved will go to confession and receive communion, though other members of the family and the *padrinos* often do not.

Although the priest complains mildly about the people and what he considers to be their ignorant facade of Catholicism, he is himself of only moderate religiosity (though he is religious) and is as easygoing as his situation demands. Characteristically, the most blasphemous and obscene jokes imaginable are told in the company of the priest, but only by people of *categoría*. Such jokes are greatly enjoyed by all, though they are initially puzzling to the outsider because they seem to question through ridicule some of the central points of Catholic doctrine, such as the Immaculate Conception and the miracles of Christ.

Although the church does not participate in the resolution of conflicts, it does enter into conflict with the village itself. Priests and members of the church hierarchy are criticized and cursed without reservation. The bishop in Cuernavaca was criticized for his modernity. The priest in charge of the municipal seat, who is superior to the priest who served our village, was greatly disliked by religious villagers because he is said to extort all the money he can get from those who must pay for priestly services—for any extra masses, baptisms, weddings, funerals, all sacraments—and to be forever asking for money for special funds. The honesty of priests in handling these funds is openly doubted (it has been cited earlier that a priest was alleged to have been "bought" with masses paid for in advance), and when their chastity is not being questioned, their masculinity is.

In 1959 there was a major controversy between the church and the village over the Easter dramatization of the Passion (such performances, which date from the beginning of the colonial period, have become traditional). Two years earlier our village had performed the Easter play with great success, evoking an unusual degree of cooperation among the villagers. The Passion had been performed as part of the processions on the three days before Easter, with each scene enacted in a different part of the village. When they wished to repeat the play in 1959, the bishop and head priest of the municipality opposed it on the grounds that village plays were poorly done and were comic and disrespectful, often involving obviously drunken actors in central roles. According to the priest, in one village Christ staggered more from intoxication than from the weight of the cross.

Finally, with our intervention on the village's behalf, it was agreed that the play could be put on in a single day, not as a three-day procession, and that it must adhere to the official scriptural text, without the village's usual apocryphal additions of various miracles along with a greater role for the Mother. As the preparations proceeded and the play was performed, however, all that the church had wanted deleted was reintroduced, and the

"The Miracle"
as proclaimed in
the Passion Play

Mojiganga masks for procession during Passion Play intermission

Passion players in procession through the village

three-day processions were held with full enactment of the Passion in advance of its approved stage performance. The conflict was renewed even more bitterly the following year.

The birth control issue provides another illustration of the relationship between village morality and the church. While I know of no sermon during our stay that dealt with the subject, villagers all know that the church condemns birth control and abortion. We believe, along with the village doctor (who often treats the consequences of what women claim to have been miscarriages or the results of falls), that abortion is common, though it is usually kept secret. Midwives and special practitioners in other towns will perform abortions, and some women are known to abort themselves. Abortion runs against popular opinion—it is a double sin, as one old woman put it, because it is a sin *"tirar un niño"* ("to throw out or discard a child") and also because bearing a child "cleanses" one of sin—but it brings only mild criticism from most other women.

Women often do provoke abortion, in any case. Aside from neglect leading more or less directly to the death of a child, for most women it is the only way to limit the number of their children. Some women who abort have inadequate means to feed or care properly for their children; their family situations may be extremely insecure, or they must work either in the fields or as domestics to support their offspring. Others who favor abortion think in terms of improving the social and educational status of their families and children. The first set of motives has more force for women; the second, for men, as it is common for men to want to help their children toward a career above the level of day laborer. The men were quite interested in birth control and were aware of some of the modern techniques. There seemed to be no moral objection on the whole, though Don Aniceto, a religious man and political conservative, was doubtful.

Aniceto was proud of having ten children—eight males, four educated beyond the village level, and two normal school graduates (his three oldest sons had helped in the education of the next three)—and proud, too, that he, an *ejidatario* and owner of a small grocery store, had managed to bring most of his sons to a higher social status. Others, he thought, were simply less hardworking and frugal than himself.

Federico, on the other hand—who had educated two sons and three daughters beyond the village level and who had two large families—was strongly in favor of birth control because it enabled people to have fewer children and to provide more adequately for those they did have. Federico believes that the church will inevitably have to accept birth control as a necessity and hopes that the archbishop of Havana can influence the church toward this more enlightened viewpoint. (This is another illustration of the ambivalent attraction toward Fidel Castro. The attraction is inhibited by anti-Communist doubts, but many would like to see the Castro position on social issues realized through the acceptable channels of the church.)

Eight men asked me directly for information on birth control; others spoke to me in the company of their wives. Gabriel said that a doctor had told him some years ago that there are no means of birth control. Alfonso said that he would take his wife to the family planning clinic in Mexico City that I had told him about. Two women obtained the necessary means of birth control from nurses in Cuernavaca, but they had mixed emotions about its use. One said that she knew that her church regarded birth control as a sin, but she had already told me earlier that if she became pregnant again she would have an abortion. Her husband had a mistress in the village, whose conspicuous affair humiliated her, and they had had a son just as her own baby had been born. She finally decided that, church notwithstanding, God would understand. Her greatest concern (and that of the other woman as well) was that no one else should know about her use of birth control. Both women were largely morally independent of the church, and to a certain extent both would act in spite of community disapproval; but they were still afraid of arming the village women, their judges, with this information.

This brief discussion has intended to shed some light on the subject of village morality in relation to the church but not on religiosity itself. All, or most, of these people consider themselves religious in the sense that they call themselves Catholics and subscribe to the beliefs of their religion. Their moral independence, variability, and irregularity in the use of its rituals or sacraments may be taken as qualifications of their religiosity, but this is not to underestimate the kind of religiosity that remains in the popular forms of the religion—especially in the street processions that combine religious commemoration, drama, and fiesta. Almost everyone turns out for these processions, and they are both respected and enjoyed regardless of the church's approval or disapproval.

There is no doubt that the villagers regarded the processional drama-tization of the Passion as their own moral concern and resented the church's interference in the matter, though they accepted the acquiescent participation of the local priest gladly enough. Similarly, we were im-pressed when we accompanied the village on its annual pilgrimage to the shrine of *El Santo del Sacromonte* by the size of the turnout and the enjoyment of the occasion, as well as by the totally autonomous organiza-tion of prayer and singing around the shrine—priest neither needed nor sought. After the communal prayer and singing, the group dissolved into the individual, each with his own approach to the "saint," his own prayers, requests, and personal needs. We were impressed again afterwards by the festive spirit of the excursion, indistinguishable from a purely secular excursion. (The saint in the beautiful shrines at Amecameca is, appropriately enough, not officially canonized by the church.)

The priest feels superior to all this, but he accepts it. Occasionally he feels bitter about being relegated to a village parish. He wished to continue his studies but complained that all favorable positions and the privilege of advanced study go to those who have wealthy families and influence ("The church, too, has its proletariat").

---

[1] Charles Leslie, *Now We Are Civilized: A Study of the World View of the Zapotec Indians of Mitla, Oaxaca* (Detroit: Wayne State University Press, 1960).

[2] Lewis, Oscar, *Life in a Mexican Village*, p. 73.

7

THE CATALINO CASE

The case of Catalino versus the *Sociedad Pro-balneario* illustrates how formal institutions are used in a situation of conflict at a time when an *ejido* village is in the process of defining a new, postrevolutionary morality for itself. The Catalino case has provided the central social, moral, and legal issues that have been discussed throughout this study as they have animated the people of the village and influenced the village's development. Everything that happened during my stay was affected by it, so that it has been mentioned repeatedly, though fragmentarily, in the preceding pages.

This chapter offers a brief history of the case, with illustrative detail from one of the village assemblies in which it was debated. It is beyond my immediate purpose and competence to try to explain fully or decide the legal issues involved; there is, in fact, great legal confusion among the various agencies that have offered opinions or decisions. We will not expound the law, then, but will show how it is understood and used by our villagers and how it relates to general morality. Our intention is also to show the various levels of access to those agencies beyond the village to which the village has recourse in conflict.

BACKGROUND

In the sixth edition of the *Codigo Agrario*, under the heading "Individual Rights" (Article 165), it is stated that "those farmers settled in an *ejidal* population nucleus, who have peacefully possessed a parcel, or who have cultivated it personally during two or more years, will have the right to have it legally adjudicated to them, even when they have not been included in the census."[1] This law (not given here in full) is the basis for Catalino's claim to the disputed land around the San Ramon spring.

Catalino claims that he rented land when he first came to the village in 1928 but that he was given a parcel of four hectares in 1929 (the right to this parcel is not under dispute). The parcel bordered on a small plot of communal land that contained the village's largest spring of sulfurous water, which was used to irrigate adjoining parcels. Catalino began to work this land, too, almost immediately. It had previously been put to some use in grazing the animals of some villagers but was generally regarded as *texcal* ("stony, unworkable").

Catalino claims that since he and his large family (sixteen children, of whom twelve survived) worked this land fully, he had the informal right to develop it. He says, too, that he had relinquished a corresponding amount of land in another field as a sort of exchange. At the commencement of our fieldwork, he and his sons had worked this portion of land for about twenty years and had rendered it cultivable. He had also built a dam many years ago that had raised the level of the stream coming from the spring and thereby allowed the water (most of which left the village *ejido* without having been useful) to be redirected in part to his own parcel, following which it continued on a route to neighboring parcels.

In the course of time, Catalino's dams formed two pools which villagers and visitors to the village used for bathing. He says, however, that when he had asked other men to cooperate with him in making the dams, and also a sluice that carries the water at its greatest height over the original stream to the fields, the others—including his brother-in-law Federico—had scoffed and refused. With much familial and hired labor, he succeeded nevertheless, and there have been complaints since then that his rerouting the water causes the sulfurous water to mix with the village's supply of sweet water, which comes from more distant sources. Until the present dispute arose, however, the dams and the rerouting were allowed

Don Catalino, his wife, and youngest son

Ted Schwartz

to persist. In addition, Catalino's work on the spring led to the extension of his claim to the land surrounding the spring on all sides.

It will be recalled that from 1950 to 1953, Catalino led a movement against the management of the sugar cooperative to protest what most thought were corrupt practices—i.e., making illegal profit on every aspect of cane planting and harvesting processes on the basis of an "exchange" between the cooperative and the *ejidatarios*. At the beginning he had the support of most of the village *ejidatarios*, including most of those who would later form the core of the opposition in the present case. But after three years of vain petitioning for a presidential investigation, which was often promised but never materialized, Catalino found himself alone. His supporters and friends gradually withdrew, either having been bribed, hoping to be bribed, or anticipating the futile end of the affair. That he refused a bribe from the cooperative manager no one denies, though some suspect his motives. There was bad feeling between him and Federico, who had been the intermediary in the attempted bribe, but he claims he did not have bad relations with the village. As proof, he has a letter signed by Don Pio and other village leaders naming him as their representative to head a commission sent to Mexico City to further a village petition.

After 1953, however, Catalino withdrew from political activity, though he remained a member of the cooperative, and from active participation in village affairs as well. Returning to the San Ramon mineral spring, he began secretly to take legal steps that would give him a federal concession to develop and exploit a public bathing resort as a private commercial enterprise. Under Mexican law, all such natural resources are federal property and must be so registered—i.e., "nationalized" before they are concessionable. For three years, as the spring and the land for twenty meters around it were being nationalized, Catalino filed the numerous documents needed for the concession, including an architect's plan of the finished resort, aerial photographs, and much else, all of which cost him a great deal of money.

In these and his subsequent moves, Catalino had the aid of an influential lawyer and politician who had a weekend residence in the village (it had been the lawyer and other wealthy visitors from Mexico City who had originally suggested the bathing resort to him). Although he spent everything that he and his family earned and went heavily into debt, he did not have to pay for the legal services of the lawyer and his office, and he admits that he could not have survived against his opposition, which was formed as soon as his plans were known, without this assistance. According to Catalino, the village discovered his plans only when Federico, who is postmaster, opened his mail and found a notice published in the official gazette of the nationalization of the spring.

The opposition claims that the idea of a bathing resort at San Ramon had been under consideration by the village for a long time—the water and springs are beautiful but somewhat cold, with an almost year-round constant of sixty-nine degrees Fahrenheit—and that they had been planning to undertake the project at the same time that Catalino was working secretly. Federico says that Catalino knew of these discussions but confided his own plans to no one. (It is also said, though Catalino denies it, that the small group of men, including Catalino, Abel Arquillos, Federico Garzelas, and the schoolteacher, that attempted but failed to buy the hacienda in 1938 had also hoped to build a bathing resort, using another large spring on the hacienda property.) Some years later, the village group went to the office of water resources in Mexico City, where they learned, ostensibly to their total astonishment, that an individual claim had already been entered.

To oppose Catalino, they formed the *Sociedad Pro-balneario,* which they say represents "the people of the village" against its "enemy." The *sociedad* actually has only thirty-nine members from the village (five of them women), plus five members from outside the village, including the manager of an *ejido* bank and a functionary of the sugar cooperative. The *sociedad* "reached" the water resources officials by marshalling their political contacts with appropriate payments (for, as they often complain, paper costs money, and each movement of a paper from desk to desk costs more money) and had themselves declared the concessionaires. At the same time, Catalino obtained an injunction recognizing his right to continue his legal proceedings.

The struggle then turned to the question of rights to the land in which the bathing resort was to be situated. The *sociedad* argued that Catalino was entitled to only his original parcel, which was not in dispute, and that he had gradually and insidiously encroached on communal land, ignoring all complaints and orders to cease by village officials. No one disputed that he had worked the land for many years or that he had improved it; it was denied only that he had done this with approval and without protest as he claims.

Asked why he had been permitted to continue working for so long a time, they reply that he is stubborn and that they are peaceful people who do not resort to violence; besides, they say, the encroachment was gradual enough to dispel the force of the protest. If he had only gone on peacefully cultivating the small plot of land that he had reclaimed for his family's benefit, they say, they would probably not have taken strong action against him, but they were angry that he had taken advantage of them so far as secretly to plan a private commercial exploitation of what was, except for the school parcel, the only communal land of the *ejido.*

Incidents approaching violence began to occur. The *sociedad* repeatedly tore down Catalino's fence around the disputed land and caused one of his sons to be incarcerated for taking down a fence that it had put up. Each claimed the land and accused the other of trespass and property damages. Several acts of vandalism were committed against Catalino's property, including damage to his dam, fences, and irrigation ditches. Catalino himself was shunned; he and his family were insulted on the streets, primarily by women. His mentally retarded son, who watches his fields, came home badly frightened when Gustavo fired a bullet through his shirt as a joke and a warning. (Gustavo had been one of Catalino's closest partisans in the campaign against the sugar cooperative. An extreme *macho* type, he fancies himself a "revolutionary" partisan of just causes and often threatens to settle things by killing Catalino to prove that there is someone in the society with *cojones* ("testicles").

Each side presented its case and used whatever influence it could on agricultural department officials on the regional, state, and federal levels. Catalino visited them all and presented many affidavits to the effect that he had worked the land peacefully for many years. Initially, eleven men of the village supported him openly and signed papers as his witnesses, but there were an additional nine whom Catalino claims helped him secretly (one, a member of the *sociedad* tells him of the proceedings of their secret meetings). Some who were with him at first withdrew their support once the seriousness of the opposition had become manifest. Others were threatened, pressured, or otherwise persuaded to join the opposition.

In one case, Lamberto and another youth who had signed as witnesses for Catalino needed the signature of Mateo, the village *comisariado ejidal* and a member of the society, on a document stating that Lamberto was not an *ejidatario,* was unemployed, and was therefore permitted to work as a *bracero* in the United States. By coincidence, I was in the office of the Executive Secretary of the Governor of the State when Lamberto presented this document, and I witnessed the *comisariado's* refusal to sign it on the grounds that Lamberto had turned "against the people" by "siding" with Catalino. Lamberto had only attested to what no one disputes—that Catalino and his sons had worked the land for years— but it was useless to protest. The secretary, who knows both the village and the situation well, put the papers aside with embarrassment and told Lamberto that the matter had to be decided by the people of the village. (The governor had taken the same position on his visit. After hearing the *sociedad's* argument and seeing the disputed site, he had said that while he thought the people of the village should have the land, he could not interfere in a federal matter.)

THE HEARING

On 25 October 1959 two representatives of the federal secretary of agriculture held a public hearing of the case in the village for the purpose of reaching a decision about the land rights. Catalino asked us to tape record the hearing, but we explained that as our position in studying the village required the strictest neutrality, we could take no action on his behalf. Our right to be at the trial at all was challenged by Alfonso and Victoriano, but their objections were overruled by the rest, led by Catalino and Federico.

One of the agents summed up the complaints of both sides. Declaring then that the legality of ownership of the land depended upon whether a *comisariado ejidal* had given the land to Catalino with the approval of an assembly of *ejidatarios,* the agents called on all the past *comisariados* in turn. The first man to be called testified that he had been *comisariado* in 1930 and had given Catalino his legitimate parcel of 40 *tareas* (40,000 square meters) but denied having given him the disputed additional portion.

This much of his testimony is true, but it should be noted that this man, who now appeared among the opposition, had also been one of Catalino's initial witnesses. A total alcoholic, he had not worked his own land (one of the largest parcels in the village) for years but had illegally rented it out to others in what amounted to virtual alienation in return for minimum support and drink. Although his "benefactors" were among the leaders of the *sociedad,* the illegality of his own position, or of those who were cultivating his land, was not, as he testified, at question.

Pio, who had been *comisariado* between 1930 and 1938, was not present, and the next to be called, who had been *comisariado* between 1938 and 1943, gave similar testimony. Manuel (a *compadre* of Catalino, who used this term at the hearing) said that Catalino had begun the illegal extension of his land use during the period from 1943 to 1945, that he had not been given permission to do so, but that there were some who thought that it was all right for him to do so anyway.

Fencing was an important issue. One of the first requirements of a man who wished to receive a parcel was that he be able to fence it, and some had not received parcels because they had been unable to meet this requirement. Federico—Catalino's brother-in-law and *compadre* and *comisariado* from 1948 to 1952—offered as proof that Catalino had not claimed this land the fact that he had not fenced it by 1952. At that time Catalino had asked him if he could extend his fence to keep animals out, but Federico had refused on the grounds that people would believe he had given Catalino this right because they are relatives. He added that the men of the village had discussed building a bathing resort there as far back as twenty years ago, that they had used the spot for outdoor banquets for visiting officials, and that on one such occasion an official of the sugar cooperative had even remarked on the suitability of the site for a resort.

The next *comisariado* to testify, now an alcoholic and a marijuana smoker, felt guilty about having withdrawn his support from Catalino, as his son had been one of Catalino's witnesses. He now gave a confused testimony, stating that he had given a part of the disputed land to Raul Guevara, the schoolteacher, who had left the village. Asked whether he had then given it to Catalino, he replied that he had not, because the land was *pedregal* ("uncultivable").

The next *comisariado,* who has himself been involved in several illegal acquisitions of *ejido* lands, was executive secretary and one of the most active members of the *sociedad.* This man testified that between 1954 and 1958 an assembly of *ejidatarios* had protested Catalino's enclosure of the spring behind his fence and ordered him to keep the spring outside the extension of his fence. Although all of the opposition group insists, and Catalino denies, that such an assembly was held, there is no official record of it.

When Federico described this meeting, however, it became evident that it had been held on the eve of their discovery of Catalino's plan (according to Catalino, they had gone to Mexico City only pretending ignorance of his plan, which they had already discovered by opening his mail). Federico said that Catalino had begun his action toward nationalization four years before they discovered it, and the opposition has often asked why, if Catalino believed he had a right to the land, he had kept his actions secret for four years. I have asked Catalino about this. On one occasion he said that he had kept it secret because he knew that the other *ejidatarios* would oppose and hinder him out of envy; on another occasion he told me that he had not planned to keep the bathing resort for himself but had planned to announce it once his moves were completed and then ask all of the village to join him. This seems unlikely and is probably his defense against the charge of *egoísmo.*

When the testimony was completed, the agent declared it evident that no one had given Catalino the right to the land around the spring. It was evident to me, however, that he had come prepared to decide in favor of the *sociedad,* as he had questioned the witnesses only superficially, had glossed over many issues, and had accepted casually the fiction that the *sociedad* is identical with the "people" of the village.

Catalino then rose to speak, heckled, hooted, and constantly interrupted by those who had always feared his power and persistence as a speaker. Those who had given testimony knew that they had "exaggerated," he said, that his claim was just, and that if they drove him to it—i.e., if it appeared that they might win—he would reveal all of the illegal activities in which his opponents were involved (a frequent threat, as Catalino knows every detail of every illegal action that has occurred in the village over the past thirty years). When the agent declared that he accepted the testimony of the *comisariados,* the assembly cheered; he added, however, that he had no say about the water rights but only about the land. Catalino replied that the disputed land had been given to him not by the *comisariados* who had testified but by Don Pio, who was absent from the assembly. (At this, the women shouted that to name one who is absent is to speak of the dead.)

Catalino then handed the agent a familiar affidavit stating that he has worked the land peacefully for twenty years (though it is not the length of time that is disputed but only that he worked it legally and without protest. Those who deny this have no proof but only their mutually supportive testimonies). The agent returned the paper saying that proved nothing because it was not signed by the man who had been *comisariado* at the time and because under agrarian law the assembly must give the land in any case. Catalino replied correctly that partition had never been conducted in this manner in the village, that it had always occurred informally and without documents, and that no one could prove his right to his own parcel if the village chose to testify to the contrary. In other words, the rights are secure, except against collusive perjury of a majority of the assembly, including the *comisariado* of the period in question.

In an attempt at conciliation, the agent reminded the members of the assembly that they were themselves partly to blame in this matter because they had allowed Catalino to work the land for so many years. To Catalino he added that while his case was outside the law, he personally sympathized with him morally. Addressing the assembly again, he said, "Perhaps Catalino Arquillos is guilty of *egoísmo,* or rather he shows his more than the rest of us." The assembly did not like this trend. To loud applause, Victoriano accused Catalino of having besotted one *comisariado* to get him to sign the affidavit. There were shouts of "Shameless!" and "Dirty old man!"; one woman cried, "Let's shoot him!" and Doña Isabel added, "And he is not even from here." At this point, Victoriano ran out to find Don Pio and returned winded to report that, although Pio was not at home, his wife had said that he had not given away anything belonging to the village. Amazingly, this was accepted as evidence.

During an intermission, the women told me other stories about Catalino, all greatly distorted by their hostility toward him. One said that he had been responsible for much of the illness in the village for years by having mixed the mineral water from the spring with the sweet water they drank (though it is the "sweet" water that is contaminated, as it arrives in open ditches from its source ten kilometers away). Federico's mistress claimed that Catalino had taken her aunt's house site (though, in fact, the aunt had sold it to someone else from whom Catalino bought it, and he also took care of the woman until she died years later). Another woman said that they had petitioned ex-president Cardenas, still the hero of the farmers of Morelos, to have Catalino removed from the village (although they hoped he would intervene on their side in the dispute, he had not acted).

Next, the agent read out an act stating that although Catalino had been unable to prove his legal right to the land, it was recommended that the village give it to him anyway. This was shouted down, the assembly was adjourned to the disputed site, and I stood next to the agent, the leaders of the *sociedad,* and Catalino as the latter pointed out the boundaries. Catalino attempted to explain to the agent that half of the land in the adjoining plot—which belonged to one who had testified against him, and whose son stood next to us—was rented (which is illegal and grounds for the loss of the parcel). Alarmed, the son began to stammer about lies, but this was unnecessary as the agent ignored Catalino's remarks (such practices are all familiar but cannot be examined closely without endangering the remaining fictions of the *ejido* land system).

The hearing was over, and, as the agents at the meeting were direct representatives of the federal secretary of agriculture, it seemed to Catalino's exultant opponents that he had lost. The assembly banqueted the two agents, and a dance held later that night (which we did not attend) was said to be unusually gay. Even the older women danced, who ordinarily do not.

On 9 March 1960, however, Catalino obtained a district court order for the arrest of the four nominal officers of the *sociedad* for damages and trespass upon his *ejido* (the real leaders, Pio and Federico, were not officials). State police came to the village and arrested three of the four, and three lawyers and a state politician then in the Morelos State Chamber of Deputies got the men out of jail on bail, though they remained technically prisoners. Their stay in jail had shaken them and, if possible, increased their hatred of Catalino, while Catalino's appearance in court was jeered by the approximately forty people who had come from the village in several trips in Pio's truck.

Not long afterwards, these men pulled down a stone fence that Catalino had erected to replace a wire fence that had been removed, though both sides had been ordered to refrain from all action on the disputed land until settlement of the land rights. Then, ten days after the leaders of the *sociedad* had been jailed, the result of the department of agriculture's investigation came in the form of an order restoring the disputed land to the village and ordering Catalino to cease work on it. Although the opposition regarded this as the final victory, their jubilance lasted only three days, for Catalino's lawyers in Mexico City (from the office of the lawyer who owned a residence in the village) obtained an order rescinding the previous one.

AN ATTEMPTED SETTLEMENT

Around 25 April 1960, Theodore Schwartz and I, who lived in the village as anthropologists, attempted to arbitrate a settlement of the dispute, which seemed to us extremely destructive to village interests and to the development that its people desired. It had dragged on for years, draining the resources of both sides in bureaucratic and legal expenses. Catalino was virtually bankrupt and was suffering mentally and physically from his obsession with the case.

The lawyers, who also wanted it to end, were doing their best to persuade Catalino to accept a settlement in return for ceding the *balneario* concession to the village, and it seemed to us an opportune time to attempt to use our own influence, along with that of the lawyers, to seek an end to the conflict. We had never intervened on behalf of either side and had succeeded in taking a neutral position (even though villagers would not accept neutrality, both sides forcing a "for" or "against" decision from everyone). We had limited our public relations with Catalino, and, though we spent time with him at his family festivals in a public way, we avoided private visits to his house which might be taken as collusive.

In a mild mood once, Catalino told us that he had come to the idea of the *balneario* at the instigation of some wealthy "friends" (really patrons). He had been doing exceptionally well in agriculture, which he genuinely enjoys; his irrigation project had successfully reclaimed what had hitherto been useless land; his avocado orchard had flourished in his own large house site; and he had been the only man in the village to undertake a fish farm, where he successfully raised Israeli carp. He had a small tractor and his son had a truck (which in their present impecunious position they could not maintain), and his other sons were being educated.

But all of that was being neglected now. He was deeply in debt to the bank with a mortgage on his house and sought a buyer for part of his beloved house site and orchard. Even his children had suffered—from their isolation, from tension, and from the sacrifices they had to make. One son wanted to go to the United States to escape involvement in his father's endless struggle, which, with its demands upon the family's collective earnings, frustrated his own strong ambitions. At times Catalino wavered, wishing that he were out of it or regretting what he had sacrificed. His wife never yielded, however, and told us that it was she who kept him resolutely on his course to protect the rights of his labor and enterprise.

Catalino was also sensitive to the moral criticism of his opponents; it was the area of his greatest vulnerability because the criticism was incompatible with his view of himself as a revolutionary, an admirer of Zapata (whom he is said to resemble and whom he portrayed in a village theatrical during the 1940s), and a fighter for just causes. The charge of *egoísmo* wounded him especially. Admitting that he had acted in secrecy for years, he nevertheless did not like to see himself as making a private commercial exploitation of a scarce public resource, and he denied that he had wealthy prospective partners.

In Catalino's private fantasies he saw himself triumphing over his opponents and then turning the whole thing over to the village, but it is hard to believe that this was more than a fantasy. On other occasions he said that he would turn the rights over to the village once they had conceded the rights but that they would pay him in return some 150,000 pesos (or $12,000) for the work he had done on the land and waterways and for his legal expenses as well. They would compensate him, moreover, for his house and grounds, and then he would leave the village. He would particularly enjoy, he said, seeing his opponents restored to their normal condition of fighting among themselves, as his absence would dissipate the solidarity of the opposition. Then the village would see who would profit from the *balneario*—possibly the few top leaders, especially Pio and Federico, but possibly none of them. They would soon be so divided and distrustful over their funds that they would never complete anything.

At the same time, Catalino's lawyers told us that they were tired of the case, weary of its complicated maneuverings and also of the exercise of costly influence in the Federal Supreme Court and the presidential Office of Complaints, in both of which they had connections. As they explained it to us, the future of the case depended upon who reached which office with money or influence. The other side had "pull," too, based on politics rather than on personal contacts; and the question of authority in the case was chaotically confusing, the Agrarian Code giving a long list of agencies having some authority in either the land, water, or legal aspects of the case. The president of the republic alone had the final authority, and while Catalino's main lawyer had influence with the president, he was reluctant to use it in Catalino's behalf. Such influence cannot be used for trifles without diminishing its effectiveness; but without presidential intervention, the struggle might go on indefinitely through the bureaucratic maze. Catalino's file in their office was huge, as he went to Mexico City at least once a week, always with some new paper that had no legal value in practical procedures.

Catalino's lawyer was fond of him but found him annoying because he haunted his weekends in the village (he also told us that Catalino had offered him a partnership in the *balneario,* which he had refused). He had not anticipated the village's resistance upon his initial encouragement of Catalino and had himself lost something that he had greatly valued— namely, his position as "benevolent patron" to the entire village. He had done much for the village—such as paying the schoolteacher for a year when the state had failed to do so, buying a set of books for the school, making many donations to public works, obtaining scholarships for some of the children of the upper-status families, giving annual Christmas parties, and even making his pool available to village children on weekends, when they were free to mingle with his guests. His position had meant a great deal to him, but now he was also an "enemy of the people."

In April, Catalino said that he was willing to seek a settlement. He offered to drop charges against the leaders who were out of jail on bail and to cede the rights of the *balneario* in return for compensation and a guarantee that he could pursue his agricultural labors unmolested; his lawyer wanted to persuade the village to give Catalino a share in the *balneario* cooperative in return for his concessions. On this basis, we invited fifteen members of the *balneario* cooperative to our home, explaining that Catalino was ready to settle and cede the rights they sought. Everyone appeared to be in a conciliatory mood—Federico most of all, Pio least of all—and agreed to meet with Catalino's lawyers. It was suggested that the meeting be kept small, that a commission be named by the *sociedad,* so that the discussion would remain calm, but Pio insisted on a full assembly of men and women, saying that he would make no concessions for the people of the village (this characteristic stance serves his purpose of preventing a conciliation).

The meeting was a total failure. The lawyer, who was supposed to offer to cede the rights in return for some compensation and guarantees, acted instead as if the other side had called the meeting to make an offer. Neither side would concede anything, each expecting concessions that were not forthcoming from the other. The hooting and heckling began at once, the women, and others as well, playing the roles that Pio had expected of them. Doña Carmela, who was in good form, said that though it had already cost them all of their money, they would go on fighting with the money they would make from the chickens the study had promised them (i.e., a family chickenhouse plan that had been stalled for a year). The calm, conciliatory attitudes of the previous small meeting were replaced by open anger, ridicule, and jeering. Catalino (who, by previous agreement, was not present) said afterward that he would have repudiated any settlement made in his name that did not involve his having either the rights to the *balneario* or full compensation. The opposition ridiculed the idea of compensation but agreed to allow him to continue to work his own parcel; others, however, wanted him out of the village.

For four months through the summer of 1960 there were no new legal developments. Catalino still had his counterorder from the presidential Office of Complaints; pressures were being brought by both sides on the Department of Agriculture; and final settlement of Catalino's damages suit was still pending. The opposition group had meanwhile enlisted the support of a "retired general," said to have presidential influence, from the village of Tilzapotla, and once again, having a new patron, its members were exuberant and hopeful.

In an act of retaliation for the jailing of his opponents, the *sociedad* had planted stakes to put up a fence of its own around the disputed area. Catalino had sent his son to pull up these stakes, with the result that on 16 September 1960 he was suddenly arrested and jailed by the district court. His lawyers came from Mexico City and had him released in two days, but he refused to believe their reassurances that he was not subject to rearrest and hid in a hotel in Mexico City for weeks, visiting the law office almost daily, before he felt it safe to return to the village.

But Catalino's opponents had rearoused the lawyer's flagging interest in the case by this direct attack upon Catalino, and now, through his influence, the presidential Office of Complaints issued a *dictamen* ("opinion") strongly in favor of Catalino. This was sent to the secretary of agriculture, who approved it with a strong statement of his own that the case was decided beyond any doubt by Catalino's long period of work on the land. Local authorities were ordered to protect Catalino and his rights, and over the next six months the village was unable to reverse this decision.

Opposition officials were afraid that they might yet be made to pay the damages Catalino had asked for and feared as well that they would not receive money and support from the rest of the *sociedad* if they had to pay. Some were ready to concede even as the group sought another injunction and a reversal of the decision, while others muttered about recourse to violence. Federico assured us that Catalino would never be permitted to work unmolested, but Catalino disregards their threats as he believes them too cowardly to carry them out. He may be right, as the leaders of the *sociedad* do not relish spending more time in the district jail, but our contact with the case ended at this point.

SUMMARY

Probably never before in the village's history has there been such a concentration of public opinion against one person, or a situation that has allowed the village to sustain so much cohesion together with so much intensity. The nature of the Catalino case is such, however, that many of the village's more general issues, tensions, resentments, and frustrations have attached to it. The case is, in short, in some ways larger than its issues; and although both sides see themselves, sincerely or deludedly, as defending high moral *principales,* if not the Revolution itself, other motives are abundantly apparent.

It is apparent, for example, that Catalino's character, *categoría,* and moral nature threaten other villagers and the village system itself. Outsiders impressed by his personal qualities, especially his intelligence and superior ability to express himself verbally, find it natural to sympathize with Catalino's individualism and middle-class aspirations. Villagers, however, see him as the opposite of the benevolent patron and his success as antagonistic to theirs and threatening to their welfare.

His *categoría* greatly differentiates him from both his peers and potential lower-rank supporters—he is self-educated far above the level of most of his peers, reads much, and speaks well—and these achievements are respected only when they are not regarded as pretentious. That he is also intrepid, self-confident, and a progressive farmer of superior ability is recognized even by his enemies. The point is, however, that he is now resented for the same qualities for which he used to be admired. His refusal to be bought off by the sugar cooperative, for example, is now given a negative interpretation because it set him in particularly painful moral contrast to all the rest.

Beyond a certain point, morality is itself regarded as a pretension to *categoría,* and Catalino's insistence upon joining the real and the ideal in his own life is threatening to the real system. He alone among the better known men of the village lives above the infracode principles that describe and often govern what is real life for most people. His familial and marital relations are true to the letter of the general moral code, and rumors of sexual felicity, plus the fact of his sixteen children, preclude any challenge to his manliness. Physically, he even looks as a man should look—i.e., he is not only considered white but is believed to resemble Zapata or Carranza. It has been seen, too, that the social and economic system of this village is extralegal in its functioning, is maintained by massive collusion, and is for the most part voluntary in its nature. Catalino threatens such a system— threatened it literally, in fact, by exposing the illegalities in land use.

Insofar as calls for violence went unheeded and this was not called cowardice, the case also demonstrates that the *macho* code is at least on the decline. For his part, Catalino feels that his opponents are basically cowards, but his wife has stated, and he agrees, that it was she who kept him on the course of intransigence; on the other side, likewise, it was the women who shrilly challenged the men to kill Catalino. Only the *macho* Gustavo wants to prove that at least one man in the village is not a coward. Perhaps someone will do the bidding of the *macho* code at last, but the inhibitions are plainly there, the result of those forces instrumental in reducing the high rate of homicide.

It has also been seen that the networks of friendship, kinship, *compadrazgo*, and patronage offer less solidarity than does a common hostility, that these multiple bonds can be cut by the lines of conflict. Though motives vary, this can lead to a temporary suppression of other conflicts, which nevertheless remain as latent weaknesses of the group. The outcome of this conflict will depend upon the political and economic resources of the antagonists' networks. Pooling them may bring the needed resources, but even a smaller network may reach into high places, finding a single but crucial connection. Indeed, much of the action in this case has involved building these networks and seeking the critical intervention of a multitude of competing authorities.

Finally, we have seen that a number of moral and legal codes have been operative in this case, providing the shifting bases for attack and defense, evaluation, rationalization, justification, and criticism. The anti-Catalino group shifts from legal to moral argument as this suits its needs—i.e., when legally wrong, they emphasize morality, and vice versa.

Each side, in fact, uses whatever it can against the other. Although villagers are basically individualistic and distrustful of cooperatives, for example, the opposition to Catalino took the form of a cooperative—ostensibly to defend the village's communal rights, though I regard this as a facade and not a serious or sincere revival of earlier agrarian ideas.

For, in truth, both sides distrust the agrarian solution to the problems of the lower, and aspirations of the higher, strata. The prize they want is not land in the older sense but the right to exploit urban leisure commercially. The village has progressed from the Revolution (in which most were passive participants) through those agrarian hopes that led to the new community's formation, through the strivings for community development that led to its achievements in village planning and public works, through its hopes and disappointment in the sugar cooperative, to the costly and corrupting dissipation of community potential of the Catalino case—the latter, a considerable drop in the moral level of conflict. The hope is frail that a just settlement might leave a lasting residue of village unity and moral force for the accomplishment of those ideological ends that the contestants evoke in their own justification.

---

[1] Mexico, Leyes y Codigos de Mexico, *Codigo agrario* (Mexico: Porrua, 1960), p. 63.

8

SOME CONCLUSIONS

The conclusions offered in this chapter on morality, selected features of social structure, and the occurrence of violence and murder are based upon the foregoing analyses of these topics in the general context of social solidarity and conflict, which were themselves based upon my own observations of village life.

MORALITY.   The village exhibits no single, or unitary, moral code but rather a number of moral codes, arranged horizontally as they relate to different institutional spheres or to different areas of behavior, and hierarchically when they relate to the same areas of behavior—i.e., the behavior approved by one code is less approved, or of "lower" morality, than that approved by another. Thus, there is a general moral code reflecting various social, religious, and legal principles that is higher than the other codes, and there is also the locally-weighted code that reflects the relative importance of these principles to our villagers. Both codes have infracode levels into which most actual village behavior falls, and if this is not explicitly approved, it is nevertheless expected and accepted.

This system of moral codes is operative in the evaluation and rationalization of behavior and serves as a referent for assigning moral status to each individual. The concept of moral status—treated here as a component of general status with such other components as sexual, socioeconomic, political, and categorical status—is useful in describing and accounting for the sharply differentiated positions and actions of villagers in the moral sphere. The systems of moral and categorical status as reported here are important but are not well-known.

A full discussion of political structure and morality exceeds the scope of this study, but its outlines have been suggested. Systematic, institutionalized political corruption is well-known on the national level, and in this respect the village is but a microcosm of the nation. A real, infracode system develops and works under the stabilizing and protective cover of the relevant code. Both are maintained by the massive collusion of their participants and are threatened by the occasional "moral" person who wishes to act according to the code itself.

SOCIAL STRUCTURE AND CONFLICT.   I found no groupings or relations notably free of conflict in the village; indeed, the cohesion of some important but unstable social groupings depended upon the presence of conflict or shared antagonism. The mother-child relation (particularly between a mother and her sons) and relations of patronage were those most capable of surviving conflict. On the whole, however, family, kinship, friendship, *compadrazgo,* and patronage relations were so conflictive that it became ultimately practical to describe social solidarity as simply the capacity to survive conflict.

Each individual's security system—i.e., the set of social resources that enable him to meet crises or unusual needs—lies in a relational network peculiar to the individual. The links of such networks are based singly or severally on kinship, friendship, *compadrazgo,* or patronage, which are described as composing a single rather than a fourfold network because of their very extensive, though not complete, functional inter-changeability as social resources. Thus, though one or more relations of a network may be disrupted or made inactivable through conflict, the extensiveness of the networks of others tends to guarantee the survival of some lines of social recourse.

Certain internal structural features were found to characterize this social organization, among them a relative weakness of horizontal relations (among persons of roughly equal age and status) compared to vertical relations; a confining of symmetrical friendship to the horizontal, with any degree of patronage tilting relations toward the vertical; and finally, the decidedly asymmetric structure and generalized exchange in the *compadrazgo* relation.

VIOLENCE AND HOMICIDE. Paradoxically, violence and murder reflect and precipitate much less of the total amount of conflict than might be expected. Violence, particularly in its more extreme forms, is usually "unmotivated" or at least unpremeditated and is often conspicuously absent just where it would be supported by one or another of the moral codes, as in vengeance or against an "enemy of the people," for example.

There is a marked disjunction between conflict and violence, and there has also been a drastic reduction in the village's rate of homicide. This is partly because the *macho* code, with its associated group of violence-prone alcoholics, is on the decline, but also the result of various selective and acculturative changes in recent village history through revolution, immigration, the village's increasing involvement in commercial, industrial, urban, national, and foreign contacts, and of certain mechanisms, formal and informal, for the avoidance and resolution of conflict and the elimination of violence and the violent. Still, the level of violence remains high, and, in spite of its downward trend, I believe that there is no reduction in serious interpersonal conflict.

There seems to be a trend in social anthropology to study the brighter side of social conflict[1]—Simmel has even spoken of the "positive" and integrating role of antagonism[2]—but I feel that the village pays dearly for its conflicts and "immoralities" in terms of their impact on the lives of given individuals and their frustrating or impeding effect upon village development.

The reader has, hopefully, gained sufficient basis to see how conflict and immorality affect the workings of village organizations, even though the successes and failures of these organizations could not be fully considered here. The situation studied does not provide an example of equilibrium or of stable tradition. The older people in the village have never known stability or security, and though some have attained a measure of these, most care more about status. They tend to define their actions as immoral but neither rationalize this nor recast the general moral code by which they harshly judge themselves and one another. They condition themselves to expect betrayal, yet they continue to hope. They have committed and codified much violence, but they seem relieved now to be able to call their nonviolence "culture" rather than cowardice.

---

[1] See Max Gluckman, *Custom and Conflict in Africa* (Oxford: Blackwell, 1955) and Edward Evans-Pritchard, *The Nuer: A Description of the Modes of Livelihood and Political Institutions of a Nilotic People* (Oxford: Clarendon, 1947).

[2] George Simmel, *Conflict,* trans. Kurt H. Wolff (Glencoe, Ill.: Free Press, 1955).

AFTERWORD

Several years ago I was in Mexico City and pondered the possibility of making the three hour drive to the village. I hesitated, afraid that I might not negotiate well the memories (theirs and mine), possible changes in the village, and my own overpowering desire to avoid offending anyone by not visiting them, for lack of time. More important, perhaps, was the fear that my analyses, with their inherent prediction, would be correct. This would not be felicitous for my friends in the village. The alternative, that I had *not* seen it correctly, would please me for the village's sake but make me feel less than adequate as a field anthropologist, let alone an analytical and theoretical one. Had I structured the events correctly? Would the mechanisms that caused and perpetuated social stratification still be operant or perhaps even amplified? Would the family structure remain the same in spite of incursions of bits and pieces of urbanization which must surely have seeped into the village from returned migrants from Mexico City or the United States? Would violence still be a last resort, or fear of it used to facilitate conflict resolution? Would the notion of accountability still be a mute and unwelcome muse unnoticed in the corner of the village meeting hall?

Furthermore, I did not feel inclined towards revisitations, having had one instanced for me by Margaret Mead's 1964 return to Pere village of Manus after many years of absence.[1] The tears of the old women, the friendly amazement and stunned smiles of the men made me ask Margaret to interpret this reception, and she said indifferently, "It is because they and I have aged." This did not ring true to me, for the natives throughout Manus did not feel tearful about old age but were rather quite Aurelian about it. Furthermore, it was highly relevant to an interpretation of Margaret's reception to have known that some natives had asked me whether white people died. For them, the ghosts of the dead disappear beyond the reef and the cargo ships sent by the dead come by the same route, so who knows about pale people appearing and disappearing from those coordinates in space? They really had not expected to see Margaret again.

Now the expectations of these Mexican villagers would not be so startling, nevertheless, I could not know what they might have expected of me. Ted Schwartz had stopped there briefly several years earlier; they had eagerly asked for news about me and he did tell them that two books had been written about them. Would they now wonder why they had not seen them? It is true that neither Erich Fromm nor I had sent them a copy of either book; even though I had fictionalized names, they would certainly have recognized the characters, and in a truthful account they could not all emerge as admirable.

My husband rented a car and we began to drive out of Mexico City and to the state of Morelos, in and out of Cuernavaca, past the canyons and *barrancas* and then past fields of cane and rice to the dirt road that led to the village. Despite my ambivalence, we both wanted to learn about the resolution of the dispute over the rights to the *manantial*, and learn whether or not a *balneario* had been built, bringing prosperity and happiness to the village in its new found wealth.

Huge pines still lined the entrance, but there were now new houses under them where there had been only forty building lots for sale when I had lived in the village. New residents were living there, not from other sections of the old village, but from other places in the state of Morelos and the country. Most came from Zacatepec, Xochitepec and Cuernavaca, the villagers resentfully told me, and had jobs in those other places. There were a few new weekend residences of people who lived in Mexico City. For who else in the village, other than Octavio, had money to build a better house? Octavio, cool and peripheral in all village events of all kinds during my stay there, had been a young entrepreneurial type who had allied himself loosely with the older leaders, but focused on his own possible future opportunities. I recalled something else about Octavio. He had been secretive and seldom talked to us, except with a perfunctory politeness about meaningless trivial matters. I hadn't liked him, because he was not "open" and because his wife wept often in my presence about her many children, her continued pregnancies and about his mistress, an attractive young woman classified as *mestizo negroide* from the poorest family in the village (the Anclillos). The mistress, too, regularly bore Octavio's children; and the humiliation that his wife experienced when both she and the mistress bore sons on the same day prompted her to tell me that this was particularly devastating, rendering them all "like animals." He had also been the last person who had handled a significant sum of money that was meant for the purchase of chickens to raise money for school expenses. At one meeting at which someone asked about the "chicken money," he glared icily at the interrogator and replied in a controlled and quiet but thoroughly menacing voice, "That money was for school expenses and it was thus used." This ended all future queries about the chicken money. He had not been unfriendly to us, particularly as we had helped his brothers get proper documentation and the invitations to work in Arizona on rose-growing farms. He simply did not share with us his thoughts and aspirations, as did most of the others.

Now, the *Zocalo* had a cement court for basketball; such new constructions gave the village a more prosperous appearance, which I found to be totally incongruent with the core village. For these villagers, except of course for Octavio with his splendid two-story house, were economically where I had left them at the end of research period alluded to in this volume.

We drove to the house in which I lived, a house that used to be called *la tontería de Deigo* ("Diego's stupidity"), for the village had not much appreciated Diego Rivera's idea of what a country house should be. There had been a tree growing through the middle of the large living room which I had found delightful. The house was no longer there but the tree remained, reflecting perhaps my own sense of loss. Across a dirt alley was Lina's house site. I wanted to see Lina and Filomena first, for they had been most open with me, and most informative. Since my visit was to be brief, I wanted to start making inquiries with those who had been my most factual and meticulous reporters. Filomena, unfortunately, had died of cancer four years earlier. My other close neighbors, Don Pascual and his wife were both dead. Lina's young daughter Cari was dead and so was her baby. Cari had been hit by a speeding car as she alighted from another car on her way back to the village.

Lina had two small houses on her *sitio* now. She said that I could build a vacation house on her land if I wished, near her small house made of stone. She explained her "better situation" to me by telling me that she had a "husband" whom she would marry soon. He worked in Monterey, sent her money and also sent her bus fare to go up and stay with him from time to time. She now had beds, mattresses and a sewing machine on the porch of the older house. Living with her were her daughter Sirena and Sirena's two small children, as well as her son and daughter-in-law. She showed me with pride a rabbit pen with two fat healthy rabbits, several *guacolotes* (turkeys), a pig, several chickens and two scrawny puppies. Then I had to see the fresh water spring on her *sitio* from which she draws water for all their needs. We laughingly recalled the undrinkable sulphur water spring, useless for our needs, on our house site next to hers. She pointed to the spring and said to me, with piety and pride, almost as though this small miracle was the only evidence she had of her worth, "Ah, this, look, this does not fail me even yet," but her voice was quiet, subdued, as though if overheard, someone or an evil spirit might get an idea of how to destroy her thoroughly. (Her daughter Sirena had been my daughter's best friend when they were nine years old in the village. They used to play games that Sirena invented: Debbi on a white horse as "leader of the crusades" while all the village children were the "crusaders"; Debbi as the Lady of the House, while Sirena was a maid and her cousin the cleaning lady. Sirena used to announce guests and add with great terror, "*han dicho comida*," meaning, "Ah, dear Lady, what are we to do?, they have come for dinner!")

As I stepped on to the *sitio* I had asked a little girl (Sirena's daughter) if Lina were there. "Oh, yes," (scurrying off) "and whom shall I say is calling?" Village children are so polite, even as I remembered them. Lina was overcome with emotion; so was I. She burst into tears as we embraced.

"You are my dearest friend" she said, "even absent from here. I wanted to write you many times, especially when my daughter was killed by a car, but I could never find you in the world."

She told me how Cari and the baby were killed, and dragged by the car that hit them. The driver or drivers were never found, since they had abandoned the car and fled. Lina and I discuss why they fled. If found guilty of having killed someone with a car, they would have been imprisoned, hounded and bled for every cent, into perpetuity. This does not mean the people who had suffered from it would ever have been remunerated for their loss. "So what difference to me," said Lina, "if they were caught?" Later she showed me how far the victims had been dragged and then where they had been buried. Because the driver was never found, Lina got nothing, not even funeral expenses. So little had changed,

I thought, in spite of more cars, more traffic, more smog, more noise. The apperance of complexity, but only more decibels.

I asked about Don Catalino, the protagonist "against the village" in litigation over the *balneario*. He had gone off to the South, having epileptic fits before he went (she described these rather indelicately as "biting off bits of that rash tongue of his as his eyes rolled around in those fits he had begun having, the old *cabrón*"). I asked about Don Pio and Don Federico . . . ("old, poor, forgotten, now being screwed by Octavio, just as they screwed poor people in the village for years").

Sirena's husband had left her with two small children. Most of the young girls now have babies, but they don't bother marrying as they did in the past to "legitimize" a relationship and a status. They don't even bother pretending that there is a "husband." Why go to the bother and expense of pretending the pregnancy is legal? Lina named a number of young women I had known as children who were in the same situation.

Sirena's husband does not support her or the children. Lina does, for her daughter has no way of earning money. I did not ask Lina where her son was, since she did not say; but in fact Lina was the head of the household with two young mothers and three little grandchildren: a residential compound with a grand matriarch, almost an intensification of what I had described in earlier years. The matricentric family was now the core of cultural continuity.

Lina's estranged husband had died, but not before leaving his celibate state, abandoning Lina, to run off with Leticia for awhile. It seemed that he ended up in a wheelchair before his death. (Lina told me that several times to be sure I could create for myself the visual impression of her former husband in his *silla con ruedas*.) Lina's former lover had now left his wife (this was the man with whom Lina had had an affair *du coeur* and who used to help her out financially), but she did not tell me who he was living with, even though I asked. (Probably no one, probably still helping Lina out). Octavio, she told me, had built two houses—each magnificient by village standards—one for his wife in the village, and one for his mistress in Cuernavaca.

"How can he afford all that construction with all those kids he has had with both women?" I ask.

"That *cabrón!* When he is sober, he tells everyone how he makes a good living with his tractor and his business, but when he is drunk he brags that he is worth twelve million pesos because of his connections."

I ask by what "road" he has connections.

"The *manantial*, you know, the *balneario.*"

"Good heavens. The *balneario*. No. No. I don't know. Tell me!" She not only tells me, but, with her daughter, we rush off so that I may see it.

"Well, Lina continues, "You remember about the *cooperativa?* Eh? You always used to go around with that recording machine, and with your pencil to get the story? Okay! Well, somehow, Octavio really wanted to be President of the *Socios*, so they finally said, 'Okay!, we will vote for Octavio as President.' So they made him President. Then money began rolling in for the *balneario* to be built. Some money came from the *Socios* they said, but hell, they can't kid us, right? These poor church mice couldn't have that much money, and I ask you where did it come from? Wherever it came from, they are cleaning up and so is Octavio, their dummy and front man for the village, for the fiction of the coopertive, for the *Socios.* "

Now, I thought, I will tell her something I had never told her when I lived there. "Lina, do you know that Don Catalino told me that this is what would happen if he lost the case?"

"He did? How did he know? Ah! How stupid of me. How did we *not* know? People here are all the same, these old ——! Of course one of them, the foxiest, would do everyone else in. Well, I don't care about all those old selfish ——! They all got what they deserve."

"Perhaps," I said, "but I am sorry, because the villagers did not get anything."

"You can say that again. We used to be able to wash up in the spring water, now if we want to take a dip, we have to pay ten pesos. Can you imagine, we have to pay ten pesos in a place where we all used to bathe freely after working in the fields." I agreed this was lamentable beyond belief, while Lina continued.

"Well, co-op members have no power whatsoever. Octavio collects all the money, handles all the transactions, tells everyone that their investment was too small, and costs so great, that it will be many years before they realize any profitable income from the bathing place. He keeps it all to himself. Look you here, who is working here collecting tickets and selling soft drinks, and collecting tickets for the rock band? All Octavio's brothers, right?"

I wondered about Pio and Federico.

"Ah, those old bastards, after having screwed the *pueblo* for years, they are at last screwed by Octavio. They get nothing from the *balneario*. They now *are* nothing. Pio isn't even in it."

This was very sad, even though it was a logical outcome of the system that I had described. It is what Catalino predicated; it was what I had predicted as I hoped it would not happen. The *Manantial de San Ramon!* The *Balneario de San Ramon*, it is now called. It had been one of the dreams of the village for a good life for all, *ejidatarios* and *peones* alike. As sure as the visible ghost of Zapata in the hills at twilight, or the dreams of finding lost gold in the hacienda left by Montezuma (wailing dead babies assured them of this), the *manantial* would save them from the wretched cycle of brutish life in the fields.

A double entry brick archway lead to the *balneario*. There was a park band shell featuring a loud rock band that Sunday, and hundreds of social dancers from Cuernavaca or from Mexico City, from other *pueblos* nearby, a sailing pond with two small boats in it, and *cabañas*. There were two large pools with no one in them. (I remembered how very cold the water was and still has to be.)

"Look," said Sirena sadly, "We have our own *xochimilco* ('floating gardens') of the village." She repeated that all of Octavio's immediate relatives were getting some sort of income, however small, from the *balneario*.

Gustavo, a macho, who had been called *el toro del manantial* because it was said he was the only one who had testicles enough to fight Don Catalino for the *pueblo* openly, was found dead in a canyon several years ago. He had last been seen accepting a lift in a car containing several men. All believed and said quietly that Octavio had arranged the abduction, that these men had bound and gagged Gustavo and threw him into a canyon, and his body was to have fallen into the river. It was found by an American girl four months later; she had lost her way while exploring the canyon.

Gustavo had been fighting Octavio and openly decrying the fate of the *cooperativa*. I am sure he was the only person in the village foolish enough to do both things. I had always (aware of my total subjectivism) considered Gustavo quite insane. Neither Ted nor I were able to make contact with him and he once fired bullets through the shirt of Don Catalino's mentally retarded son as this son worked the land which in now the *balneario*. This had been an act the village *did* find reprehensible, even though he did it *"por el pueblo."*

I note that under the *ejido* law, Don Catalino should have received the rights to the land. This had not been in question very much (see p. 168). Problematic was the fact that this very land was where the *balneario* would have been build, and the fact that the spring belonged to the whole *Ejido* of the *Pueblo*. I had watched with great interest politicians and lawyers from Mexico City observe and discuss this Catalino case over the years, explaining points of *ejido* law public and private ownership and rights of usages.

Lina told me, responding to a question, that Octavio wanted Gustavo to sell a *sitio* that was near the *manantial* to one of his (Octavio's) brothers and Gustavo refused to do so; that is why he lost his life. Octavio's family was able then to purchase the *sitio*.

Conversations during this recent visit with Don Pio, Don Federico and Octavio verified what Lina had told me. Octavio allowed as how lending out his tractor and some small, undisclosed businesses had made him prosper. Pio and Federico sadly admitted that the *socio* investments in the *balneario* showed no returns, because the investments were too small and the costs were so large. They said it had not been a good investment for the village and, besides, the water was much too cold.

One more question: "What," I asked, "did the village people think about Fromm's book?" Yes, they had heard of it from Ted Schwartz and also from other visitors before him but had not seen it. There seems to be a sense in the village that I had, at least, told "the truth" in my book, although they had not seen that book either. What they meant by that, of course, is not that Fromm did not, but that I dutifully had recorded every secret of the bad behavior of "the others" that each had brought to my attention. They had liked the idea that the guilt, shame and moral failure of others might be in print. But "in print" does not mean much to a group struggling daily to negotiate the layers of fiction and reality that surround every endeavor no matter how trival. No one requested from me a copy of either book; nor was it ever mentioned for the rest of my visit.

The *balneario* and the rock band filled me with sorrow for the passing of the village I had known. This village now had more cars, more tourists, more people; here was a superficial intrusion of urban culture, but structurally and functionally nothing had changed. What was gone was the tranquility, which had not been replaced with well-being.

I shall remember Lina's little grand-daughter sitting with knees crossed and hands folded, along with her brother looking like small adults, attentive to all that was said. They would rush for a pencil when someone asked for one and were ready to smile when glanced at. I recalled that this was my first impression in the village: the little girls, precocious in their adult roles, washing dishes in the *apantles*, covered with rebozos, imitating their mothers in anguishing over abandonment by the father and the prohibitive cost of everything. What was gone were rebozos, stored in the closet of costumes, but the script—at least in this village—was unchanged.

Don Catalino, the single protagonist, had lost. He had predicted to me that if he were to lose, those who had fought for the village invoking Agrarian Revolutionary heroes such as Zapata would then fight among themselves. The winners, he had prophesied, would be men from Mexico City with significant sums of capital for investment in the enterprise.

The outcome was interesting for several reasons, but to me not the least interesting facet was that the village information from women was always considered gossip, even by Erich Fromm who discouraged me from paying attention to it! And yet it was the women from whom the information I gathered was the most reliable. Men, I had noted in my field notebook, had to do much footwork with facts, since these facts were used to reinforce male images. Women here were inconsequential and hence free to be truthful. I had not been in the village long during my early research when, in reply to a question on the status of women, they taught me the following verse on the ages of womanhood:

> *A quince, una rosa*
> *A viente, esposa*
> *A treinta, vaca*
> *A quarenta, caca*

(from rose to bride to cow to dungheap by age 40)

As in the immunological response of a system to the cell that does not belong, Don Catalino was ejected from the social system of the village as though he were an agent for disorganization and disaster. The process by which this was brought about had already begun in 1960, when women bragged to me that some of them had gone to Mexico City to hand-deliver a petition to Lazaro Cardenas to get this person, a threat to Revolutionary ideals, out of the village. At that time, many in the village had had themselves incarcerated to protest Catalino's attempt to develop the *balneario*.[2] "We are as one man," they had said, all of those who had pitted themselves against Don Catalino. Because of the barrage, through the years, of village petitions to oust him, Catalino may have had no choice but to leave. At least he had managed with help from his lawyer friends to get himself installed as an *ejidatario* in Chiapas, a long way from the village. What had propelled affairs to the point where the delicate balance of Catalino against the village ended in system breakdown?

Catalino had played an important role for the village; he had defined his adversaries and given them an identity within the remembered glory of the Agrarian Revolution of the early decades of this century. With this linkage in their minds between a dubious current event and an ideology, he also gave political office-seekers and office-holders who visited the area something to say about ideology, so that their rhetoric rang with authenticity and present urgency. In his person villagers had an enemy to fight. Their hatred galvanized the different groups in the village around the concept of *el pueblo*, by which they meant both the village and "the oppressed people," and allowed them to relive the struggle against the callous landholders of the past, now resurrected in the unlikely personage of Don Catalino. They had their arguments about his claim to his land, although these were somewhat shaky. It was rather a multileveled antagonism, because in a practical here-and-now sense he threatened, in his defense, to expose them for their actual daily flagrant violations of the laws about *ejido* usage. But more importantly, he threatened their notion that it was not possible to merge real and ideal in one's life, that corruption was a fact that had to be accepted, that a person could survive only in a petitioning stance and even then only if others permitted him to survive, let alone prosper.

In this battle of belief and action, of the one against the many, the village had once more experienced one of its customary and familiar historical defeats. Once more thay had learned that those politicians, who assured them a strong faith in the cause of *el pueblo* must surely triumph, deserved but a passing glance and a cynical distrust. I have alluded in this volume to other earlier disillusionments, for there were many. Each time the villagers were disillusioned, they held endless discussions, or what might be called group debriefings, in an attempt to understand the causes of their failure. It seemed, then, that they despised their own inability to judge those who led them and those who seemingly opposed them. They felt that this poor judgment, along with constant internal dissent, prevented them from joining the rest of the world in the march of progress. In this, their latest failure, it seems that they recognized that they had followed blindly those whose corruptibility was never in doubt, and made an enemy of the people the one whose integrity had never been in question. This is not to say that they now felt that Don Catalino was not wrong; they now thought rather that their actions and reactions were not wise.

We noted, in the preceding sections on morality (pp. 93–94) that the road to a good moral record was paved with proscriptions, and that concern with guilt meant the guilt of *others*, not one's own. Behind moral choices there was not only an ethic, but an aesthetic as well. How, I wondered on this visit, had deeply embedded and intricately contextualized social images affected social roles and village behavior in this Catalino case, whose outcome did not surprise me? How did those images sustain the emotional tone and shape social actions?[3] In terms of aesthetics behind moral behavior and the social action to implement it, how was Don Catalino transformed in the minds of the villagers from the paragon of true manliness imbued with the best of tradition and thoroughly praiseworthy, to that acerbic, intemperate *macho* who could now be destroyed with no one having any pangs of conscience about his destruction? Interestingly, in a parallel of role reversals, while Don Catalino became the despicable *macho*, Gustavo, a contemptuously viewed *macho*, became for them, for a brief time, an Agrarian Revolutionary hero and village savior.

During the three years of my living in and having close contact with village events and persons, I had observed a gradual but perceptible transformation in villagers instancing of Don Catalino's behavior that were indicators of their changing attitudes. When I first moved into the village, all were genuinely concerned that I should appreciate his traditional virtues, even though his plans to build a bathing pool annoyed many (but not all) of them. For he had been a Zapatista (pp. 14–20), even though the other men in his original village had been against Zapata. In my family typology (p. 59) he had earned the highest regard as a present, influential and fine disciplinary father, which classified him with only seven other men in the village. He was strict and authoritarian with his children whatever their sex or age (a greatly admired traditional trait). His relationship with his wife was close, confidential, loving and respectful; this was a relationship admired by all, particularly the women who later bitterly and vociferously hated him, and all claimed it was unique. He had been a hard worker for the village and a great fighter with words (*pleitista*) when he had argued on behalf of the village. Morally and physically, they told me, he had resembled Emiliano Zapata (p. 19). He was a man of *categoría*, fair-skinned, well-spoken and literate, who lived in a modern type of house rather than a lowly *jacal*. True, his wife was rather *mestizo*; but she had given birth to many children, had raised them well, and she was loyal to her husband—speaking on his behalf to politicians when they came to the village. She was the "injectionist" pumping all patients who came to her full of penicillin for aches and ills. They used to recall that he had been generous in all things, that he fought to get water for the village, and that he allowed an old woman to live in his house when she had nowhere to go. Also, he was the only one who could not be bought off by the politicians.

Now in transforming their image of him the villagers did not change these characteristics, but rather, as though caricaturing them in a spiteful cartoon, simply colored them with negative hues. New instancings and their derivative character indices became the following: he had too much to say to his sons, and was mean to them, even those who were grown and married, e.g., he did not want them to immigrate to the United States. (Two of them did so anyway, and one of them had been in the U.S. for many years.) Yes, he helped bring in water for irrigation into the village but that was so he could steal it for his own use, and mix it with his sulphurous spring water so that villagers could become ill. By the end of my third year in residence, Don Catalino had become the major cause of illnesses in the village. He was not exactly accused of bewitching, but this was slyly implied by tone and gesture. His rhetorical gifts in arguing a case in a cogent and compelling manner were demoted from having accorded him the title of *pleitista* to having him referred to as *pleitoso*, a trivial bickerer. His ability not to be swayed from fighting for righteous causes later earned him the reputation for intransigent stubborness, as *terco*, *revoltoso* and *caprichudo*. He came to be seen not as a man of initiative and imagination, but as an *egoísta*, one who is so selfish that he cannot be swayed by community concerns or the public interest. His *catergoría* was transmogrified to *orgullo* (small-time hubris) and a kind of *anti-indigenismo*, meaning that it was offensive to the more indigenous or "native-looking" types of the village! (I had usually heard *Indigenismo* ridiculed except in pompus orations on national holidays.) His generosity with the fruits of his agricultural activities was now seen as an attempt to buy the goodwill of former friends, acquaintances and visitors. He had taken in the old woman, it was said, so that he could have her property at her death. (Actually, that property was purchased by another individual who much later sold it to Don Catalino, as the property was adjacent to the Catalino's house site, which meant that the old woman had been his neighbor for years before she could no longer take care of herself.) His incorruptibility was now described as pigheadedness, for moral compromise was actually the "rule" (p. 153). What he had earned from his hard work and initiative was now attributed to the fact that he had always been an *aprovechado*, one who takes advantage of others and situations. Finally, he was one who was not *de aqui*, not from here, an outsider and alone.

A man whose character had been the core of village traditions and the ideal of male identity had become peripheral and then ejected. His place had been filled temporarily (almost as a spur-of-the-moment *commedia dell'arte* by a repertory group) by a person whom no one had ever respected. All of this happened over a three year period, as Don Catalino, the "unbound" individual conflictant (pp. 28–29) was pitted against the "bound" group; that is to say, those whose alliances kept coalescing, creating a group that referred to itself as *el pueblo*. The bound group "became" the village as it absorbed more and more persons into concensus that the lonely protagonist was an enemy of the people. This process was aided and abetted by office-holders and office-seekers on tour to gain or bolster their grass roots political support. While being feted as *patrones* by all who thought of themselves as petitioning *peones* (another traditional behavior-determining image), these politicians took up the cudgels for "*el pueblo*" against the sole individual who sought a fair hearing to what he considered his constitutional rights. This unvarying stance by visiting politicians had the strong tendency to override any and all attempts at destabilization of alliances within the bound group. Villagers who belonged to the bound group peered expectantly into the eyes of these same politicians to see a future of hope for themselves. There was a symmetry in eye-gazing, as "the people" and politicians gave each other promises of future victories by sacrificing Don Catalino.

Whenever anyone in the village recounted the facts that had never been in dispute, about Don Catalino working his land, said person was swiftly, summarily and severely punished. Retaliation often reached such individuals, sadly, by way of village influence on lower level bureaucrats in Cuernavaca who refused them visas for temporary jobs in the United States, or agricultural loans which should not have been denied them. They were, oddly enough, even told the reason for denials of their request, that is, that they were adversaries in the battle of the people in this very important case. (I had been present at several of these denials, having been asked by the petitioner to accompany him.) Such denials were meant to assure that there would be total silence in future inquiries as to whether Don Catalino and his sons had worked land for the necessary amount of time.

There were multiple amplifying mechanisms widening the chasm between the antagonistic parties. The first of theses was the use of petty officialdom by the group that referred to itself as *el pueblo*, in the manner exemplified above. Secondly, Don Catalino also assured maximum cohesion in the bound group by going outside the village, and outside other local arenas of possible arbitration, in his continued attempts to have his case adjudicated in Federal courts of jurisdiction. To go outside an arena where members of the cooperative had some influence was unforgiveable. Disengagement had become unthinkable, and on both sides there had been a rush to resolution of this conflict, *venga lo que venga* (come what may).

Another amplifying effect on the conflict was the fact that the village was integrated into the bureaucracy of the rest of Mexico through petitioning systems. (p. 124). Many Mexicans from diverse socio-economic groups and backgrounds had mentioned to me with pride during my stay that in their country one worked through *personal* contacts, understanding and influence, and not through interpretation of the law or constitutional principles. The generally held belief appeared to be that the latter were ludicrous, since interpretation is endless and must ever be arbitrary. (I do not present this view to belittle it, for it has its merits, else why do Americans have such concern with which President of which political persuasion selects the individuals who will interpret our constitution?) I had, on many occasions, conversed with Mexican lawyers who had just returned from the United States and who, in disbelief and amusement, noted to each other and to me that "up there they really try to resolve litigation by applying the law." This is not to say that Mexico is a country where the law is never applied, but rather that what people say and believe does have a behavior-determining potential which can be demonstrated to influence behavior.

The people of this village had been led by men who were skilled petitioners, men of words gifted in the obsequious cultivation of those above them. Catalino, too was skilled in such things. So the system and method in which they had believed failed them all. This outcome, I learned on my return visit, left them stunned and confused. Nor were they pleased to remember that having presented themselves to me and others as people who abhor violence, they had resorted to violence against a defenseless "adversary," Don Catalino's retarded son (pp. 171–72). Villagers also now felt some shame about their collusion in having received as comrades certain persons who, before the revolt against Catalino, had been held in contempt. Their defeat once more confirmed the notion they had always had of themselves: incompetent, undiscerning and ever bound for failure.

One of the aims of our study had been to arrive at an understanding of the relationship between social character and the possible courses of community development. We two anthropologists who lived in the village had noted an interesting correlation between the type of crop planted by an *ejidatario* or by a person who "rented" land for planting and his personal characteristics. For example, the more speculative crops such as tomatoes or rice did not attract those who wanted little risk and were content with small gains. There were many who wanted to feel secure and gain something for their efforts, even though they were going to be cheated at every step from seed or plant purchase to marketing. These persons would plant sugar cane for the sugar cooperative in Zacatepec (Schwartz 1963). But no one wanted any of their children to have to make such choices. When asked what they wanted their children to become, they would give a reply that included a class of occupations, mostly clerical or professional, none of which were agricultural. Now, in their own lifetimes and perhaps for their children, in this hope for the *balneario*, they had wanted to exploit urban leisure commercially, and this right, too, was taken away from them by those who have long known how to go about this.

Where to go from this shattered enterprise and latest disenchantment? Other young men, since my stay, had gone away to the United States and some young women had gone to work in Cuernavaca or Mexico City. What remained were the old people, and some very young, a few *ejidatarios* still working the land, and a rather significant group of people who had purchased lots in the widened confines of the village, but who "are not from here": not from the village in any sense of the word. The reassemblage of the village included many who had shared neither their history nor their painful past.

As I used to discuss their "system" with them in the abstract, they professed an objective and thorough understanding of "how things work" (there are many examples of this given in the text). But their consciousness of culture, year after year and project after project, does not seem to have had a didactic influence on their behavior within events. This is a village that has had much stimulation for change, as the text documents, but has seldom succeeded, and never succeeded spectacularly. However, one small partial success will cause all failure to be forgotten for the moment and will reinforce the patronage-peonage pattern of interpersonal relations with its concomitant corruption, collusion for conformity, and continued inculcation into passive-receptive attitudes.

The emotional tone of the village remained similar to that of the village I had known earlier. All appeared superficially cheerful and lively, but after a brief talk one found insecurity and depression underneath the cheer. When Ted Schwartz and I had noticed this in earlier years we had called it "institutionalized depression," meaning that the use of counter-depressive strategies helped them to stop just short of *experiencing* the depression. They lived and still live in an environment which offers frequent sources of deprivation and frustration. Life is one of long, hard work with little reward and insecure survival, where interpersonal relations led and lead to disappointment. They do not seem to live by the notion of the "limited good," an attitude toward resources described elsewhere (Foster 1967). In my idiom, using models from economics, they are not wage-fund theorists, but rather opt for a Keynesian notion that "pump priming" from the outside is possible, that is, that "the good" both in quantity and quality can and must be made to appear from outside sources. But they admit that they simply do not have the formula to succeed in such endeavors. Therefore, their reference levels for expectations, both positive and negative, are set so low that real life experiences, however harsh, will not fall below these previously set levels. This results, of course, in a generalized constriction of social patterns, and all social behavior is based on discounted expectations. Social fantasy, almost totally pessimistic, provides an immunizing and buffering effect. Songs, movies, stories, jokes and *dichos* (sayings) were often repeated, their fatalistic weight being balanced by the lightness with which they were performed or pronounced. Songs were and still are of betrayal, abandonment, solitude, inebriation and nothingness. These generate not only reference levels but strategies for behavior as well. Expecting to be abandoned, one abandons. Fearing isolation, one isolates oneself. So, as new ethnographic facts greeted me on this visit, I was not surprised to learn that many young mothers have dispensed with the marriage ceremony altogether, in awareness of the statistical probability of the outcome of marriage in such a setting.

The matricentric family, however, is stronger than ever, with all that it entails. There is, for example, the ease with which a man can abandon a "wife" as he becomes ever closer to his mother. That is to say, a man's devotion to his mother makes it almost imperative that he distance himself or separate from his wife as the two women compete for his affection. Only later does he realize that the centripetal force of maternal affection is also an entrapment, more subtle and complete than that of marriage. Men are still caught between rebellion and hostility against maternal authority, although it is referred to as the deepest of loves. What continues, too, are the open conflicts between people in complementary roles, such as wife and mother-in-law.

During the recent past, immigration has provided a vista for change for the immigrant, and in a very attenuated way these immigrants provided a small window to the world for the village. Education, too, might have provided such a view, but family relations influenced the young scholars so pervasively with notions of obligation and duty that several young people who had gotten as far in their schooling as to be in Cuernavaca, would invariably drop out because they would experience *ataques* in school. To me, the village physician described such "attacks" as pure hysteria engendered by alienation and fear of loss of family ties. Returning home (with vitamin pills as placebo medication) invariably effected a complete cure for the *ataques*.

Anthropologists are consumers of the experiences of others, and subsequently brokers of those experiences as they structure information for their analytic goals. The problem I had set for myself of how a system evolves and maintains itself is a serious and difficult one. I said in the introduction that I developed the themes of this work through intimate knowledge, over three years, of many events and trajectories of personal lives and many personal and group interactions. In presenting the early finished manuscript for review I was interested to learn that many professionals (some known and some unknown to me), who were encouraging and sometimes complimentary, nevertheless asked that I delete those sections that aimed to make the *process* by which I had learned all that I knew visible and open for consideration by the reader. Some suggested that I delete completely all references to persons (which I refused to do). My field notes had not been written in a manner that might be called indexical or topical. I rather recorded the flow of events, trying to understand my own reactions and the possible decontextualization of what I was observing, because I was part of the observation. I tried to learn their attitudes toward me, and certainly to feature what they featured as important, not what I though they should have considered of importance, such as kinship ties or *compadrazgo*. These people were obsessed with conflict, violence and mortality, and these became central also to my concerns—a method that one might have called "phenomenological," except that this was not a label then applied to such endeavors. Because I accepted their own ethnographic facts and the manner in which they were given to me as part of the data, I was as astonished here, as I was later in Melanesia, by the gap between the analytic constructs and discourse with which I had been prepared to receive the living data and the manner in which my informant-colleagues transformed what I wanted to hear by presenting me with their reality. I chose their world on which to structure the information that I wrote about in this text, as I have much more graphically and pointedly in a recent work (Romanucci-Ross 1985).

Perhaps I had to put years between myself and my work in this village in order to be objective enough to understand one aspect of the unfolding of the Catalino vs. "the people" theme. Just how much did our presence provoke polarization and activate the repertory theater aspect of this social group to play out roles they knew so well, even to the destruction of one cherished ideal—that together "the people" would win any battle? We, too, might have had an amplifying effect on the desire for ethical and aesthetic meaning in the trajectory of a life, or the life of a village. We were there with our pencils and notebooks, our cameras and tape recorders, and did we not surely want a performance? Dr. Fromm, who they had heard was very famous, brought many visitors there, and surely he must have expected something.

If I imply that all the above amplifying effects on the major village conflict created their own reality, I do not mean to imply that it was therefore a false reality. But exposition of the process of how such a reality was created will validate the manner in which it is true (Romanucci-Ross, 1985, p. xi).

A culture is always the product of a historical moment and the sex and temperament of the describer and the described. In the act of collecting data over time, one evolves a consciousness of self and other. It is questionable whether one can ever learn about self without knowing the other. Anthropologists have engendered skepticism when they have tried to address what some were pleased to call "universals" among the problematic, and chose sites such as the South Seas or other geographic spots as laboratories to solve problems for everyone. Social structures and webs of relationships in cultural groups studied as though in laboratories should never been tapped for answers to questions that those groups never asked as they developed such structures and relationships (Romanucci-Ross 1985, p. 207). What emerged from my three years of research in this village in rural Mexico was dictated not by my questions about universals but rather by the events that I observed, and by the immediate and daily concerns of the villagers themselves. It is suggested that this approach can make a more authentic contribution to our understanding, not only of a specific society, but of human behavior in general.

Lola Romanucci-Ross, 1986

---

[1] I was told that, in an earlier visit, the villagers had deluged Ted with questions about me—then realized that their curiosity about me was too great and that this caused him to "be pained" (as they saw it). Ted told them we both remarried but gave no details. Lina hinted to me that the village was very curious as to who remarried first. I merely told Lina that Ted remarried first and very

quickly. Then she gave a long look at my husband, "This one is good, one can feel that. Yes, this one is better—well, at least, one can hope."

² They regretted this act, and later asked me to photograph and write about the jail—one small room housing forty persons, with no beds, no tables, no chairs, only one toilet (the non-flushing kind) and no food. Food had to be purchased from a restaurant across the street from the jail and paid for from a fund of the *cooperativa pro balneario*. This had all begun when several persons were jailed for destroying Catalino's fence, and others wanted to be jailed also, especially some of the women who had acrid comments for every occasion, and who seemed to be full of hostilities in search of persons or situations on whom or on which to alight.

³ The *dicho* quoted at the beginning of this book, *el macho vive mientras que el cobarde quiere*, could conceivably mean that the *macho* lives while the coward just wishes or desires to live (see Hunt 1975, p. 948). But in this village, it was from analyses of the paradigmatic from which I learned meanings as syntactically presented, and here the meaning is as I translated it: the *macho* lives as long as the coward wills it.

REFERENCES CITED

Hunt, Eva. Review of *Conflict, Violence and Morality in a Mexican Village* by Lola Romanucci-Ross. *American Anthropologist* 77, no. 4 (December 1975): 946–48.

Foster, George. *Tzintzuntzan: Mexican Peasants in a Changing World*. Boston: Little, Brown, 1967.

Schwartz, Theodore. "L'usage de la terre dans un village à Ejido du Mexique." *Etudes Rurales*, pp. 37–49. Paris: Ecole Pratique des Hautes Etudes; Sixième section, Juillet-Septembre 1963.

Romanucci-Ross, Lola. *Mead's Other Manus; Phenomenology of the Encounter*. South Hadley, Mass.: Bergin and Garvey Publishers, 1985.

FILOMENA'S HISTORY

During the witchcraft affair, Filomena asked me to record the following on tape.

"I have suffered much since I was a little girl. They put me to work when I was eight years old. Before that, I felt so much jealousy toward my mother because she had lovers. As soon as I was aware of it—we were still in Guerrero—it made me so angry. My father had died, so that I never knew him. I was three years old when he died. When he died, he left me some land and some animals and some other things of value—some for me, some for my little sister. The first thing my mother did was to sell all my part of it. She said it was to support me, but actually she needed and used the money to run around and have a good time, to go to Acapulco.

"By the time I was eight years old I could stand this jealousy and chagrin no longer, and I left home to live with others. So then I had a foster mother. This foster mother beat me for anything at all; if I broke something, I was beaten until the marks were very visible on my body. Sometimes the pain was so great that I could not even fall asleep at night. I went from there to another home, and then to another. I used to earn one peso and twenty-five centavos a month working the *nixtamal* [the mixed ingredients from which tortillas are made]. I used to get up at two in the morning to grind the *nixtamal* in the container.

"The people fed me; they gave me a bed of twigs. In some of the places I lived they treated me well, but in some places they treated me badly indeed. My mother left the scene when I was twelve, and she would not return. My brother, seeing me alone in the world, took me into his house. He was a Zapatista. With my brother I suffered greatly because he was always fighting. There were always bullets being shot, and we were walking in their midst. We were always hiding either our things or ourselves. We used to hide in the hills. Often we would eat nothing for several days running but grass and a kind of sweet potato, but then someone would run to bring us things to eat. The 'government' was always after us.

"Then my brother wanted to have me put in jail for stealing. This was a calumny. My mother went to jail in my place. This was about the land I told you about that was to be mine, but my mother took it over to sell it. My brother took it, said it was rightfully his, and that *I* had stolen it!

"In those days I earned $1.25—you could buy a dress for $1.80—but worse than that, they gave the $1.25 to my mother. She wasn't so poor, for she always had corn to sell. My mother hated me. When I would go to her house I would see her eating fruits, wearing nice clothing, and even jewelry, and I could not understand why she made me work for so little money. When I was fifteen, my friends used to say, 'Don't be stupid, don't work so hard; your father left you something to live on.' This used to make me capricious, and sometimes I wouldn't work.

"My mother married again, and I, out of spite, refused to give him his meals. Then one day the old man [age thirty] tried to seduce me, and I threw him out. I threatened him. I went to my mother and I thought she would scold me, but she did not scold me. That is how I began to sell *maiz,* and I said to my mother that I would never want [to love] a man.

"Now, about this black magic. Chucho's wife is working at it, and I am working at it by lighting candles for saints, but she is not winning because the Devil is stronger than anyone. I pray to Saint Anthony, and I have even resorted to the prayer of death. This is praying to Jesus Christ to help you win out over someone and to never give them peace. I will give you this prayer.

"Well now, back to my life. The world was now turned around, I had control; I was fifteen. In 1915 my dear grandfather died of hunger. There was such great need. The government and the Zapatistas went around undressing people who were decently dressed. I used to go hiding with the girls in the caves and fields. Once we went to hide in a church, and the government men found us. We didn't know what to do, so we began to pray. We told the government men that we just wanted to get out of the range of bullets.

"We just didn't know where to stay. Once we slept in the trees so they wouldn't see us. They had stolen some twelve-year-old girls to have as wives. It was like that all the time—'Here comes the government,' and everyone taking to the fields; at night, grasshoppers and snakes in the caves. Once we were told, 'Don't sleep in there; there are scorpions, and they are poisonous.' We could go back to the *pueblos* when we could learn that the government men were gone—all sorts of people, not just young girls but all the *'pacíficos.'* Government men stole not only the daughters but the wives of just anyone. Once they stole one of my girlfriends, who died after eight days of being constantly screwed. Then they threw her dead body into her house. They did it for all sorts of reasons. Sure, I guess they needed women, but they also did it to be mean. Many children were born of unknown fathers to girls who had been raped.

"I got married when the Revolution was over. I knew Diaz because they had cows and were selling milk. I had a *novio* ('intended') who was planning to ask me to marry him, but a mule dragged him along the ground, killing him. I loved him very much. He was tall and slender with blue eyes. I cried so very much. This was my first love. No, it was another, the first one. I had had another *novio,* and he died from an infected leg. Just from that he died. What rotten luck! My fate has been really bad. Another boyfriend wanted to marry me, but I told him I was too young. He said it didn't matter, I could learn everything later. But I said no, so he looked for another and took her away.

"Why does Chucho keep seeking me out now? Last night he came here with his *palomilla* ('gang') and said he wants to give it to me. Only Cecilio kept him from doing something foolish. He told some of his friends here in the village that he is jealous of me and doesn't know why—much more jealous than he is of his wife. But he's been separated from her for eight years; she only decided to start fighting for him since he became interested in me. Do you know why I went to Mexico City yesterday? I went to look into this black magic, and it is true that Barbara [his wife] practices black magic.

"Yes, Diaz was selling cheese, and that is how he got to know me. He used to come to my house to sell cheese, cream, and cottage cheese. He said he would take the place of my dead *novio.* We were *novios* for two months, and then he asked for my hand. My mother beat me up for this because she didn't like him. They all said he was a bad sort, a drunkard and a womanizer. Once my mother beat me because he brought me flowers and I accepted and hid them. I lied about who gave them, but she found out and beat me.

"But my mother didn't even want me to have girlfriends. She said that girls would give me bad advice and that I would begin to come apart. Then he asked to marry me, but she took a long pole burning at one end and told me to tell him that I did not want to get married. A married couple in town said to my mother, 'Why do you beat her so? You run around with lovers and things like that, and she is, by her behavior, setting the best example in the village.' My mother used to lie to me. She used to tell me that she was going somewhere to sell or buy cloth, but I knew about her all the time.

"The Diaz family had cows, even though poor. My mother-in-law liked me from the start. I began to be a good housekeeper. The family was this: me, my husband, a brother of his, and my mother-in-law. In the beginning, everything was fine, but then my mother-in-law began to slander me. She told my husband that I had lovers and named especially the *padrino* of our marriage. He did not believe his mother because actually he spied on me. We lived like this for two or three years with all those calumnies, but then we had to look for another house. Then the mother-in-law really got angry with me, said ugly things to me, and started to beat me.

"We went to another *pueblo* because of this *agrarismo* [political movement for land repartitioning]. My husband wasn't an *agrarista,* he was a merchant. There was so much fighting and killing, because some persons would sell land to others and then the *agraristas* would come to reapportion these same lands that had been purchased. Now here we were again running and hiding in the hills. His mother lost her mind finding herself alone and seeing that her sons could not be with her because of this *agrarismo.* She was insane, and she would run out into the street and shout and insult everyone. She would call everyone 'whore', 'son of a bitch', and so on. She threw rocks at people, and when I brought food to her she would throw the dishes and utensils at me and tell her son and everyone else that I did not feed her. At night we had to tie her down so that she (and we) could sleep. She had a brutal strength. Her sons did not commit her to an institution, because the closest one was in Mexico City and that was too far away.

"One day he began to beat me because his sister told him I would not feed their mother and he believed her. Now I told him I would leave because I was tired of suffering. He begged me not to leave, but then he beat me for having said I wanted to leave. I could bear it only because his uncle gave me moral support, and he was the mayor of the town. Children? No, I couldn't have children—but I had several miscarriages. How did he feel about it? He said, 'It is better not to have children so that no one will suffer. There will be that much less suffering in the world.' And, after all, I was just more or less a maid for his mother . . . . "

APPENDIX 2

VILLAGE NICKNAMES

Sex	Nickname	Reasons
F	*La Apretada* ("the constricted one")	Because she is not "open" and does not like people
M	*El Barbon* ("the bearded one")	Because he is bearded
F	*La Boa* ("the serpent")	Because at the Saturday night dances she interacts with just anyone (people are particularly judged on these occasions)
F	*La Bruja* ("the witch")	Because she is a "real" witch
F	*La Calzonera* ("the trader in trousers")	Because she reputedly pulled the pants off a man she coveted
F	*La Camela* ("the camel")	Because of her curved spine
M	Carranza	Because he has a mustache like Venustiano Carranza

M	*El Chicote* ("end of a rope or cable")	Because he is very thin
M	*El Chilaquil* ("a flying insect that stings and flies away")	Because he is a gossip
M	*Chiva, El Toro del Manatial* ("goat," "the bull of the spring")	To prove that he has the *huevos* ("testicles") for the village versus Catalino
F	*La Cochinera* ("the trader in pigs")	Because she kills pigs, a butcher
M	*El Coton* ("the cotton")	For his *"camisa de Indio"* ("Indian shirt")
M	*La Cuecla* (no meaning, nickname for a lazy person)	Because he is lazy
M	*El Diablo* ("the devil")	Always said jokingly with the implication that he likes this to be said of him; it is more to indulge than to describe him.
F	*La Frijolera* ("the trader in beans")	Because she used to pick the beans that others left in the fields
M	*La Gabiota* ("sea gull")	Because like that bird, he has no definite habits
M	*El Gigante* ("the giant")	Because he is tall
M	*El Governador* ("the governor")	Because he would like to govern
F	*La Gorila* ("the gorilla")	Because of his looks
M	*La Gringa* ("American female")	Because they think he looks like an American girl
M	*El Guante* ("glove")	Because of his delicacy in "handling" others

| M | *El Lambiscon* (nickname for a flatterer) | Because he "butters up" those who might do him favors |
| F | *La Llorona* ("the weeper") | Because she cries in school |

Sex	Nickname	Reason
M	*Manito Mario* ("little brother Mario")	So-called by his younger brothers and the villagers but not to his face
M	*El Metrero* ("the trader in meters")	Because of a defect, he walks as if he is measuring distances by the meter
M	*El Mielero* ("the trader in honey")	Because he steals and eats honey
M	*Mula,* or *El Alacran* ("mule" or "scorpion")	Because he thinks himself very *macho*, because he is recalcitrant and a misanthrope
F	*La Muñeca Chocolatera* ("the chocolate doll")	Because she talks to drunks in her mother's bar
M	*El Muñeco* ("the doll," masc.)	Because he walks like a girl
M	*El Niedo* (no meaning, just a nickname)	Because he likes everyone
M	*El Patatas* (an augmentative form of *patas,* meaning foot and leg of a beast)	Because he has big feet and walks peculiarly
M	*El Prieto* ("the dark-colored one")	Because he is dark
F	*La Putaniera* ("the trader in whores")	Because she trades in whores
M	*La Rana* ("frog")	Reference to his appearance

M	*El Ratonero* ("the trader in rats")	Because he partitioned *La Colonia de la Rata Muerta*
M	*El Sapo* ("toad")	Reference to his appearance
F	*La Treca* (no meaning, just a nickname for a debtor)	Because she makes debts and does not pay them
M	*Todo Eso Es Mio* ("all this is mine")	When he walks, he draws a circle with each foot, as if to say, "All this is mine."
M	*El Zopilote* ("buzzard")	Because of his very dark skin
M	*El Zurcador* ("furrow maker")	Because of a defect, he walks as if he is making furrows

BIBLIOGRAPHY

Aramoni, Aniceto. *Psicoánalisis de la dinamica de un pueblo*. Mexico: Universidad Nacional Autonoma de Mexico, 1961.

Banfield, Edward. *The Moral Basis of a Backward Society*. Glencoe, Ill.: Free Press, 1959.

Calderón de la Barca, Mme. *Life in Mexico during a Residence of Two Years in That Country*. reprint ed., Mexico: Tolteca, 1952.

Caso, Alfonso. "Land Tenure among the Ancient Mexicans." Paper delivered at the American Anthropological Association Meetings, Mexico City, December 1959.

Cosío Villegas, Daniel. *Historia moderna de Mexico*. 5 vols. México: Editorial Hermes, 1955.

De la Fuente, Julio. *Cambios socio-culturales en Mexico*. Mexico: Escuela Nacional de Antropología e Historia, 1948.

Devereux, George. *Mojave Ethnopsychiatry and Suicide*. Bureau of American Ethnology Bulletin, no. 175. Washington, D.C.: Smithsonian Institution, 1961.

Diez, Domingo. *Bibliografía del Estado de Morelos, no. 27.* Mexico: Monografías Bibliograficas Mexicanas, 1933.

Edmonson, Munro S.; Carrasco, Pedro; Fisher, Flen; and Wolf, Eric. *Synoptic Studies of Mexican Culture.* Middle American Research Institute Publication, no. 17. New Orleans: Tulane University, 1957.

Eisenstadt, S. N. "Ritualized Personal Relations: Blood Brotherhood, Best Friends, Compadre, etc.; Some Comparative Hypotheses and Suggestions." *Man* 56, no. 96 (July 1956): 90–95.

Evans-Pritchard, Edward. *The Nuer: A Description of the Modes of Livelihood and Political Institutions of a Nilotic People.* Oxford: Clarendon, 1947.

Foster, George. *Empire's Children: The People of Tzintzuntzan.* Mexico: Nuevo Mundo, 1948.

—————— . "The Dyadic Contract: A Model for the Social Structure of a Mexican Peasant Village." *American Anthropologist,* 63, no. 6 (December 1961): 1173–91.

Friedrich, Paul. "Assumptions Underlying Tarascan Political Homicide." *Psychiatry* 25, no. 4 (1962): 315–27.

Fromm, Erich and Maccoby, Michael. *Social Character in a Mexican Village.* Englewood Cliffs, New Jersey: Prentice-Hall, 1970.

Garibi Tortolero, Lic. Manuel. *Catecismo sintetico Guadalupano.* Mexico (n.p.), 1932.

Gluckman, Max. *Custom and Conflict in Africa.* Oxford: Blackwell, 1955.

González Pineda, Francisco. *El Méxicano, su dinámica psicosocial.* Asociacion Psicoanalitica Mexicana Monografías Psicoanaliticas. México D.F.: Editorial Pax, 1959.

Gruening, Ernest. *Mexico and Its Heritage.* New York: Century, 1928.

Krader, Lawrence. "Person and Collectivity: A Problem in the Dialectic of Anthropology." Transactions of the New York Academy of Sciences II 30, no. 6 (April 1968): 856–62.

Leach, E. R. *Political Systems of Highland Burma: A Study of Kachin Social Structure.* Cambridge, Mass.: Harvard University Press, 1954.

—————— . *Rethinking Anthropology.* London School of Economics Monographs on Social Anthropology, no. 22. London, 1961.

Leslie, Charles. *Now We Are Civilized: A Study of the World View of the Zapotec Indians of Mitla, Oaxaca.* Detroit: Wayne State University Press, 1960.

Levi-Strauss, Claude. *Les structures elementaires de la parente*. Paris: Presses Universitaires de France, 1949.

Lewis, Oscar. "An Anthropological Approach to Family Studies." *American Journal of Sociology* 55, no. 5 (March 1950): 468-75.

——————. *Life in a Mexican Village: Tepoztlán Restudied*. Urbana, Ill.: University of Illinois Press, 1951.

——————. *Tepoztlán: Village in Mexico*. New York: Holt, Rinehart & Winston, 1960.

Magaña, General Gildardo. *Emiliano Zapata y el agrarismo en Mexico*. 5 vols. Mexico: Ruta, 1951.

McBride, George McCutcheon. "The Land Systems of Mexico." American Geographical Society Research Series, no. 12. New York, 1923.

Mexico. Acusacion fiscal de la Suprema Corte de Justicia. *En la causa instruida a varios reos, por el asalto, robos y asesinatos cometidos la noche del 17 y mañana del 18 de Dic. de 856*. Mexico: Imprenta de A. Boix, 1858.

——————. Gobierno del Estado de Morelos. Cuernavaca. *Codigo de procedimientos penales y exposicion de motivos: ley organica y reglamentaria del ministerio publico*, 1946.

——————. Estado de Morelos. Secretaria de Hacienda, II. *Estudios historico-economico-fiscales sobre los estados de la republica*, 1939.

——————. Leyes y Codigos de Mexico. *Codigo agrario*. Mexico: Porrua, 1960.

——————. *Constitucion politica de los Estados Unidos Mexicanos*. Mexico: Porrua, 1961.

Mintz, Sidney and Wolf, Eric. "An Analysis of Ritual Co-parenthood (Compadrazgo)." *Southwestern Journal of Anthropology* 6, no. 4 (1950): 341-68.

Mosk, Sanford. *La Revolución Industrial en Mexico*. Berkeley: University of California Press, 1951.

Muller, Florencia. "La historia vieja del Estado de Morelos." Unpublished thesis, Departamento de Historia e Antropologia, Museo Nacional, Mexico, 1948.

Murdock, George Peter. *Social Structure*. New York: Macmillan Co., 1949.

Parkes, Henry Bamford. *A History of Mexico*. Boston: Houghton Mifflin, 1938.

Parsons, Elsie Clews. *Mitla, Town of Souls.* Chicago: University of Chicago Press, 1936.

Paz, Octavio. *El laberinto de la soledad.* Mexico: Fondo de Cultura Economica, 1959.

Peterson, Federik A. *Ancient Mexico: An Introduction to the Pre-Hispanic Cultures.* New York: Capricorn Books, 1959.

Portes Gil, Emilio. *Historical Evolution of the Territorial Property of Mexico.* Mexico: Alteneo Nacional de Ciencias y Artes de Mexico, n.d.

Potter, Jack M.; Diaz, May N.; and Foster, George M., eds. *Peasant Society: A Reader.* Boston: Little, Brown & Co., 1967.

Pozas, Ricardo. *Juan Perez Jolote: biografía de un Tzotzil.* Mexico: Escuela Nacional de Antropologia e Historia, 1948.

Quirk, Robert E. *The Mexican Revolution 1914-1915.* Bloomington, Ind.: Indiana University Press, 1960.

Ramirez, Santiago. *El Mexicano; la psicología de sus motivaciones.* Asociacion Psicoanalitica Mexicana Monografias Psicoanaliticas. Mexico. Pax, 1958.

Redfield, Robert. *Peasant Society and Culture: An Anthropological Approach to Civilization.* Chicago: University of Chicago Press, 1956.

Sahagun, Bernardino de. *Historia general de las cosas de Nueva España.* 5 vols. Mexico: Robredo, 1938.

Sainte-Croix, Lambert de. *Onze mois au Mexique.* Paris (n.p.), 1897.

Schwartz, Lola Romanucci. "Conflits fonciers a Mokerang, village Matankor des iles de l'Amirauté." *L'homme* 6, no. 2 (1966): 32-52.

_____. *Morality, Conflict and Violence in a Mexican Mestizo Village.* Ann Arbor, Mich.: University Microfilms, 1962.

_____. "The Hierarchy of Resort in Curative Practices: The Admiralty Islands, Melanesia." *Journal of Health and Social Behavior* 10, no. 3 (September 1969): 201-209.

Schwartz, Theodore. "Systems of Areal Integration: Some Considerations Based on the Admiralty Islands of Northern Melanesia." *Anthropological Forum* 1, no. 1 (July 1963): 56-97.

Seigel, Bernard J., ed. *Biennial Review of Anthropology, 1961.* Stanford: Stanford University Press, 1962.

Simmel, G. *Conflict*. Translated by Kurt H. Wolff. Glencoe, Ill.: Free Press, 1955.

Simpson, Eyler. *The Ejido: Mexico's Way Out*. Chapel Hill, 1937.

Simpson, Lesley Byrd. *Many Mexicos*. Berkeley: University of California Press, 1952.

_____ . *The Encomienda in New Spain: The Beginning of Spanish Mexico*. Berkeley: University of California Press, 1950.

Tannenbaum, Frank. *Mexico, the Struggle for Peace and Bread*. New York: Alfred A. Knopf, 1950.

_____ . *The Mexican Agrarian Revolution*. New York: Macmillan Co., 1929.

Tweedie, Mrs. Alec. *Mexico as I Saw It*. 2d ed. New York: Macmillan Co., 1902.

Weber, Max. *Max Weber on the Methodology of the Social Sciences*. Edited and translated by Edward A. Shils and Henry A. Finch. Glencoe, Ill.: Free Press, 1949.

Whetten, Nathan. *Rural Mexico*. Chicago: University of Chicago Press, 1948.

Wolf, Eric R. "Types of Latin American Peasantry: A Preliminary Discussion." *American Anthropologist* 57 (1955): 452–71.

Womack, Jr., John. *Zapata and the Mexican Revolution*. New York: Alfred A. Knopf, 1969.